PLOTTING THE COURSE

LIFE LESSONS FROM THE SPORT OF SAILING

To Jeniffer —
Thank you so much for all that
you do — what a beautiful finished
product!

Smooth sailing always,

Rick

PLOTTING THE COURSE

LIFE LESSONS FROM THE SPORT OF SAILING

RICK ARNESON

FOREWORD BY
ANNIE GARDNER

 MAKAI PRESS

MAKAI PRESS

Makai Press
PO Box 3058
Rancho Santa Fe, CA 92067

Plotting the Course by Rick Arneson

First edition trade paperback print run February 2014.

ISBN 978-0-9893790-0-7

Library of Congress Control Number: 2013918270

Cover & Interior Design: Monkey C Media
Editor: Mary Altbaum

Front cover photograph: Sharon Green
Back cover photograph: Onne van der Wal
Interior illustrations: Rick Arneson

Media or Specialty Sales:
STRATEGIES Public Relations
PO Box 178122
San Diego, CA 92177

To my mother, in loving memory.

CONTENTS

A New Look at an Old Sport | The Wide World of Sailing |
The Elements of Achievement

Dare to Dream | Find the Right Fit | Follow Your Desires |
Set Goals | *SMART Goals* | Develop a Winning Mind-Set |
Confidence | *Visualization*

Gather and Manage Your Assets | *Take Inventory* | *Make Your
Wish List* | *Consider Alternatives* | *Conspire to Acquire* |
The "Arms Race" | *Manage Complexity* | *Make a To-Do List* |
Mind the Little Things | *Make the Most of Your Efforts* |
Take Care of Your Toys | *Consider the Pros and Cons of
Fixer-Uppers* | *Control Excess*

Build a Winning Team | *Let Everyone Know Their Roles* |
Artists and Scientists | *Trust Them to Do Their Jobs* | *Develop
Communication* | *Supporters* | *Mentors*

Get Plenty of Practice | *Dedication to Preparation* | *Get Your
Homework Done* | *Scheduling* | *Make the Most of Practice Time* |
Show Up | *Mind the Time*

FOREWORD

THERE ARE LESSONS TO BE LEARNED in the things we love, lessons to be shared through the anecdotes they provide.

I've been a sailor my whole life. It defines me. In my 20's if I saw a palm tree swaying, my whole body would ache, just yearning to go windsurfing and feel the power of the wind propel me and the board through the water. It's a passion so deeply ingrained that it is more than a sport to me—it's a way of life. So it is with all of us who have found the simple pleasure of going down to the dock and taking in the familiar smells of salty seas or freshwater lakes, or musty sails in bags and lockers, of hearing the twang of halyards banging against masts and reliving the memories of experiences on the water that leave large imprints on our souls.

There have been times, sometimes months, sometimes years, where I've put sailing on a shelf because kids were born, or being a team mom for baseball or soccer games ruled. But the beauty of sailing is that it's always waiting right where you left off. And no matter how young or how old you are, it's a sport that welcomes you in or welcomes you back.

My love of the sea has taken me to so many places around the world. I've been a skipper and captain for racing and cruising yachts. I've raced catamarans and sailboards against the best in the world, and have been honored with five world championships. I brought home a medal after competing in the 1984 Olympic Windsurfing Exhibition. I sailed as part of the afterguard of the America³ women's team in the America's Cup trials. I've gotten to be a commentator and TV host for sailing and adventure shows. All in all, sailing has brought me some incredible experiences.

The thrill of competing at the highest levels and sometimes being victorious is only a small part of why I love it. The cliché that it's the journey, not the destination that matters most, holds true. Whether I'm driving an 18' catamaran at 20+ knots, a 100' yacht at 12 knots, crewing on a J105, or captaining a 58' cruising cat in the Caribbean, I am always learning new things, new techniques, and better ways to handle challenging situations. Preparation, dedication, and the development of interpersonal relationships with teammates, coaches, and competitors represent just a portion of what makes racing sailboats so dynamic. There's so much that this sport can teach us through lessons we carry off the water into our lives ashore. That's what Rick Arneson has brought out in these pages.

Rick has combined his knowledge and background in coaching, sailing and business to deliver information that is well organized, easy to read, and quite frankly the best book I've read about sailing in a very long time. He has approached his subject matter with such detail and insight that I wanted to get the yellow highlighter out and mark up every page!

While quiet and soft-spoken, Rick's influence in the sailing community is apparent. He has won his fair share of regattas and championships, but it is his personal style and his approach to the sport that his competitors, teammates, and longtime friends admire most. Sailors have been heard to say: "I love sailing with Rick", "He's wicked smart", "He never yells no matter what the situation is", "He's well-respected for his sportsmanship", "He jumped in the class and placed 2nd against guys who'd been at it for years!", "He'll always do penalty turns, unless he knows the other guy is wrong".

Rick's reputation for sportsmanship reminds me of a legend in our sport, Paul Elvstrom. Paul has four Olympic gold medals, and has medaled in world championships in eight different sailing classes. But even more important is how highly respected he is by his peers. Paul is the source of my favorite quote: "If by winning the regatta you lose the respect of your fellow sailors, you have not won at all." It's this type of sportsmanship that Rick exudes. Both on and off the water he is a gentleman by anyone's standards.

In *Plotting the Course*, Rick shares valuable lessons for people from a broad range of backgrounds. Sailors, business leaders, parents, students, and so many more can benefit from this book. It is truly inspirational and is packed with wonderful examples not only from the world of sailing, but also history, business, politics, philosophy, and even everyday situations that we all might encounter.

Now that you have this book, take your time and read it cover to cover. Then put it next to the bedside table and open it to any page for reminders and valuable nuggets of information that will not only help you to win in sailing, but also in life, work, and love. I only wish I'd had it when I was twenty, but since I'll never grow up I'm grateful to have it now. It's timeless.

—Annie Gardner

PREFACE

PASSION BREEDS INSPIRATION IN ANY FIELD of endeavor. When your mind, heart, and soul are devoted to anything important to you, there will always be some degree of overlap between the way you pursue your passion and the way you see the rest of your world. At some point, everyone meets someone who just can't get off their favorite topic in a conversation, or who seems to compare every situation to their greatest passion. It could be the life of a historical figure, or perhaps a favorite film, or it could be a particular sport.

I've been sailing since early childhood, and over time I found that my love of the sport grew to a level at which its presence was just about always felt in the back of my mind. It was eventually instinctive for me to face a scenario on the water and apply it to situations on land. Sailing, or specifically sailboat racing, had opened up new perspectives for me as a youth. It taught me about matters such as teamwork, self-discipline, preparation, focus, assessing risks, setting and pursuing goals, keeping success in perspective, and recovering from defeat. As much internal guidance as my sport provided at first, it was brought into a new light by the time I reached college.

I set out in my freshman year to start a sailing team at Pepperdine University. What I found along the way was that I was setting out on what was essentially my first sailing campaign. The logistical challenges kept piling up: I would need to write bylaws, recruit and train the team members, raise the funds for the fleet, manage the budget, run team meetings and practices, coordinate travel, maintain the equipment inventory, and incidentally, race.

As it turned out, I was basically starting a small business. So when it came time to choose a major, I selected business administration, in part for the skills that I felt I most immediately needed to develop to run the team. This worked to my benefit twofold. I like a good metaphor, and as my sailor's mind absorbed a completely new subject in the classroom, the parallels between sailboat racing and business became apparent to me. My sailing experience drove home classroom lessons on business, and business lessons were aptly applied to my sailing. In the end, pursuing both of these fields together in college reinforced both of them for me.

For about a ten-year span, starting in those university days, I coached various sailing teams and programs. I've had the opportunity to coach sailors from the beginner to the advanced racer, and while the details may matter more the further up the ladder you go, many of the principles for winning a sailboat race bear constant reinforcement at any level. In the process of bringing sailors back to those basic tenets of success, it continually occurred to me how valuable they could be for application in everyday life. The discussion may have been about taking the time to prepare, communicating with your teammate, asserting yourself when it counts, keeping an eye on the competition, adapting to your environment, or playing the odds, just to name a few, but all these topics and more struck a chord as valuable advice in any case.

Subjects such as war and sports are often applied to lessons for success in business or in life. Sailing is a sport that, while global in its reach, is admittedly not at the forefront of the majority of the world's sports fans' minds. Nonetheless, it is a fascinating sport that can provide inspiration to people from all walks of life. What follows is a sailor's perspective on some of the lessons that can be drawn from this complex sport and applied to life's challenges. It will be a tour through a sailor's racing experience, starting with the planning that goes into the quest for victory, passing through the trials and tribulations of the regatta itself, and tying in the learning phases of the aftermath of competition and the buildup to the next goal. In each of these steps, there will be principles that successful sailors apply to their racing that can be duly applied to life off the racecourse as well. There will be situations that crop up that mirror everyday challenges to some degree, and can offer possible solutions as inspired by a racing sailor's methods.

The success principles of sailing herein can be demonstrated in a wide range of situational applications in life as well as historical and present-day contexts. These principles will be explored with comparative application to everyday situations as well as other sports, business, finance, politics, war, and historical events. The lessons that apply to winning in sailing not only apply in many situations on land today, but have proven true over time as well.

Life's challenges take many forms, and it is often easier to put a difficult or unfamiliar situation into perspective by comparing it to a more familiar one. Using the sport of sailing as a setting, the following pages will paint a picture of the cyclical nature of life's challenges and provide some suggestions from the sailor's standpoint as to how to pursue and achieve success and personal growth. It is my hope in assembling this material that the reader may draw inspiration for their own life from the sport that has so often and so profoundly inspired me and my fellow sailors around the world.

PART ONE

THE INSPIRATION OF SAILING

*It is not the ship so much as the skilled sailing
that assures the prosperous voyage.*

—GEORGE WILLIAM CURTIS

SAILING HAS EXISTED IN VARIOUS FORMS for thousands of years. The sailing vessels of the ancient world included such different designs as the oared ships that traveled up and down Egypt's Nile River, Chinese junks, and Polynesian canoes that traversed the South Pacific, to name a few. Ancient artifacts uncovered in the Middle East suggest the existence of sailing vessels as early as the fifth millennium BC. With the invention of the sailboat thousands of years ago, new worlds opened up. Not only did a new form of travel emerge, but in time a new form of recreation; sailing wasn't just useful—it also turned out to be fun. Sailboat racing was an inevitable evolution of this once utilitarian discipline. For millennia, sailing ships carried people and goods, for commerce as well as warfare. The sport of sailing as we know it today, however, didn't officially emerge until the seventeenth century in Europe.

The first regatta on record was held on England's River Thames in October of 1661. The race was between two yachts, one belonging to King Charles II, and the other to his brother James, the Duke of York. The course was to be down the river, from Greenwich to Gravesend and back again, the prize being one hundred pounds sterling. The king himself drove his yacht to victory, and the sport of sailing thereafter began to catch on. It would be decades before the common people began to host regattas of their own, but this was the era in which racing yachts, sailing regattas, and yacht clubs found their origins. By the nineteenth century, America had established its own yachting prowess on a global scale in winning the "100 Guinea Cup" from England's Royal Yacht Squadron (later to be named the America's Cup). The sport of sailing has grown by leaps and bounds over the last few centuries, and continues to be a part of millions of people's lives anywhere that there is water to be raced upon (and even in some places where there isn't, where iceboats and land yachts are employed instead).

This widely beloved sport has been enriching the lives of its participants in numerous ways since its birth. It has brought people together from all walks of life to share a common passion. It has driven passionate and ambitious challenges that have tested people's will and intellect to the highest degree. It has created new industries and careers. And, like so many other sports, it has inspired people to succeed off the water with the lessons inherent in its nature. Organization, teamwork, decision making, discipline, and problem solving are among the valuable life skills that a sailor cannot help but develop, all to their benefit off the racecourse as much as on. This sport has an endless horizon of possibilities ahead of it, and will continue to thrill and inspire people for many generations more. As long as there is wind in the air, there will be sailing. And as long as there is sailing, there will be sailors and sailing enthusiasts to enjoy and learn from it.

A NEW LOOK AT AN OLD SPORT

Sailing is often a misunderstood sport, partially because it usually takes place far away from most observers' eyes. For the average person, various mental images may come up when somebody mentions sailing. One may imagine the tall ships of yesteryear out on the open sea with huge, billowing sails. Or, perhaps an image of an elegant cruising sloop, with brass hardware and teak decks, gliding over the waves off some island paradise. Still another image could be that of high-tech America's Cup yachts jockeying for position before the start of a race.

These are all parts of the sport, to be sure, but the sport of sailing is so vast in scale and diverse in scope, that there is no one-size-fits-all description that will do it justice. There are sailboats of all shapes and sizes, from little dinghies that could fit inside the bed of a pickup truck to superyachts that overshadow everything on the water short of a military vessel, oil tanker, or cruise liner. There are cruisers who just enjoy being on the water occasionally with friends and family, there are professional racers who compete year-round, traveling the globe from one regatta to the next, and there is a large number of those who are somewhere in the middle.

Much of my own sailing career has been spent racing small boats and various one-designs. I enjoy being on boats and going for the occasional cruise, but by and large I can't seem to be in a boat for very long without starting to think about how to optimize performance. Even if there's nobody to race against, I know that there's a right way and a wrong way to sail a boat, so you might as well do it right. Racing sailboats is a way to take things to the next level; when you've gotten your boat performing well, what better way to keep improving than through competition? Competition in general gives benchmarks for performance, quick and measurable results, and extra opportunities for learning. In this case, the fact that you're on a sailboat just makes it even more fun.

To know what it's like to be a part of this scene, most people would have to drop a lot of assumptions about sailing. Here are some common misconceptions and criticisms sailors have heard over the years:

Myth #1: "Sailing isn't physically challenging."

Sailing's a tough sport, and requires a lot of physical strength and endurance. Some boats are more demanding than others, and at the Olympic or World Championship level, the sailor's physical conditioning counts even more. High-performance boats in particular require aerobic ability, strength throughout the core, legs, and arms, flexibility, and the endurance to keep your concentration up under great strain for an hour-plus long race. In sailing, as in life, being in shape not only keeps the body running strong, but keeps the mind sharp, as well.

Myth #2: "Sailing's just luck—it's the wind, not the sailor's ability, which determines the outcome of the race."

The wind is always changing, and sailors need to watch weather patterns before and during races to see where the next puff of wind or favorable wind shift will come from. We can't force the wind to do what we want, but we can take advantage of the changes in conditions to make them work in our favor. That's not luck—that's opportunity. An opportunity can be squandered by the sailor who doesn't know how to make it work in his or her favor. When a sailor is well prepared for a race, then they are well suited to handle any eventuality, whether it's potentially positive or negative. As two-time Olympic medalist and America's Cup winner Buddy Melges said, "Sailboat racing becomes a game of chance only when you are not prepared." The methods of successful sailboat racing, like many decisions we face in life, are based largely on anticipation of probable outcomes and smart consideration of risk.

Myth #3: "Sailing's just for the wealthy."

There are sailors from all walks of life, enjoying the sport together the world over. Learning to sail doesn't have to break your bank account. There are many fine sailing academies and clubs throughout the US and around the world that charge very reasonable rates for lessons. More and more schools and universities are offering sailing classes as part of their physical education programs. Many sailors also learn by joining a boat owner's crew and picking up skills along the way. There are boats of all sizes available to fit any budget, and the used boat market is usually full of terrific finds. Anyone with an interest in the sport shouldn't let a limited budget stop them. Just meeting some of the sailors in your area can present opportunities to get onto the water. The right approach for your budget will present itself. Sometimes there are creative ways to meet our goals with the resources we have.

Myth #4: "Winning a sailboat race just depends on who has the fastest boat."

The fastest boat in the world won't help you if you don't know how to get the most out of it. It takes a lot of skill to get a boat around a racecourse, and many times a more talented team has managed to beat a superior boat. That being said, a faster boat does make winning races much easier, assuming the crew makes no mistakes, the boat doesn't capsize or have any equipment breakdowns, and the skipper plays all the wind shifts intelligently. Indeed, the serious competitor should be taking every step to ensure that they have the best equipment going into a contest. Preparation is the key to success in competition on and off the water. As the saying goes, you don't bring a knife to a gunfight.

THE WIDE WORLD OF SAILING

Sailing, in its many forms, can present numerous formats of competition. The largest racing yachts may primarily compete in ocean races, traveling down a coastline, across an ocean, or even around the world. Small one-design boats typically race around courses designed to take about an hour to sail, and generally incorporate multiple laps. Boards and skiffs may use a slalom course to put a premium on maneuvering. Besides the variety of course layouts, sailboat races can vary the contest between the players. There's fleet racing, with large groups of boats racing together; match racing—one-on-one contests running through a bracketed round-robin series; and team racing, with two small groups of boats facing each other for a best combined tally of their individual finishes. Most races have stationary start lines, but some races use rabbit starts, which are begun in motion with the fleet ducking behind a boat on the opposite tack (the "rabbit"). The more sailing a person does, the more likely he or she will get to experience more of these formats, and the more they will broaden their knowledge of the sport. It's common for the top sailors in any given class to have a broad background in the types of sailing they've done in the course of their career.

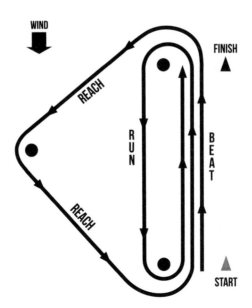

LAYOUT OF AN "OLYMPIC" COURSE

Whatever the format, every sailboat race is designed to challenge the sailor on certain factors. The design, condition, and use of the sailor's equipment will be determining factors in any race, so it is up to the sailor to make sure his boat, sails, and gear are all state of the art and ready to function. The human factor is what makes the sport an ongoing challenge, though. The sailor will need knowledge of the weather and the tides, and their effect on the course; an understanding of the racing rules and how to incorporate shrewd racing tactics within their boundaries; methods of tuning and driving his boat for optimal speed; and a natural, instinctive feel for the motion of the boat to enhance his reaction time. Some boats are primarily a challenge of strength, and some are a challenge of smarts, but all boats reward a healthy dose of both.

Competitive fleets can be tough to navigate during a race, and there is some potential for collisions if everyone isn't on their toes. Any time two or more boats come into close quarters on the racecourse, the right-of-way rules come into play. For some events, there are umpires following in motorboats to judge any rules infractions on the water, but most of the time, sailing is a self-policing sport. Fouls can usually be absolved by some means, such as penalty turns or a temporary stop. If the two boats disagree on who was at fault, however, they can protest and discuss the matter on shore after the race with an impartial jury. It's a bit like a court of law, with each side presenting a case, calling witnesses, and questioning each other. Since protests slow down the ultimate result and put both parties at risk for disqualification, most sailors do what they can to avoid protests. Protests, like lawsuits, can wind up costing you more than you gain, even when you win.

Risk is an ever-present factor in the tactics of sailing. For most decisions that offer a reward, there is a risk that accompanies it. A skipper may want to call for a lighter and larger spinnaker for more speed, but must consider that a sudden unexpected puff could tear it to shreds, costing him much more speed, not to mention money. He may want to sail a higher course on an off-wind leg that will offer more speed, but sacrifice position and distance to the next mark. He may believe that one side of the course is favored, but finds that he'll have to split from the rest of the fleet to get there. Boats in the lead will generally seek to position themselves between their competition and the next mark of the course. If the opposition should split off in different directions, the leader

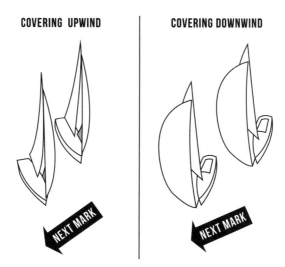

COVERING UPWIND   **COVERING DOWNWIND**

NEXT MARK   NEXT MARK

will need to determine how to respond. Trailing boats also face decisions that balance risk and reward. If a skipper of a boat that's behind decides to blanket the wind of his nearest opponent on an off-wind leg, he'll need to remember the defensive tactics that may be used against him in response. Engaging with the leader can start a battle that is more costly than it's worth, so some forethought is required before making his move. In the ongoing push for better results, it takes some mental discipline to recognize the risks that accompany the sought-after reward, to create a plan suitable to the situation, and to act on that plan decisively.

While anyone looking for success on or off the water will seek out high reward for low risk, there's generally no way to eliminate risk entirely. Preparation can address the factors that you can control, or at least address, but there will often be something waiting to challenge even the most thoroughly prepared. When you look at the big picture, sailing around a racecourse includes a lot of potential obstacles and snafus that can slow you down:

- Opposing currents
- Big waves
- Kelp patches
- Other racing boats
- Chop from passing motorboats
- Spots of windless holes

- Crew mistakes
- Equipment failures
- Missed wind shifts
- Late or slow start
- Marine life

Every sailor goes around the course with the ambition to sail the course perfectly. As it turns out, none of them will. There are too many factors happening all at once for a human being or a team of human beings to avoid any slowing effects whatsoever. The boat that wins the race is the one that made the fewest mistakes, or avoided any major obstacles that may have slowed down the other boats. Nobody can do it perfectly; they can just do it the best they can and make sure it's a little better than the other guy.

It's taken hundreds of years for this sport to evolve to its current state, and it continues to branch out into new formats and variations, each advance in technique or technology making it more inclusive to newcomers and all the more interesting for the experts. Sailing's challenging nature provides benefits beyond the sport itself; it provides the opportunity to bring out the best in people. It introduces people to those with whom they'll compete and those with whom they'll cooperate. It teaches people to accept some degree of uncertainty, but it also teaches how to reduce the chance of nasty surprises. It demonstrates not only the importance of the little details that make a difference, but also the importance of understanding the bigger picture. It rewards thorough advance preparation as well as smart adaptation when the game changes. It can also reward daring ambition as fast as it punishes greed. It is a sport that will not gladly suffer fools or cheats, and it both demands and rewards persistence, creativity, reason, and patience. In short, sailing can be a lot like life.

THE ELEMENTS OF ACHIEVEMENT

There are three big-picture elements of achievement that will be covered as we move ahead, encompassing many elements of sailboat racing as the basis for valuable takeaways that can apply in the way we live our lives in other ways. These elements, the three stages of an ongoing process to grow and achieve, are Planning, Performing, and Learning. A successful result for any important effort depends greatly on these three elements, each as necessary as the others.

They act as a cycle over the long run; we make a plan for success, take action to accomplish our goals, and then use the experience to learn and build a foundation for the future as we begin making new plans for success. The cycle can end when we stop making an effort to succeed (but why do that?), or it can speed up with each new effort and each learning experience.

Planning involves setting goals, allocating resources, preparation and practice, surveying the field, building a team, and preparing body and mind. Sun Tzu wrote in *The Art of War* that the victors of any battle win first and then go to war, while the defeated go to war first and then seek to win. This lesson has held true over time, as the outcome of any contest is generally determined well in advance as a reflection of the superior planning of the eventual winner. When the time for the competition arrives, the time for plans is past—now it's time to perform.

Performing at a higher level means execution of the success you've visualized for yourself. It can also mean building up your standards of success through competition, either with others or against yourself. Of course, you can't win them all, and there are always opportunities to improve. That's why learning, both through competition and as an ongoing personal habit, is so valuable.

Learning involves an honest evaluation of performance and an optimistic outlook. After all, learning is just the first step in planning for the next time. You make your plans, perform your best, learn what you can, and set plans again. Growth from any challenge depends not only on what is learned from the experience, but on how you go about gathering new knowledge in order to improve in your future efforts. Life just keeps presenting new challenges for us, whether it's in sports, career, academics, or anything else.

This cycle of achievement can be represented visually as a training course, not unlike one commonly used by a novice sailor to practice boat handling. The drill is simple, consisting of laps around a course of three buoys, allowing him to practice steering and sail trim through each leg of the course. It may be an awkward process at first to go through the whole circuit, but with every lap the sailor completes, he performs better and better. Such is the cycle of achievement off the water. Imagine that each leg of the course represents one of the three achievement principles of planning, performing, and learning, in that order. Each leg leads into the next, in a cycle that repeats, and is completed each time more proficiently. Your planning dictates your performance, which in turn will provide opportunities for learning, which will influence your methods of planning for the next contest. The more you go through this cycle, the smoother your "sailing" will become, and the higher your ultimate achievement will be.

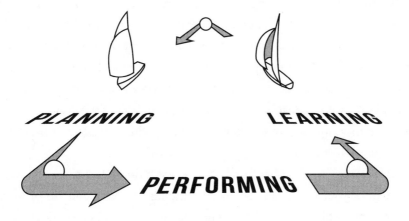

PART TWO

PLANNING

I'm a great believer in luck.
The harder I work, the more of it I seem to have.

—Attributed to Coleman Cox

The planning that goes into any endeavor is a significant measure of its outcome. This process includes the aspects of mental preparation as well as physical preparation for action. Throughout any challenging effort, there will be turning points at which the deciding factor between the correct course of action and the incorrect one is derived from efforts made in the planning process, usually long beforehand. Sailing is a sport that rewards thorough planning and preparation. Watching *Stars & Stripes* continue its domination of *Kookaburra III* in the last race of the 1987 America's Cup final, Star World Champion and Cup contender Tom Blackaller commented to Walter Cronkite, "This race was actually won by *Stars & Stripes* about two years ago." The benefits of thorough preparation are neither new nor unique to sailors alone; just as Sun Tzu wrote centuries ago that every battle is won before it is ever fought, the worlds of business, sports, politics, and other professional pursuits have showcased planning's value by rewarding those who dedicate themselves to it.

Preparation before taking action includes gathering and managing resources, which can pertain to finances, materials, or a support group of talented people. Training for action is another crucial element of this process. This means not only devoting time and effort to practice, but getting the most out of that practice time. Before and throughout this planning process however, is the foundation of intellectual preparation: goal setting, visualization, and developing a winning attitude. When each of these planning elements are brought together, the battle is nearly won, dependent only upon the plan's successful execution as plotted out from the beginning. Planning is built on the lessons of the past as much as on the dreams of the future; when lessons learned can be incorporated into the planning process for each successive endeavor, the cycle of achievement gains momentum and each success builds upon the next one.

MIND MATTERS

The mind is everything. What you think, you become.

—BUDDHA

EVERY GREAT ACHIEVEMENT BEGINS IN THE MIND. It's within our own minds that brilliant ideas are hatched and plans for success are made. The mind's power for generating great success comes not only from its role as the inspiration for a master plan, but also as the guiding force for the plan's implementation. In short, when you can see your own success in your mind's eye, you reinforce its chance of becoming a reality. The ever-imaginative Walt Disney could speak from experience when he said, "If you can dream it, you can do it."

DARE TO DREAM

The Jules Verne Trophy, inspired by Verne's story *Around the World in Eighty Days*, is a prize awarded to challengers who sail a boat nonstop around the globe in eighty days or less, starting and finishing in England. The challengers are unrestricted in the design of the boat or the size of the crew, and the winners of the award hold it until their record is beaten by a new challenger. To sail completely around the world in under eighty days sounded ridiculous at first … until Bruno Peyron of France actually did it in 79 days, 6 hours, 15 minutes, and 56 seconds! Since then, the record has been bettered multiple times, and twice by Peyron himself. In 2005, eleven years after setting his original record, Peyron set a stunning new record of 50 days, 16 hours, 20 minutes, and 4 seconds. What had seemed impossible at first quickly became not only possible, but nowhere near good enough. The record has subsequently been cut to less than 46 days, and will likely be shaved down further. With time, patience, resources, and planning, even the "impossible" can be achieved.

The great success stories that we know and cherish are those of the people who dared to dream beyond their perceived boundaries. There's a great deal of courage required to actually pursue the lofty dreams we may have, but time has shown over and over that "impossible" is often more opinion than fact. There's an old saw that it is technically impossible for bumblebees to fly, considering the relatively small size of their wings compared to the size of their bodies. The bees of the world must not have gotten the word, because they seem to be flying around without any problem. "Impossible" has been thrown around for human beings over the years, too. It was just a matter of decades between the time that man achieved his "impossible" dream of getting an airplane to fly, and another "impossible" dream of walking on the moon. A medical procedure as complicated as a heart transplant sounded impossible until it was successfully performed. An engineering feat like the Great Pyramid of Giza seems impossible for an age before bulldozers, but remains a testament to looking beyond what *is* in order to embrace what *could be*.

It takes a lot of bravery to look at something that's never been achieved before and set about doing it. Nobody who has ever accomplished anything of the "impossible" realm ever had a guarantee of success. Pioneers of the past have faced the risks of ridicule, financial ruin, and even loss of life and limb to go after their dreams. The path over the "impossible" hill is rocky and fraught with danger. But without the ability to visualize success, to think outside the bounds of accepted reality, the first step into a new frontier could not even be taken. It takes much more than just imagination and self-confidence to reach astronomical new heights, but belief that the impossible is possible is the foundation of revolutionary goals. You must *believe* if you want to *achieve*.

The mind is a powerful tool in getting over the "impossible" hill. It takes an absolute belief in yourself and tremendous determination to do something that you've been told can't be done. Part of the process is *seeing yourself* doing it, and accepting the possibility of the accomplishment. Walking across red-hot coals without injury or breaking bricks with a single punch doesn't sound plausible, but there have been people of incredible mental and physical discipline who have actually done it through mental mastery.

Self-doubt can crush your chances of breaking any records, but when you're both physically *and* mentally up to the challenge, "impossible" barriers begin to crumble. Arnold Schwarzenegger recalled in his memoir *Arnold: The Education of a Bodybuilder*: "I talked to weight lifting champions and they told me the same thing: it's in the mind ... If they have lifted it mentally, they will undoubtedly lift it physically. There's no two ways about it, because they've done all the training, their bodies are ready; now it's only in the mind ... For years, weight lifters could not lift more than 500 pounds. Nobody could. They did 499 ½ but never 500 ... They stood in front of the weight thinking, 'No one has ever lifted 500 pounds. Why should I be the one?' Then in 1970 [Vasily Alekseyev] of Russia lifted 501 pounds. He broke the barrier. A month after that, three or four guys lifted 500 pounds. Why? They believed it was possible."

One famous stunt that made other feats sound safe by comparison was Philippe Petit's high-wire act between the twin towers of the World Trade Center in 1974. Petit was so fascinated with the towers, which were yet to be built when he first read about them, that he took it upon himself to set up a wire between their roofs and walk the wire 1,360 feet above the street. Petit spent years preparing for this stunt, particularly because he had never walked a high-wire before. The first time he visited the towers to scout the location, he gazed up from the street and took in their immense size, thinking what an impossible task this would be, but determined to go for it anyway. When the towers had been completed and his day had come, Petit didn't simply walk the wire, but went back and forth several times, dancing, lounging, and frolicking on the wire for forty-five minutes! Since he had no permission to perform this stunt, the authorities detained him after he returned to the roof. Luckily for him, his performance generated such goodwill among the public that all charges against him were dropped.

Years later, as he recalled taking those first steps onto the wire, Petit reflected on the thrill that struck him as he embarked, "Whenever other worlds invite us, whenever we are balancing on the boundaries of our limited human condition, that's where life starts." For Petit, his high-wire act was a profound personal achievement not simply for its novelty, but for its destruction of the "impossible" barrier. He undertook an original and seemingly impossible challenge that required him to immerse himself in its preparation with the ultimate commitment and zeal, and succeeded not only to survive the experience, but to find a new appreciation for the potential that we have to accomplish incredible things.

FIND THE RIGHT FIT

One of the great things about sailing is that there is something for everyone. There are boats for kids, adrenaline junkies, casual cruisers, tall people, short people, light people, heavy people, the big and brawny, the quick and agile, and even the handicapped. Each boat has a design that will appeal to certain personal styles: some are for those who love technical development, some for those who love a tough physical challenge, and some for those who want a close, tactical race. Fleets have their own personalities that attract different people, too. Some fleets consist mainly of serious, solitary competitors, while others are much more social and easygoing. It's this kind of versatility in the sport that can make it appealing for anyone, at any age, of any shape or size, who can make their way to a body of water. When getting into the game, whether for the first time ever or just to try sailing in a new fleet, sailors must decide what setting is most suitable for them.

As Socrates wisely and concisely advised, "Know thyself." It takes an honest look at oneself to really be able to choose the direction that's most suitable to one's nature and abilities. We must ask ourselves who we are, where we want to go, and whether one direction or another will bring us ultimate satisfaction according to our personal priorities. A sailor, for instance, will need to ask questions like:

- *What kind of sailor do I want to be?* (i.e., cruiser, club racer, international competitor)
- *What kind of sailing would I enjoy?* (ocean racing, fleet racing, match racing, team racing, all of the above)
- *What kind of boat fits my lifestyle?* (affordability, storage capacity, maintenance needed, etc.)
- *What characteristics of a particular boat matter to me?* (the athleticism of windsurfing, the speed of a catamaran, the maneuverability of a dinghy, the stability of a keelboat, etc.)
- *What kind of people do I enjoy being around?* (a serious crowd, party people, younger people, older people, a mix)

- *What are my priorities and where can I be flexible?* (e.g., Do I need to stay close to home, or am I free to travel? Do I need a boat that will be good for the whole family, or just for me?)
- *Do I realistically have the potential to thrive in this particular fleet? What would I need to change?*

Such questions draw out the personal traits of the person asking them in order to help them find the niche that will make them happiest. This isn't to say that anyone needs to pigeonhole themselves into one particular area of expertise. While many sailors graduate from little dinghies into progressively larger, faster, and more technical boats over the years, they are often content to bounce around and compete in a wide variety of classes; the skipper of an oceangoing sled can always return to sailing the little eight-foot dinghy that he first learned in if it suits him. These questions are rather to help point a person in a new direction when a new course of action is called for.

Self-analysis of this kind can be of use to people looking for a new direction in any number of fields. Similar questions to those above can be of value to those in search of a new career, for example:

- *What industry do I want to work in?* (consumer products, technology, entertainment, etc.)
- *What kind of position suits me?* (finance, legal, marketing, etc.)
- *What kind of position fits my lifestyle?* (hours required, work attire, length of commute, etc.)
- *What characteristics of a company matter to me?* (large corporation or small start-up?)
- *What kind of people do I enjoy being around?* (a casual, creative work environment or a more conservative, professional setting?)
- *What are my priorities and where can I be flexible?* (salary, promotion potential, benefits, title, corner office, relocation assistance, etc.)
- *Do I realistically have the potential to thrive in this particular position? What would I need to change?* (Do my interests, experience, and education match? Do I need more school or training?)

Besides athletic and professional pursuits, self-analysis questions can help with personal and social growth. Whether you want to be a better employee, student, athlete, or spouse, you'll need to know what your positives and negatives are, what kind of lifestyle you enjoy, how much you're able to commit of your time and energy, and where you can see yourself down the line. Knowing who you are and what you want might not be obvious at first. Some have a good sense of direction early in life and others spend years working it out. Often, it takes a number of ventures into new territory in order to find a good fit. It's common for a person looking for their niche to get there by process of elimination, finding along the way what doesn't work for them. It's not necessarily failure to take a new road when your current efforts aren't working out. Thomas Edison had a long journey toward the completion of a working lightbulb, but he maintained an optimistic outlook, remarking, "I have not failed. I've just found 10,000 ways that won't work."

FOLLOW YOUR DESIRES

To succeed in sailing, as in anything in life, it takes a deep and genuine desire to achieve your goals. The desire to win is the fuel that keeps the fire in your belly burning when the climb to the top begins to feel particularly steep. This is called "staying hungry" in many sports, as in "hungry for victory." The longer or tougher the challenge ahead, the hungrier you will have to be to keep chasing your objective. But, if you've committed yourself to the challenge and the desire to achieve your goal has rooted itself in your heart, then your motivation will be strong enough to withstand the hurdles along the way.

Training to sail in the Olympics is a long and arduous journey today. As the bar continues to rise in international sailing competition, just qualifying for the Olympics is a quest that can demand years of sustained effort. A sailor looking to qualify for her country's one and only berth in her sailing event must be prepared to match and exceed the efforts of her fellow countrymen seeking the same spot. This could be a four-year stretch of campaigning, or it could be more. It will definitely entail an enormous amount of travel. There will be equipment to develop, acquire, maintain, repair, and replace over time. There will be times of training when she doesn't feel like it and times on the road when she'd do anything to get back to her own bed. There is pressure, frustration, and exhaustion to cope with time and again on the campaign trail, and this is all just to be given the opportunity to race for a medal. If not for the burning desire in the sailors' hearts to get to that Olympic podium, no campaign would even last up to the trials.

Desire is made up of love and energy. There are many people who love something but lack the energy to pursue it themselves—these people make enthusiastic spectators and supporters. Others have energy to burn and leap into the fray, only to drop out down the line because they lack the love of the game that it takes to sustain them through the tough times. With both love of what they do and energy to do it better, winners in any field can attribute their success to their own desire.

Bill Clinton was politically inclined as a youth, holding student offices and volunteering for various political campaigns. A highlight of his boyhood that gave his love of politics an even greater boost was the opportunity to meet John F. Kennedy at the White House. Clinton not only had a love of politics, but boundless energy as well. Always chasing another problem to solve, Clinton often would conclude his response to each of his staffers' laundry lists of problems to solve with the question, "What else?" Bill Clinton's desire to succeed in politics not only made him the youngest Governor in the US when he won the governorship of Arkansas at the age of thirty-two, but it later helped him to become president of the United States as well.

When you are planning to take on a difficult challenge in your own field, ask yourself:

Do I really love what I'm doing?

Have I got the energy to sustain the kind of effort needed to win?

If you can honestly say "yes" to these questions, you've got the desire that it will take to win. It won't always be easy, of course, but what you've got going for you is the foundation of motivation that you'll need when the going gets tough. Some sailors show up on the start line entirely indifferent to winning, and they seldom do. The sailors who have the desire to win have much better odds of crossing the line first. How could a sailor keep concentrating when they're mentally exhausted? How could they continue to hike outboard when their muscles are screaming for relief? How could they keep coming out to the start line when it's cold and damp (and there's hot chocolate and a football game on back at the clubhouse)? The answer: Desire.

If you find that you haven't got the love and energy to give you the necessary desire to win at a particular challenge, don't feel bad … just pursue something else for which you truly do have that desire. You'll save yourself time and frustration if you put your attentions into something that suits your personal pace and that gives you satisfaction. If you have found a mission that you've got the desire to pursue, then it's time to make some goals for success.

SET GOALS

We can dream outside the box, but the process of achieving a dream can be long and sometimes frustrating. To make a dream a reality will take a more realistic, analytic approach in order to plot the course to success. This means reframing the dream as a goal.

SMART GOALS

SMART goals are taught today in all kinds of venues, from sailing schools to business schools. SMART is a helpful mnemonic device to help us remember the five qualities of effective goals: Specific, Measurable, Attainable, Realistic, and Timely. Each of these tenets is a qualifying aspect of a SMART goal. Before embarking on any endeavor that will require significant investment of time, energy, and resources, it's a good move to step back and look at the goal ahead and determine whether it is a SMART goal.

Be Specific

Nonspecific goals are unachievable, because there's no real destination set. You can never be sure if you've reached your goal if you never determined exactly where you were going in the first place.

Nonspecific goals:

"I want to be rich one day."

"I want to be a good sailor."

Specific goals:

"I want to earn a million dollars by the time I'm forty-five."

"I want to win our club championship next year."

These examples, being rich and being a good sailor, are subjective goals. What's "rich"? What's "good"? It depends on whom you ask. If you can narrow your objective to a specific accomplishment, you're on your way to making a workable plan for success.

Make it Measurable

There has to be some quantifiable parameter to make your goal measurable. If your goal is to run faster, what time do you want to set for the specific distance? If your goal is financial, what specific amount are you seeking to attain? If your goal is to succeed as an actor, what's the role you're looking to land? A measurable goal is one in which you can actually chart your progress to see how close you are to reaching it. World record holders for everything from the longest distance swum to the longest beard have numbers to back up their claims.

Keep it Attainable

Is your goal actually attainable under your current circumstances? If you were suddenly told to bake a cake from scratch in three minutes, any reasonable person would know that it just wasn't going to happen. Attainable goals are those that can be reached using the resources that are on hand, or that are available. Considering the time you've got, the skills you have, the tools available, and the limitations facing you, is there a way to get it done? Remember that difficult doesn't mean unattainable. SMART goals are attainable, even if some creativity is needed to get around some of the roadblocks that may stand in the way.

Do a Reality Check

When we've been caught up in a dream we've held for a while, it becomes more important to do a reality check. Reality checks aren't meant to be harsh or crushing; they're an honest way to look at whether a goal truly is a realistic one so we don't frustrate ourselves over the long run by putting our best efforts forward in the wrong direction. Of course, there are risks when starting off in any endeavor, and you may find some long odds ahead of you in your own quest. The real question is, even though there are risks, and the odds may not be in your favor, is your goal still within the bounds of reality? Be sure to answer this question for yourself honestly and objectively before starting off on a long journey.

Set the Timetable

"Someday" isn't a word to be used with SMART goals. Time is sometimes the quantifier itself, but it's also a necessary parameter to motivate us to accomplish what we set out to do. Procrastinators are often heard to say, "There's always tomorrow," but that's the whole problem. Tomorrow's got a tomorrow of its own, and the next thing you know, you've missed tons of golden opportunities to get going and achieve what you want that much sooner. To make your goal timely, set a schedule and make it a reasonable challenge. Know how much time you can commit to the goal, and translate that into how long it is likely to take to accomplish it.

For instance, a traveling sailor could say, "I want this boat driven cross-country in three days." A person starting a weight loss plan could say, "I want to lose ten pounds by the end of May." A business owner could tell his sales team, "Let's reach twenty million dollars in sales by the end of next quarter." An artist could say, "I want to finish this painting by Friday."

The goal itself will help you to grow if you make it a bit of a stretch. Sometimes we set deadlines for ourselves, and sometimes they are thrust upon us, but by rising to the challenge, we come out of it more confident and more accomplished than we went into it. Leave "someday" for things you *might* want, and start after what you *do* want today.

Write it Down

Committing a goal to memory is a good start, but committing it to paper is an effective method of reinforcement. Your goal doesn't have to be announced in the news, or even posted where anyone but you can see it, but it's a helpful mental reminder to see that goal staring back at you from time to time. A common place where people like to post goals is on their bathroom mirror; it's one of the first things they see at the beginning of the day, and one of the last things at the end of the day. There are all kinds of places a motivated person in any profession can put their goals in writing: on their desk, their dashboard, a notebook, or even hidden away in their wallet.

Take a moment to spell out the specifics of your own SMART goal and make sure it is something that is specific, measurable, achievable, realistic, and timely. You can put it into a drawer and look at it when you wish, or keep it out in front of your eyes to motivate you each day. You might even use this technique on your next New Year's resolution, which is something most people tend to decide upon, pursue briefly, and then abandon. If you're shy about anyone else seeing your goal, think of a "code" or symbol that means something to only you that you can post out where you can see it. There's a story of a politician who kept a broom in the corner of his office to remind him of his goal: he wanted his next election to be a clean sweep.

DEVELOP A WINNING MIND-SET

The essence of competition lies within the competitor's mind. Successful competitors are able to think themselves to victory just as the unsuccessful may think themselves into defeat. When a person's self-image is that of competence and success, they become competent and successful. It takes a strong positive mental image to form a foundation for success before any action is taken in a worthy endeavor—a visualization of the contest and its ultimate outcome. In preparing for a successful effort, no competitor can afford to ignore the value of mental preparation and the cultivation of a winning mind-set.

The winning mind provides us with the drive to be a part of the contest and to push ourselves to new levels of success. It is the spark that lights the fire in the competitor's belly as well as the fuel that keeps the fire burning through the ups and downs of the effort. It suppresses despair and injects determination to keep going when things look hopeless. And, it tames the lofty highs of victory to keep winning in perspective and soothes the pain of defeat with mature understanding and hopeful persistence.

Under the strain of competition, a person's inner reserves must be called upon to sustain them through the challenge. Moments of self-doubt may creep up when the going gets tough. A full plate of details to attend to may be a constant series of distractions. When things go wrong, a winner needs to know how to deal with it and keep moving. When things go right, he needs to appreciate how things are going and keep his focus. The development of a winning mind is a journey with no final destination, and one of the key steps along the way is confidence in one's self.

CONFIDENCE

Sailors can often tell who the stars are just by looking around on the dock. Regardless of how one's boat looks, what clothing they're wearing, or what brand of sails they have up, there's a certain air about someone who knows how to win and is planning on doing so. It can be seen in the sailor who makes fewer trips between the boat and locker because he knows exactly what needs to go and what needs to stay. He may be in a hurry, but there is no panic in his tone or his body language. Rather, he projects an energetic enjoyment of the race ahead, which later gives way to straight-faced focus when race time arrives. In short, he knows what he's doing and isn't particularly worried about much.

There's great value in maintaining an air of confidence in any situation. A confident person is noticed sooner in a crowd, is respected more readily by their peers, and is perceived as a winner even before they have been given the opportunity to demonstrate their expertise. Pushed too far, however, an effort to appear confident can instead come off as haughtiness, arrogance, or rudeness. Grandstanding betrays a lack of true confidence, while the general affect of a genuinely confident competitor is one of comfort in their surroundings, respect for those around them, and an air of purpose in the way they carry themselves.

The sailing world includes some very accomplished sailors who are soft-spoken and relatively modest while remaining confident in their abilities. There are also sailors of both greater and lesser ability who have been obnoxious in their cocksure trash-talking and/or self-congratulation. The latter group does itself no favors by carrying around a bad attitude with which to alienate their fellow competitors. We all encounter some characters like these at some point in our lives. People with a tendency to say, "I'm not in this to make friends" will find that they seldom have many. Overly aggressive and destructive attitudes can often betray inner insecurities in a person. The true winner does not have to antagonize or belittle his competitors, nor need he sing his own praises boastfully, because his accomplishments can speak for themselves. A competitor with high self-esteem and great self-confidence who can project it *without* tearing down his competitors and peers will establish himself as a rightful "leader of the pack" in the minds of the field before the race is run.

When you're wading into new surroundings, it's not always easy to carry such confidence off, but time and experience can help you to gain a winner's bearing in due course. That being said, first impressions matter, and you never know who you'll be meeting for the first time when you leave the house in the morning. Even though you may not feel totally confident in an unfamiliar situation, getting into the right frame of mind can help you to make a stronger first impression. Any challenge that scares us will first require getting past our initial anxieties. Public speaking is one of the most nerve-wracking activities that many people recall having had to go through. For those who make a career of performing before crowds, they must do well enough in their early outings to continue to advance in their career (you can only be booed off the stage so many times!). Anyone who spends much time on stage, be they a singer, actor, preacher, comedian, teacher, or motivational speaker, often finds early on the value of the adage, "act as if." That is, act as if you've done this a million times before and love every minute of it. Go ahead and pretend to be comfortable in uncomfortable surroundings, and after playing the part of a confident expert long enough, you may discover one day that you actually are just as much at ease as you've hoped to appear.

VISUALIZATION

Successful execution of an objective can be helped along through visualization. This is the next step after building the belief in the attainability of a goal and the determination of how this goal can be achieved. Visualization, or mental imagery, is the inner focus on the details of the accomplishment. When first starting off in the goal-setting process, it can be a big confidence booster to visualize what the fruits of victory may be—imagining the sight of a big paycheck, the headlines announcing your success, or putting your trophy up on the mantle. When the time for action comes in the planning process, though, it's important to visualize the details of the little steps along the way.

The perfect spinnaker set is a process that takes only seconds, but includes a number of precise movements all working in sync together. The crew must not only know what the final spinnaker set should look like when completed, but where to place their feet, how the halyard should be hoisted, when to trim in the sheet, where the spinnaker pole should be set, and so on. It is helpful for each team member to visualize, step-by-step, the motions of their role in this process being done perfectly, so that the image of precision is so well ingrained in their minds that successful execution feels like a habit before the fact. As new crews train together to improve their boat handling, it is natural that mistakes will be made along the way. Task imagery is a way for the crew to continue to improve their performance by reinforcing their physical tasks with visualization of successful execution beforehand. Visualization also serves as an effective way to reduce performance anxiety and boost motivation by increasing the expectation of a positive outcome. If the crew can see themselves executing the perfect set, their odds of getting it right under pressure get a boost.

Across the board in the world of sports, visualization is critical to performance. Sports that involve projectiles, whether it's a ball, an arrow, a puck, or a bullet, require that the player see where they are shooting and visualize the path. A tennis player doesn't look at the ball as it hits her racquet, but focuses instead on where she wants the ball to land. A golfer needs to visualize the path of his ball before making a crucial putt, visualizing how the slope and texture between his ball and the cup will affect the ball's path. It's more than just focusing on the journey to the target, though; it's imagining just how the club face will hit the golf ball or how the racquet will spin the tennis ball that leads into the actual performance of the task. Seeing oneself succeed at any task can entail detailed mental imagery such as this. The more complex the task ahead of you, the more detailed your visualization beforehand should be. When you can see every aspect of your performance unfolding beautifully in your mind, you are better prepared to execute with precision.

Visualization can be a constructive mental tool in business as well as sports. For an entrepreneur, it takes vision to be able to see what kind of company she wants to build; what its mission and purpose will be, the brand she wishes to build, the business model that will make it successful, the kind of people that will make it run, and the products or services that it will provide. To make any new business a reality, it needs to take form through visualization first. It's through such visualization that the process of bringing the new business to life becomes clear.

Just about anyone can imagine a situation in which their ultimate success can depend on visualization. Here are just a few more examples that illustrate situations in which visualization can be very effective:

Architecture: The architect must know what the purpose of the space will be, what sort of "look" the building will need, structural limitations, budget constraints, etc. Knowing what the parameters of the design process will be, it's up to the architect to visualize options for their client. To be able to "see" the finished product before it goes onto paper is vital and essential in the creative design process. One can imagine the sort of visualization that had to go into the design of the Burj Al Arab hotel in Dubai, which rises above the skyline like a giant sail over the desert.

Home Improvement: Whether you're adding a room, fixing the roof, or repainting a space, you need to know what you want the finished work to look like, and how you will go about each task. This can apply to the process of redecorating as well. Moving furniture is much easier, both mentally and physically, if you've got a good idea ahead of time of how the job is going to be accomplished. After all, nobody wants to move a piano more times than they have to.

Cooking: If you don't have prior experience with a particular recipe, or a picture in your cookbook to go by, preparing a new dish can be a baffling experience! You'll need to be able to imagine what your finished dish should look/smell/feel/taste like ahead of time, or in the end you may find yourself ordering pizza instead.

Retail: Businesses put a great deal of thought into the placement of items in their stores. The flow of foot traffic, the tastes of various consumers, and the sale priority of given items all determine how the layout of a store takes shape. By knowing their customers' needs, preferences, and habits, store owners can visualize the appropriate layout of their shop to move merchandise to better effect.

Fitness Training: Many people set goals of a particular weight or clothing size when getting into shape, but concentrating on the mental image of a fitter version of you in the mirror can make a difference in the training process. Imagining yourself at the end of your training is excellent motivation to hang in there when workouts begin to feel tedious, and helps to bring the fitness "dream" much closer to reality. Visualize the "after" photo of yourself now, and the current "before" version will soon be a distant memory.

The more practice you get with visualization, the more clarity you will be able to apply to each objective. You'll be able to visualize the smallest details of your goal and how its execution will affect your senses, such as the sound and feel of the ball hitting the tennis racquet after the perfect forehand, or the smell and sounds of the ocean just outside the beach house you've been wanting. Bringing the imagery close to reality in your mind can boost your self-confidence and motivate you to bring about its actual fruition. If you struggle to visualize some things, look for inspiration around you in pictures or music, or even try to describe your objective aloud to help yourself along. Visualization has driven people to excellence in everything from making better sales pitches to winning Olympic medals. By taking advantage of the power of mental imagery throughout your efforts, you will be able to give yourself a significant boost in performance.

RESOURCES

I believe when you get in a war, get everything you need and win it.

—Dwight Eisenhower

A critical part of the planning process is the acquisition of all necessary resources. Resources may come in the form of money, information, physical assets, or people. People and organizations often find themselves dealing with limitations when it comes to the amount of resources that can be acquired or managed, so the efficient use of the resources that are acquired is a critical element of success. Competitive environments may create a need (or at least the perception of need) to build up one's coffers in order to maintain an advantage, but this can be a race of negative returns if costs begin to exceed the benefits. Having the best available resources also means maintaining them to keep them working well; neglect can destroy the advantages gained by having better resources, including people as well as materials. By understanding what your most essential needs are, acquiring the resources that meet them, and making the most of their use, you will be able to establish or at least pursue a competitive advantage in your efforts toward your goals.

GATHER AND MANAGE YOUR ASSETS

As you plot your course toward your ultimate objective, you'll need to consider what resources are needed to see you through to the finish. Resources required for most endeavors often involve a financial aspect, but they also often require people, materials, and information. Sailors need a number of resources to perform in a race. The bigger the event, the more complex the organization needs to be. In an America's Cup campaign, hundreds of millions of dollars and years of preparation may be put in, making for a massive logistical challenge. Even for the amateur racing sailor, resources required could include a variety of needs:

People
- Crew and backup crew
- Training partners
- Coaches

Materials
- Boat
- Rigging
- Maintenance equipment
- Trailer
- Sail inventory

Information
- Weather data
- Current and tide charts
- Intel on competitors

Finance
- Travel/Fuel
- Lodging
- Food
- Storage/Slip fees
- Entry fees

These are just a few of the resources that are put under consideration before the race even occurs. Each of these categories can be applied in a variety of other endeavors when considering the resources required. As another example, let's say you're starting a new company that makes backpacks. For your backpack company, just some of the resources needed could include:

People
- Senior management
- Customer service
- Accounting staff
- Marketing staff
- Human resources
- Sales team
- Design team
- Factory managers
- Sewing personnel
- Warehouse staff

Materials
- Building & Facilities
- Computers
- Phones
- Desks and cubicles
- Sewing and cutting machinery
- Packaging materials
- Office supplies
- Forklifts
- Fabrics and lining
- Zippers and fasteners

Information
- Demand for backpacks in your market
- Costs of production
- Pricing of competitors' products
- Expected shifts in the economy
- Hiring regulations
- Distribution channels for your products
- New technology
- Shifts in consumer culture
- Upcoming promotional events
- Competitors' branding strategies

Finance
- Employee salaries
- Sales-team travel budget
- Marketing campaign costs
- Rent on property
- Taxes
- Shipping/Postage
- Utilities
- Legal fees
- Raw material inventory
- Production

Take a look at your goal and consider all of the resources that you'll need to achieve it. The bigger the challenge, the longer the list is likely to be; so this is a list to start writing out and keep adding things to as you think of them over time. There are some key questions to ask:

What resources do you already have?
What do you still need?
What substitutes would be acceptable?
How are you going to get what you need?

Take Inventory

Before starting off on any significant challenge, it's often natural to assume that you're starting with nothing. Chances are that you've got something going for you at the starting point. It could be just about anything helpful:

- *People* (Friends, family, or colleagues that can offer advice or assistance)
- *Materials* (A pen and paper to write that novel, shoes to train for that marathon, or just knickknacks in the garage to put into that revolutionary new widget)
- *Information* (An Internet connection, a library card, a savvy colleague or mentor in your field)
- *Finance* (Savings, donations from supporters, a scholarship, a grant, or a bank loan)

Every racing sailor is challenged at some point not only on the basis of their sailing ability, but also their ability to coordinate the necessary resources for competition. They may need to recruit a whole new crew, create a new system of rigging to keep maneuvers running smoothly, develop a network of information sources, or set up a nonprofit fundraising account to make their campaign come together. Start getting your resources organized with a list of what you've already got going for you; you'll be able to put these things to good use in time. Your next task is to determine what still is needed.

Make Your Wish List

You're not just wishing for things, you're creating more of a shopping list of what you must have to reach your goal. This list fills in the gaps of what you can foresee as necessities for success. You might not immediately think of particular resources you'll need, so be prepared to return to your list and revise as you go along. You might also be completely surprised later on by things you hadn't thought of, but will be necessary nonetheless.

To help reduce the likelihood of unplanned-for expenses or other unpleasant surprises, get out in front of the ball and ask for advice from someone who's been there before. If you haven't had the opportunity to talk to someone in person for suggestions, you might be able to read about someone who's had success in your field. However, even with valuable research or advice, put your imagination to work and consider a couple of what-if scenarios so you can find yourself prepared, even for far-fetched possibilities.

CONSIDER ALTERNATIVES

Some items on your list will be *essential*, and some will be *preferred*. It's common for people to confuse what they want with what they need. Knowing the difference will help you prioritize where to put your energy first, and point out what things you can come back to down the line. Think about what you can do as a Plan B if you bump into any roadblocks. Sailors often need to come up with substitute plans for events in order to make do with their resources on hand. If a hotel at a regatta looks like it's going to be too expensive, they might stay on a friend's couch (or floor). If they can't get their own boat to a faraway regatta, they may be able to charter a boat from the local fleet. Many a sailor's locker or toolbox is full of spare parts, bits and pieces, and odds and ends, just in case they need to improvise a repair at a moment's notice. These aren't ideal solutions, of course, but such alternatives keep the wheels from coming off the whole plan when resources get tight.

Small businesses just getting their start may refer to this initial squeeze as "bootstrapping"—making the absolute most of what you've got to build up from the resources already on hand. New companies often face challenges in the start-up phase when capital is hard to come by; but by reinvesting in itself over time and keeping initial costs as low as possible, a new company can expand over time. This is how companies like Apple, Microsoft, and Hewlett Packard grew into major corporations. It's when you've been down this road that you can tell others years later how you "pulled yourself up from your bootstraps."

CONSPIRE TO ACQUIRE

Now you're busy determining what your master plan is going to require for success, but you've still got to plot out how you'll manage to gather all that's still needed. In most cases, you can prioritize what needs to be acquired first in order to keep things running smoothly logistically, and create a timeline for all of your resources. Let's use an example of a sailor who has just moved to a new town and wants to get started racing small boats in the local fleet. He'll need a boat, sails, equipment, facilities, and clothing just to get started. He can prioritize his plan of acquisition for these resources as follows:

Facility for storage: The boat has to be kept somewhere, and he'll need to determine exactly where before he rushes out and buys one. Options may be the local marina or yacht club, or if there's space, at home. Keeping the boat at home sacrifices convenience and necessitates a trailer, but it may be cheaper in the long run if it's a possibility. He'll need to know what kind of boat he'll be getting as well, in order to determine his storage needs.

Boat: The boat itself is the next highest priority for his new sailing campaign, and likely the most expensive. When the boat has been purchased, the sailor will know what to purchase next in terms of sails and equipment.

Sails: A sailboat won't get far without sails, and the type of sails used will be a determining factor in what sort of equipment is needed. The deck layout may even need to be changed to accommodate a particular kind of rig setup.

Equipment: This could include a wide range of gear such as hardware, covers, electronics, fittings, or miscellaneous knickknacks that can be determined more easily after sailing the boat a few times and having some time to think through personal sailing preferences.

Clothing: After sailing the boat, the sailor now knows how wet he's likely to get on a typical sailing day, what the weather at his usual sailing venue is, and what kind of physical demands he'll need his sailing clothing to accommodate. If he'll be sailing in a cold or stormy venue, the sooner he gets good clothing, the better. The right clothes can make all the difference on a boat or on land. There's a saying in Norway: "There's no such thing as bad weather, only bad clothing."

This is an illustration of prioritizing the gathering of resources in order to plan the financial and logistical needs of your campaign, whether it's in sailing or any other endeavor. Before the first day of school, a student needs a backpack, then books and supplies to put inside. Before buying cattle, a rancher needs to purchase land, and then build a fence to keep them in. The more complex any project is, the more benefit can be had from plotting out the steps needed in the gathering of resources.

The "Arms Race"

There's an interesting phenomenon that is the same in sailing as it is throughout the world. It is the natural progression of technological advancement and creative experimentation that allows new leaps to be taken in any effort. Ideas are constantly formulated, limits tested, and boundaries broken. There is also a trickle-down effect that takes place when highly financed research and development creates a breakthrough and finds applications over a broader range than originally intended. For example, e-mail gained footing early on as a communication method for the US military in the 1970s, but then evolved into an essential everyday tool for civilians the world over.

Likewise, professional sports equipment tends to be developed by manufacturers for a specific purpose or athlete, and then makes its way into the open market if it proves successful. Therefore, new tools are being developed all the time for all industries the world over, and as the world becomes smaller, advances happen even faster. The result of faster technological advancements and an open global market is an ongoing "arms race" at the corporate and individual levels; a contest, either subtle or overt, to have the best resources available to excel at your field, be it a more powerful computer, more advanced sails, a faster button-making machine, or even a new method of manufacturing that revolutionizes the industry. Whether it's a better idea or gadget, a competitive world has created a need to look for an edge anywhere we can find one over the other guy.

The "arms race" can be an alluring contest within a contest that thrives on the competitor's spirit. While the term derives from the buildup of nuclear weapons during the Cold War, a matter of severe global urgency, the "arms race" referred to here can be as benign as two neighbors looking to outdo one another with lawn art. To sailors, technology that proves successful in a major competition such as the America's Cup or Volvo Ocean Race will tend to be adopted in boats everywhere, and racers often dash to put it to good use in time for their next regatta. It could be a differently shaped mast, high-tech sails, or an expensive new compass, but you can always bet that the top sailors in various classes will jump on the opportunity to try out something new as soon as it comes to market in order to keep an edge.

In the business world, the need to stay on top of new trends is even more urgent. When the Internet came into widespread use in the 1990s, businesses began looking for creative new ways to put websites to good use for their own companies. Commercial websites began as a sort of billboard or electronic brochure for many companies; they tended to show a company's logo, contact information, some eye-catching graphics, and some brief informational bits. Within ten years of their introduction into mainstream commerce, websites for many companies became fully interactive. As technology advances, companies continually find new ways to implement its use in marketing and processing their goods and services. The corporate world has learned to embrace innovation—to lead or at least keep up with new advances—in order to remain competitive in a rapidly changing marketplace.

Innovation drives our evolution in the modern world, so the "arms race" is hard to ignore. As the law of the jungle states, the strongest will survive. Since early man invented tools, people have been on an upward climb to have better resources at hand than those competing for what they want and need. The canny competitor in today's world needs to be on top of their own field by being aware of the "arms race" going on around them.

Gather Information

Keep your eyes and ears open for news in your field wherever you can find it. Read publications in your industry, sport, or area of interest. Watch what your colleagues and competitors are using to keep their edge. Talk to friends and people you trust in the field who are also looking to improve their game. While the most promising new ideas may be kept top secret, you can train yourself to anticipate new trends by educating yourself in your area of interest.

Share Information

When you're intrigued by something new and promising, such as a tool, technology, or idea, test it out for yourself and get someone you know involved.

You'll find that having someone to try a new idea with will help spur some creativity and help you determine on your own whether this hot new innovation has real promise or is turning out to be just a lot of hot air. Sailors often have a tuning partner with whom they can share ideas and test them out. The result of the honest feedback that tuning partners provide is that both parties benefit.

Imitate, Then Innovate

You can join the inventive end of the "arms race" by developing your own take on the latest innovation. Modeling your early efforts on existing standards can help bring you closer to their level, but not surpass it—to get beyond that level, you'll need to start developing your own ideas to gain an advantage. Getting to know a new method or tool so intimately that you understand it inside out will free your mind to develop new concepts based on what you've adopted already. Much scientific advancement in history has been accomplished by standing on the shoulders of giants.

Anthony Fokker, who designed many of Germany's most advanced aircraft in World War I, came to one of his most successful innovations in response to a competitor's design. At the time, aircraft designers were working on plans to create a machine gun that the pilot could fire through the propeller, but no one had yet perfected it. When a French plane was shot down, Fokker was able to study the captured wreck, which inspired his design for a machine gun that synchronized its firing with the rotation of the propeller blades, allowing the bullets to pass between the blades, rather than bounce off of them. This innovation was a leap ahead that started a period of German air superiority during the war which became known as the "Fokker Scourge." Ironically, Fokker's new designs would later be similarly leapfrogged by the French and British. The evolution of design in any area can take this back-and-forth pattern of development, with the bar being raised every so often to create a new standard to be surpassed. There's no need to reinvent the wheel while you're making your way through the ranks. It's often a question of how you can make a *better* wheel that will help you to stand out.

Recognize the Boundaries

The "arms race" can become a desperate struggle for some people, and sometimes all for naught. New innovations don't always turn out to deliver what they initially promise, and some unscrupulous people have gone to great lengths to acquire the latest new thing whether it's actually helpful in the end or not. Don't allow a tough competitive field to drive you to abandon your principles. Look for ways to improve and try to get the best resources available, but never put yourself at risk by going to any unethical or illegal lengths to acquire them.

MANAGE COMPLEXITY

When setting out on a new endeavor, one of the early decisions to be made in the planning process is how complex the workings of the effort need to be. In most cases, the budget will be a major deciding factor as to how sophisticated an approach to pursue, but it can also be a matter of personal choice. In the world of sailing, different kinds of boats offer varying degrees of simplicity or complexity to the sailor. Some sailors love getting into development classes— the kind of boat in which there is some wiggle room in the rules with which to try out new ideas. Such boats can have a variety of experimental rigging setups that create a virtual "cat's cradle" of lines throughout the cockpit, or perhaps some unusual contraptions that look like they've been borrowed from NASA. Other boats are set up very simply, with only the most essential control lines in place, offering "less to get tangled," as the advocates say. There is a need for some degree of complexity in any endeavor in order to take performance to the next level, but the simplification of complex principles is often what makes improvement to any system truly effective in practice.

Ted Turner focused on a simple approach to his successful America's Cup Defense of 1977, and it worked well for him. While the early favorite, the *Enterprise* team, spend a great deal of time and effort trying new and unconventional ideas with rig tune and sail design, Turner devoted his efforts to crew work and incremental speed gains through traditional methods. "We've been using the tried and tested way to sail," said Turner. "We haven't been relying on computers or new technology to win, just by 'get a good boat, put some good sails on it, put some good crew on it, and then go out and sail the devil out of it.'" This philosophy provided a clean, straightforward approach to a campaign that steadily improved through the trials and not only won the right to defend from previously favored American rivals, but also won the America's Cup handily against the Australian challenger.

Complexity for the sake of improvement can come with some growing pains, as the crew of *USA* discovered in the trials for the 1987 America's Cup in Fremantle, Australia. *USA* sported a radical keel configuration in comparison to the other boats in the fleet. While most other boats had a winged keel and aft rudder, *USA* had a fin keel with a long lead bulb, with a rudder in the bow and a rudder in the stern. This revolutionary concept was implemented to provide maximum lift for the appendages in a straight line and added maneuverability. The drawback was that it made the boat extraordinarily difficult to steer, and skipper Tom Blackaller compared it to flying a helicopter. The boat also had a tendency to make too much leeway sailing upwind in big waves; each time the forward rudder rose out of the water, the wind would push the boat sideways by a few feet. Despite the enormous potential that *USA* showed, and her impressive if inconsistent bursts of speed, the design created too steep a learning curve to allow the crew to get the most out of her. Sometimes, in the quest to reach the next level, it's easy to get mired in complexities that make our efforts too difficult to manage effectively.

Our place in technological development today demands complexity for the sake of progress, as well as simplicity for accessibility. The simplest ideas have been surpassed: the calculator replaced the abacus, the automobile replaced the horse and buggy, and the rifle replaced the spear, for instance. Each of these mechanical developments involved more complex inner workings, but proved more effective in accomplishing what they were designed to do through greater performance potential. The challenge for those who create and use technology is to ease the burdens of such innovations—as their inherent complexity often makes them difficult to understand—through simplifying their use in order to realize their potential. The yacht *USA*'s complexity opened new horizons for performance, but was not simple enough for human operators to use effectively in "field conditions." Driving an automobile would be a baffling and frightening experience if the driver had to manually control every aspect of the engine's functions while navigating through traffic. Luckily, the latest technologies that are introduced into our world and that actually have staying power are those that are simple enough for the end user to learn to use without an advanced engineering degree.

To truly be an expert in one's field, one must actually embrace the complex inner workings of the "machine" in which they operate. An upcoming politician must know how the political system operates in ways that the outsider doesn't. An auto mechanic must know every inner working of an engine in order to find and resolve problems. A business consultant must understand the flow of work processes in an organization in order to help maximize the business's operational efficiency. How much focus to put on those complexities, however, depends on what side of the system you stand: the user craves simplicity, while the innovator accepts complexity as a necessity for progress. Any efficient system that requires a degree of complexity must be made simpler in its execution in order to improve speed of use, reduce errors, and allow a wider pool of users to be able to operate within it. Fast-food restaurants require rapid and accurate response to incoming orders, but consistency in their operating systems allows these businesses to be run mostly by teenagers. Likewise, auto-factory engineers know the multiple steps that go into the construction of a complete automobile; their job is paramount in the planning phase of the factory and in getting any bugs out. For the line workers, however, efficiency is the priority, so their roles are simplified so that they can quickly and accurately perform the specific step that their station requires as the car makes its way down the line. Complexity has its natural place in the development phase of an endeavor, but simplicity of execution must be planned into it as well, or the wheels can come off down the road.

When innovating by developing new systems, whether it is organizing your filing system, managing a sports team, planning for a trade show, or running an organization with hundreds of employees, you will need to be able to take many little components and make them work together smoothly, not unlike a clock. Complexity is to be expected in any efficient system for its ongoing development and upkeep. Its effective execution demands simplification in order to keep it performing to its optimum. GE's former CEO, Jack Welch once said, "For a large organization to be effective, it must be simple." A product or service, no matter how complicated and sophisticated its inner workings, can also benefit from simplification for the user. When Google launched its popular web search engine, many users were pleasantly surprised by the lack of clutter on its web page. Google employs a vast and complicated computer network to provide its service, but for the end user, it is simplicity itself.

By finding the balance between sophistication and simplicity, individuals and enterprises can find success.

Make a To-Do List

When life demands our attention in multiple areas, staying organized can become an uphill battle. Keeping written to-do lists, however, can help to keep us on track. Former Laser World Champion and Olympic Finn sailor Peter Commette uses lists to organize both his sailing and his career off the water. "My mom always kept lists of things to do, and she started me when I was very young," says Commette. "There is a great satisfaction to crossing things off a list as you accomplish a task. As a lawyer, I have to keep many balls in the air at once. If one falls, it can have catastrophic repercussions for my client and my family. Without lists, those balls would be hitting the floor right and left. Since I'm not as smart as my rivals in a courtroom or on the racecourse, keeping lists and being just a little more organized than the next (guy) gives me a leg up I need to be competitive. Sometimes, it appears in trial that I have a great comeback off-the-cuff in response to something someone says, but rarely is the response truly off-the-cuff. Rather, the comeback is a product of hours and hours of more preparation than the other, and I've already anticipated an argument or testimony of the very same substance, so that the reply, if not planned exactly, at least naturally presents itself to me as a by-product of the extra work put in."

The existence of a written list can not only refocus you on the task at hand, but it can be a good motivator as well; not only to complete the objective for the moment and move on to the next, but to consider what else can be added to a new list. It's a natural response to feel a sense of accomplishment as we check off one job after another on our list, and it's also natural not long after everything's crossed off to want to start a brand-new list. Through this cycle, we are not only keeping ourselves organized, but we are holding ourselves responsible and keeping ourselves motivated in the process.

Mind the Little Things

Sailors at the top levels put enormous amounts of effort into preparing their boats and equipment for competition. There is a great deal of reassurance that comes from knowing that you've covered your bases and have done all you possibly can to ensure that your equipment is up to the challenge ahead. Meticulous attention to detail is the hallmark of many successful sailors, as well as many businessmen, doctors, attorneys, musicians, chefs, artists, engineers, and on and on.

Multiple world-champion and America's Cup winner Dennis Conner's philosophy of having no excuse to lose began early in his sailing career as a Star crew. Sailing with one particular skipper, Alan Raffee, taught him the benefits of thoroughness in boat preparation. While other, more experienced sailors spent far less time on boat maintenance and preparation, Raffee, who had not sailed his whole life, seized on every possible opportunity for even a fractional increase in boat speed, removing mere ounces of unnecessary weight and meticulously inspecting the bottom's finish for any flaw. It was this thoroughness and attention to detail that allowed him and Conner to be competitive in the high-caliber Star fleet, and it taught Conner a valuable lesson that would serve him well throughout his sailing career.

Such fastidious nitpicking can seem like overkill, particularly since many measures taken exact a high toll in labor for only an infinitesimal gain in performance. However, there are reasons to be as thorough as possible in the care and preparation of your resources:

You are eliminating potential setbacks. The corporate world has generated a valuable credo: "No Surprises." When you've put in your time and attention to cover your bases, you're less likely to be surprised later by any nasty roadblocks. More often than not, things go wrong because we never imagined such problems occurring. It can therefore take a little extra imagination at times to consider where problems could potentially crop up. Accidents, failures, mishaps and catastrophes are often preceded not by one single error or breakdown, but by a combination of little, easy-to-dismiss problems that snowball into one big problem. For example, a boat may break its mast in a gust of wind due to a chain reaction of rapid equipment failures which trace all the way back to something like one misplaced fitting that caused the backstay line to chafe. To stay ahead of potential setbacks, we need to look beyond the obvious checkpoint items and look for our hidden vulnerabilities, as well. It adds work, but in the end, a little extra attention can go a long way. As the saying goes, a chain is only as strong as its weakest link.

You gain peace of mind. A sailor needs to be able to focus on steering, sail trim, tactics, and so on without worrying whether the halyard is strong enough to keep the mainsail up. If all the equipment has been checked and double-checked, there won't be the distraction of fretting over what could go wrong. When you can check each of the items off your list that need attention, you can focus instead on making things go right.

Two-time Snipe World Champion Augie Diaz has made a habit of meticulous attention to preparing his equipment for a regatta, which not only helps his boat speed, but also his mind-set. "I'm sure I spend too much time getting the boat totally ready and taking care of every detail," says Diaz. "But the reason I do it is because then, when I have done that, when I get to the regatta I feel like I'm very prepared, and therefore I should be able to do very well in the regatta. So it's more of a mental preparation thing, and that's why you'll see me putting in such attention to the details."

You add up advantages. At the highest levels of competition, whether in sports or any other field, the difference in performance between the top competitors is rather small. It is seldom one major factor that separates the leader from the rest of the pack, but an ability to be just a little bit better in a number of areas. As Henry Ford said, "A handful of men have become very rich by paying attention to details that most others ignored." By cutting down on factors that hold you back and looking for any possible gains in areas that give you a boost, you'll start to whittle out a lead over the competition.

Another captain of industry known for his attention to detail was John D. Rockefeller, the father of Standard Oil. Although a generous philanthropist, Rockefeller was notoriously frugal by nature and put great effort into reducing costs in his business wherever possible. He regularly inspected his plants while carrying a notebook, jotting down ideas as he went for ways to perfect the plant's operations. Once at a New York plant, Rockefeller noticed a machine affixing caps to the top of oilcans, and he suggested reducing the number of drops of solder on each can from forty to thirty-eight. After finding that some cans leaked with thirty-eight drops, they tried thirty-nine drops instead. When no cans leaked at thirty-nine drops, thirty-nine became the standard number of drops of solder applied to cans at each Standard Oil refinery. Years later, Rockefeller reflected that in the first year, a reduction of a single drop of solder per can saved twenty-five hundred dollars, but in the years that followed, the savings to his company amounted to many hundreds of thousands of dollars as his export business expanded.

This is just one of the many ways that Rockefeller cut costs to plug a profit leak. Just as any sailor strives to eliminate leaks of water coming into his boat, a businessman strives to eliminate leaks of profit leaving his company. As Rockefeller proved by becoming the richest person in the world, every little bit helps.

MAKE THE MOST OF YOUR EFFORTS

The most detail-oriented, "no stone unturned" approach can be costly in terms of time and resources, so it's important to understand the value of allocating one's efforts to minding those details. There comes a time when attention to the overall mission must take priority over picayune or nonessential matters. To make the best use of our time, we need to know when to stop working on *everything* and work instead on the *right* things.

To be able to filter out the issues which need our attention from unimportant matters, we need to see early on what our priority is, what the foundation of our approach will be, and where our limitations are; that is, *what* we're doing, *how* we do it, and *how much* we can put into it. If the objective is well-defined, then it's relatively simple to come back to it as a baseline for our work by asking, *"Is what I'm doing relevant and important to my goal?"*

From the very start, it's also important to understand what the foundation of our approach to our efforts will be. The more complicated the endeavor, the more difficult it will be to make a major course change. We need to set off in the right direction early on, or we can find ourselves struggling to manage changes down the line. To make sure we're still on the right course, we can periodically ask ourselves, *"Is what I'm working on consistent with my approach to the project?"*

We also need to see what parameters we're working within in terms of time and resources, so we need to ask, *"Will the benefit of what I'm doing be greater or less than the cost?"* Nobody wants to waste time and money on work that won't matter in the end. While we can't always be sure if added work on a particular project will ultimately pay off, we owe it to ourselves to at least consider its value ahead of time.

Team New Zealand's successful America's Cup challenge of 1995 was a superbly executed program that existed on a relatively modest budget. In previous efforts, Team New Zealand had spent time and money trying radical innovations to gain an edge, but for 1995, they decided to focus on making all-around improvements to a more conventional design. In contrast, some other teams were trying radical concepts in computer tests for months on end. Due to the relatively short duration of the campaign, the design team had to get the concept of the boat right at an early stage, or the last months of development would be spent striving for major leaps in performance where only minor improvements would be possible.

The result of Team New Zealand's approach was the creation of the two near-identical *Black Magic* yachts. Having Doug Peterson, designer of the previous Cup winner *America³*, on the design team was a boon. The *Black Magic* yachts were a refinement of *America³*: a stiffer mast, slightly less flared topsides, and a narrower rudder were among the subtle improvements to the foundation on which the yachts' designers were working. Instead of devoting time to learning new concepts from ground zero, as New Zealand had with its previous tandem keel challenger NZL-20, the Kiwis were able to focus on perfecting what they already knew was working, as well as to avoid being sidelined by protests over any controversial innovations as they had in the past. Any America's Cup campaign has a tremendous amount of moving parts to it, but the Kiwis were able to find success by determining the foundation of their approach to the campaign early, avoiding distraction, and focusing on constant improvement to the platform they had established. This approach not only spared time and resources, but allowed Team New Zealand to keep its focus on the racing throughout the trials and the Cup match.

It's important to be diligent in your work and to be attentive to detail, but don't let that attention be misdirected to the point of losing sight of your project's priorities. Manage your timeline to allow adequate attention to detail, and if the time crunch is truly tight, prioritize the details into the most and least important ones to attend to. Attack the most important issues first and work your way to the more trivial ones. Prioritizing the load is particularly important, not only when time is tight, but when there are many items to address. When there is so much to do and so little time to do it, take a breath, determine what's most important, and start there first.

Take Care of Your Toys

People in all walks of life can have an unfortunate tendency to abuse their resources. They can take a lifetime to learn their lesson as well—the same guy who left his bike out in the rain as a kid may leave his tools out in the rain as an adult, only to get the same rusty result. In the interest of making the most efficient use of your resources in terms of financial investment as well as performance, it's important to take good care of what you have on hand.

Top sailing teams know that there can be an hour of maintenance and upkeep for a racing yacht required for every hour's worth of sailing. It's not just a matter of returning to the dock and fixing things that break; there's a lot to do to keep equipment functioning smoothly. For instance, boats that race in saltwater need to be rinsed well after sailing so the salt won't corrode the fittings. Sails have to be rinsed if they get salty, but stowed dry and rolled properly. If the boat is stored on a trailer, the bunks need to be designed to conform to the shape of the boat and minimize pressure on the hull. Between the preventative maintenance as well as the repairs when something does give, sailors get to know their boats quite well ashore as well as on the water.

Another sport that can relate to the need for constant equipment upkeep is auto racing. The costars of each Indianapolis 500 team are the pit crew— the mechanics who keep their machine running smoothly over a long and grueling race. These cars are built for speed and not necessarily for durability, which is why tire changes are a must in order for the driver to keep racing. Without making the pit stop, the tires can blow out, taking the driver out of the race entirely. Sailors and race-car drivers know that if you want high performance gear, it's going to mean some extra care to keep it functioning smoothly.

Everyone has an asset that needs upkeep. Simply owning a car means regular oil changes, tune-ups, and washes. Owning a house means taking care of it, not just so it's adequate shelter, but so it can be a comfortable, welcoming, and appealing home. It's crucial to have functional plumbing and a roof that doesn't leak, but it's also important to keep the yard looking good and have a fresh coat of paint once in a while. There's value in the house in terms of the comfort of its occupants as well as its value on the real-estate market. Maintenance of any asset doesn't only come down to the use you'll get out of it today, but its value when you decide to sell it later. Whether you're purchasing a used boat, car, or house, you'll have to ask some hard questions about its condition if the asking price is too low.

Taking care of your belongings not only keeps them looking and operating at their best, but maintains their resale value as well. Making a habit of maintenance can be a learning experience that teaches you more about your prized assets. A new boat owner can become an innovator in his class by spending some time familiarizing himself with the workings of his boat below decks. A car owner can learn to distinguish minor problems from major ones by attending an auto maintenance course. A homeowner can take some pride in their house by putting some extra effort into making it a home they can be proud of. It's like our parents told us… take care of your toys and they'll last longer.

CONSIDER THE PROS AND CONS OF FIXER-UPPERS

Most of us encounter a fixer-upper opportunity sooner or later. For a sailor, it can mean a fantastic learning experience and the rewards of a miraculous resurrection of a boat thought beyond recovery. It can also mean endless frustration and an ever-expanding budget to breathe life into a boat that seems bent on retirement. There are usually a number of ways to make a fix-it project that you're passionate about worthwhile, but it's worth giving some consideration to the pros and cons of a fixer-upper before diving right in:

PROS
- Cheap to start
- Learning experience
- Sense of accomplishment when done

CONS
- Can be expensive to finish
- Can be frustrating
- Time—and labor—intensive

In real estate, there may be some appeal in picking up a property for a bargain, fixing it up, and selling it for a profit. Many people that go down this path are overwhelmed halfway through the process, saying, "I had no idea it was going to take this much work and this much money!" Some people just seem to have the right personality for fix-it projects, and others are more easily frustrated by the demands these projects tend to impose. This applies much the same to one's own home-improvement projects as it does to an investment property; it's easy to fall in love with the mental image of a new kitchen, but the magic of the process begins to fade quickly if construction drags on or costs expand.

Investors seeking to flip a fixer-upper may find some difficult tasks ahead to revitalize their asset: they may find themselves thrust into the roles of landscaper, plumber, painter, mason, and carpenter, or shelling out the funds to hire such experts. However, the process of going through such an upgrade can serve the investor well over the long run by giving them an eye for detail, familiarizing them with the improvement process, and broadening their perspective for future such investments.

Fix-it projects can present headaches along the way, and sometimes the house, business, car, boat, or whatever you're working on is too far gone to make the investment of your time and money worthwhile. Before leaping forward into a fix-it project, consider how much time, money, and patience you've got to put into it. Even though you stand to reap rewards at the conclusion of your fix-it project, remember that you are bound to be inheriting some problems with the bargain that you've found. You'll need to be able to identify these problems and consider ways to address them before moving ahead. The most earnest efforts can be excellent learning opportunities that can pay off down the road through the experience gained. If you're the type that enjoys the journey, don't rule out a fixer-upper opportunity. If you're the type that is more concerned with the destination (that is, fast results), consider going for the purchase that is in the best condition that you can afford.

Control Excess

Sailors at the top levels of racing tend to become obsessive about trimming the fat, literally and figuratively. Weight is a critical factor in sailing, and can be favorable when it goes hand in hand with strength. When weight is not functional, however, it has to be cast off to help improve performance. In reference to the sailors themselves, there are some boats with large, powerful rigs such as the Star class, in which a big, strong crew is needed to help keep the boat flat and to manage the large sails. In smaller boats such as the International Moth, a one-person skiff that skims above the water due to the lift provided by its winged appendages, the skipper must be light, but still strong and agile enough to handle the boat. Some one-design classes have introduced maximum crew weights into their rules, while others have minimum crew weights. The difference lies in the nature of the boat, and whether it is more desirable to be big or small when racing. Sailors in very competitive fleets must often try to achieve a high strength/weight ratio, particularly in smaller boats.

The boat itself also needs a high strength/weight ratio for competition, and class rules regulate the minimum weight and the structural requirements of most boats. Scientific advancements and innovative developments have changed the materials used in the construction of many racing classes over the years. Heavy cotton sails have been replaced by Dacron or Mylar in many small boats, and Kevlar has given way to carbon fiber in some of the bigger boats' sails. Most boats were built of wood up until the 1960s, and now most one-design sailboats are made of fiberglass. Race boats continue to get stronger and lighter by design, but they need to be kept at the minimum allowable weight for racing without sacrificing strength where it's needed. Once the hull, spars, and fittings are weighed in to the minimum, all unnecessary weight must go. This leads to some unusual steps being taken. Many crew members on yachts in the Volvo Ocean Race have had to sacrifice some pretty standard creature comforts in the interest of weight savings. For example, you'll find no door or walls around the head (toilet) on one of these racing thoroughbreds.

It's not just in sailing where lightening your load can pay off, though. Travel by any means can often present a bit of a challenge as to what to pack. The objective for the efficient traveler is to bring what you need and use what you bring. The "road warriors" with the most travel experience tend to know just how to pack their bags with only the vital essentials, so they don't get slowed down by unnecessarily large and heavy luggage. When a sailor needs to fly to a regatta, there are a number of resources he may want to bring besides his clothing, such as tools or other equipment. He needs to consider, however, what can realistically be brought on a plane and what items he can do without or obtain on-site when he arrives. Many of us can remember a time that we brought way too much luggage on a trip and wound up with extra airline fees and a sore back to show for it. Everyone wants to be prepared, but nobody wants to drag around more gear than they have to.

Racing sailboats are something like start-up companies, in that the fastest movers are designed to be lean and mean. Entrepreneurs often need to wrestle with the problem of managing resources and eliminating excess spending. When a small business is just getting off the ground and doesn't have sufficient cash flow to support expansion yet, measures are often needed to keep costs down. All too often, layoffs are needed to keep a struggling new company in the black when it has overstaffed its operations. As hard as it is to manage large amounts of work with fewer hands, overstaffing can actually make growing pains worse for a new company. Even after going through the difficult and morale-killing process of cutting back on staff, some of the costs associated with them remain, such as a lease on a larger office space. When putting together any group of people for an organized effort, more isn't always better, since overloading can create more confusion and stress on the effort as a whole. Sailors know it's easier to leave that unnecessary gear back at the dock than to toss it overboard once you're underway. Like a racing yacht, an organization that needs to be quick and agile needs to bring aboard only the resources that are absolutely essential and leave out anything extra. Unlike some racing yachts, however, every business definitely should have walls for the restrooms.

PEOPLE

In union, there is strength.

—Aesop

Having great people around you, working together toward a common goal, can truly make a winning effort. Putting together a skilled and dedicated group that can build on each other's strengths will provide a boost to any complex endeavor. With the development of energetic and efficient interaction between individuals, a symphony of coordinated efforts can be made in the midst of chaos. Even those undertaking a solo effort can count on great people for support; mentors and role models as well as supporters such as family, friends, and fans can contribute the energy, motivation, and guidance needed to keep a long and difficult project on track. Working with others isn't always easy, but when great people come together with chemistry, coordination, and conviction, it can create a significant competitive advantage.

BUILD A WINNING TEAM

When preparing for a tough challenge ahead, consider who you want by your side to help you along the way. Sailors place a tremendous value on the ability of a team to function smoothly through adverse conditions. Winning teams in sailing are often remarkably quiet; there are no raised voices, no running around chaotically, and no sarcastic remarks. The movements and communication on board are smooth and even, and everyone is focused on the task at hand. Efficient teams like this are put together based on a few simple principles:

They have a common purpose: Everyone on the team knows what the goals are and share a firm commitment to achieving those goals. Nobody wants their time wasted on a half-hearted effort, so the team members hold each other accountable for each other's performance, always seeking to lift each other up, never to tear each other down.

They balance each other: The best teams are made up of unique individuals with the ability to play to each other's strengths and shore up each other's weaknesses. Sam Walton delegated much of the day-to-day responsibilities of running Walmart to trusted executives, but he stayed involved by reviewing operational statements and traveling to stay up to date on the latest developments in the company. "I've been asked if I was a hands-on manager or an arm's-length type," wrote Walton in his autobiography. "I think really I'm more of a manager by walking and flying around, and in the process I stick my fingers into everything I can to see how it's coming along." With a natural talent for numbers but little organizational skill, Walton focused on the end results and let his associates handle smaller details. "I think my style as an executive has been pretty much dictated by my talents," he said. "I've played to my strengths and relied on others to make up for my weaknesses."

They are compatible: People can be very professional in their conduct, but they still are just people with their own personalities. Sometimes, groups are built of individuals that go together like oil and water. Robert F. Kennedy and Lyndon Johnson never got along, but after President John F. Kennedy's assassination, Johnson asked RFK to stay on as attorney general in order to maintain continuity in the administration. For Robert Kennedy, seeing Johnson take his brother's place as president was particularly painful, and the antagonism between the two men continued. Kennedy left the administration after a year to pursue a Senate seat, and Johnson was perfectly happy to let him go, even supporting his campaign, hoping to gain another Democratic seat in the Senate. It's hard to pinpoint what may be a source of conflict between people at times other than the fact that they just don't seem to like each other. It can be hard to lose someone when they don't want to stay, but in the long run, it may be best to let people go their own way if things aren't quite flowing. This is a common issue in workplaces all over the world, and unfortunately, we haven't found the cure for personality polarity yet.

They know their roles in the big picture: Members of a team need to know what their contribution is, not only so they can have the best possible handle on the detailed minutiae of their task, but to maintain a sense of value and contribution to the group. Each person can derive more satisfaction and motivation from the task at hand when they can see how their actions help to deliver success.

They communicate well: There are different scenarios in sailing or anywhere else in life that call for a new method of communication. A top sailing team that has been together for a while knows what information is important and how to communicate it. It almost sounds like a coded language, consisting of sentence fragments and peculiar terminology, but it's delivered clearly and in an even tone during a race, and it is understood by all on board (even if the outside observer may be completely baffled). It's important to know how to communicate for any environment that you are in. There are times when candor is called for, and other times when tact is a priority. Sometimes you need to be stone-faced, and other times feelings are allowed to come out. One needs to be in touch with the demands of different situations when it comes to communication, because too much can go wrong from simple misunderstandings. Whatever the demands of delivery, strive for clarity wherever possible, and when in doubt, ask if your message has been understood.

They maintain focus: Sailing requires the ability to stay on task for long periods of time, so focus really pays off for the teams that are able to maintain it. The business world can relate to the demands of a constantly changing environment as well. It only takes a short time of taking your eye off the ball for a golden opportunity to be missed, or worse, a threat to materialize. Overnight racers work in shifts, allowing periods of rest so that someone on board is always concentrating on the salient details while someone else gets a chance to "recharge their batteries." A team that can stay mentally fresh over the long run by rotating some recovery time into the effort will be able to avoid burnout better than one that never allows any letup.

They place "we" above "me": You've probably heard the saying, "There is no 'I' in 'team.'" Good teams consist of talented individuals, each contributing their own unique strengths to the collective goal. The most efficient and successful teams are those that have no giant egos popping up to take the credit when things go well or to point fingers when things go sour. The winning team congratulates each other in success and puts their heads together after a loss to consider, "How can we do better next time? What are we missing?"

The team can not only maintain harmony through the ups and downs, but also contribute more productively to the collective good by focusing on raising the performance of the group through cooperation.

LET EVERYONE KNOW THEIR ROLES

The skipper of any sailboat knows that, for each job on a boat, certain skills are particularly valuable. Racing crews often include sailors of a variety of builds and sizes, as their particular tasks may best suit their physique. A position on a crew can also depend on one's experience more than their physical characteristics, such as the job of tactician or navigator. Assembling a top-notch sailing crew is in essence the delegation of responsibility to individuals best suited to perform in their chosen roles.

There is a wide variety of racing sailboats in competition today. One-design classes, such as those seen in the Olympics, are good examples of boats in which the selection of the appropriate crew member can make a big difference in performance. The Star, which was sailed in the Olympics for decades, is a powered-up keelboat with a crew of two. Both sailors need fast hands, sharp instincts, and plenty of strength, but the forward crew is generally much burlier in physique than the skipper, as his job is to hike outboard to keep the boat flat upwind. When you see two Star sailors standing together, one of relatively average height and build and the other more resembling an NFL linebacker, it's a fair assumption that the former is likely the skipper. In the 470, however, both sailors need to be very light, since the boat is much smaller and doesn't need as much brawn to keep it under control. The crew on a 470 spends most of the time hanging on the trapeze to keep the boat flat, and this added leverage benefits a tall, lightweight sailor in the position. The skipper, on the other hand, must be flexible and quick as well as lightweight. Since different boats sail differently and entail different jobs, sailors must be able to see what boats suit their abilities and attributes, or how they may train themselves to suit the boat they're in.

Building a solid team means having the right people in the right place, either in sailing or in other areas. For example:

Football: The quarterback needs sharp eyes and a good throwing arm. A defensive lineman needs plenty of overall strength for blocking and tackling.

To switch two of these players into the other's position usually wouldn't be very beneficial to the team.

Business: The advertising department needs creative people. The accounting department needs organized, analytical people. The employees in either department were hired because their education, experience, and personality best suited them for the position. Imagine the potential disasters in a creative approach to accounting, or how different an ad that an accountant had put together might look, and you can appreciate having the right people in the right place.

Acting: Even more challenging than casting the face in a movie role is casting a team. While casting *Star Wars*, George Lucas put a special emphasis on the chemistry between the three main heroes, Luke, Han, and Leia. Many talented actors came forward to audition for these roles, but the ones who came to appear on the silver screen were the ones who seemed to click best as a group. Who knows how differently the film may have turned out if John Travolta, Kurt Russell, or Jodie Foster had been part of the trio?

ARTISTS AND SCIENTISTS

We all know people from various walks of life with a tendency to seem either more creative or more analytical. In most cases, people are naturally one or the other and will pursue careers and interests that cater to these characteristics. While we can find ways to put either our creative or analytical skills to good use, there is great value in building a balance between the "artist" and the "scientist," either within ourselves or within our team, to find the best chance for success.

Sailing is a sport that is derived from both art and science. It has a long history of nautical traditions, from the celestial navigation of the ancient Polynesians to the Dutch shipbuilding methods of the seventeenth century. It is also steeped in science and technology, its principles being derived from aeronautics, meteorology, oceanography, geometry, and physics. Each individual sailor has a propensity toward either artistic or scientific methods in their approach to the sport. There are the "seat-of-the-pants" sailors that develop boat speed through the look of the sail shapes and the feel of the helm, and the technical wizards that pursue more of a scientific method approach, quantifying each gain through controls and variables.

Tom Blackaller seemed to take a more artistic approach, once remarking, "I think that sailing is very much seventy percent art and only thirty percent science ... it's much more an art than it is a science ... and I think that every time the scientists get into it, the vagaries of the wind and the waves and the currents foul them all up." The 1992 America's Cup winner, Bill Koch, placed a high value on technological development but still recognized the value of balancing the two approaches. "Technology has become increasingly important in formerly low- and non-technology sectors such as sailing," he wrote. "Since boatspeed is a science and sailing is an art, to win we needed to combine the art and the science." Koch appreciates a balance of both art and science in his own life: he earned a doctorate in chemical engineering and went into business, but also became an avid art collector. As success in sailing requires proficiency in both the artistic and scientific aspects of the sport, sailors with a tendency to favor one approach can find balance by developing their "other" side, or teaming up with people who take the other approach naturally. Applying this principle is also beneficial off the water.

A little bit of introspection can help you to determine whether you'd consider yourself more of an "artist" or a "scientist." Do you feel more comfortable making a decision on instinct (artist) or on quantified results (scientist)? Do you have an easier time visualizing images (artist) or processing numbers (scientist)? Do you tend to say how you "feel" about something (artist), or what you "think" about something (scientist)? This is another way to look at the traditional view of seeing someone as being more highly developed on the right (instinctive) side or left (analytical) side of the brain. By knowing whether you are principally one or the other, you gain some insight as to what your natural strengths are. Depending on your natural proficiency and the task you're undertaking, you will know whether you need to develop the "other" side, or perhaps seek assistance from someone with the skills you'll need for your effort.

For example, an "artist" with an affinity for cooking may decide to open up her own restaurant. She has infinite creativity, an instinct for how to bring ideas to reality in every dish, a passion for the work she does, and a close relationship with her customers. To open up her restaurant, however, she will need an understanding of business matters: obtaining a license, securing the right facilities, hiring and managing employees, keeping records of inventory and finances, understanding business law and liability issues, and so on. She could pursue training through school, literature, or seminars to gain these skills, she could team up with a partner with more business expertise, or she could do both. The success of her restaurant will depend on sound business decisions as well as creative flair and instinctive innovation, so it is to this entrepreneur's advantage to do what she can to bring an "artist" and a "scientist" into the decision making process, even if she needs to act as both.

Leonardo daVinci was the very definition of a Renaissance man, having made lasting contributions to the worlds of art and science. A natural painter since his youth in fifteenth century Italy, daVinci was commissioned by the Duke of Milan to create various paintings and sculptures for the public. It was during this time that daVinci also developed his understanding of science, studying mathematics, aerodynamics, anatomy, architecture, construction, astronomy, mechanics, and even weapon design, among others. The melding of science with his artistic nature gave him a remarkably productive inventive streak, and his schematics for the bicycle, helicopter, and automobile influenced the development of the technology of today. Through the balance of the "artist" and the "scientist" in himself, daVinci was able to not only deliver masterpieces such as the *Mona Lisa* and the *Last Supper*, but designs for mechanical marvels that were four centuries ahead of their time.

There's an "artist" and a "scientist" inside of everyone, and times come when the skills of one will be more beneficial than the other. To overemphasize one at the expense of the other, however, takes away vital perspective that could be called upon at any time. Effective teams often consist of both "artists" and "scientists" to provide a balance of skills being contributed to the mix, even though communication may be more challenging for the different sides at times. To seek to balance the "artist" and "scientist" within oneself broadens horizons, increases understanding, and expands knowledge that will be vital for creativity and problem solving, for sailor and non-sailor alike.

Trust Them to Do Their Jobs

The philosophy, "If you want something done right, you have to do it yourself" can have significant drawbacks for a would-be leader. Even if it is physically possible for one person to take over every task of a team effort, delegation of responsibility makes the team stronger as a whole. It builds morale as people take pride in their job, eases the burden on each member of the team as the workload is balanced, and helps breed creative solutions to problems. A less secure leader may feel the need to try to do everything himself, but the enlightened leader will understand the value of delegating tasks to team members that play to their strengths, and trusting them to use those strengths to carry them out successfully.

The action of a yacht race tends to move so fast that there is no opportunity for a skipper to micromanage every task being performed on the boat. Heavy air conditions put a skipper's trust of the crew to the test. When it's blowing a storm, the crew can barely hear one another or see very much, and the boat takes on the characteristics of a bucking bronco. When the time comes to jibe a boat in a heavy air race, the consequences of a mistake can be much more severe than in less breezy conditions. The boat could be knocked on its side if the steering angle isn't just right coming out of the jibe, the spinnaker could rip, someone or something could wash overboard, the mast could break if the stays aren't secured fast, or any number of other potential horrors. The skipper doesn't have the time or opportunity to tell everyone how to do their jobs in these conditions. To even attempt to do anything other than call the jibe and make the turn of the wheel at the right time would be useless; she must trust the crew to do their jobs in sync to get the boat through the turn and on the new jibe smoothly, because she has no choice if she wishes to stay in the race.

Trust is a key factor in delegating responsibility to others, be it aboard a racing yacht or in a business. Outdoor apparel manufacturer Patagonia espouses a management philosophy that focuses on building harmony in the workplace to increase productivity. Benefits like on-site child care and flexible work hours, even to allow time to go surfing, are just a couple of the reasons for Patagonia employees' loyalty, as well as the company's progressive style of management. While the employees appreciate the trust put in them to pursue their tasks without the burdens of a strictly regimented work environment, Patagonia's management has found that they strive to be worthy of that trust. By giving them room to breathe, the company gives its employees room to perform.

While leaders seek to be involved in the daily operations of their business, they often find themselves walking a line of being available and well-informed, while avoiding micromanaging and stifling the flow of their employees' work process. When the boss has her hands too deeply into every detail, she may find down the line that her employees have lost the initiative that got them their jobs and have started asking the boss what to do for every little task. When this happens, the business becomes unsustainable—unable to function without a single individual at the top giving out directions. As hard as it is sometimes to step back and let people handle a job themselves, they will usually appreciate the trust being given to them and the opportunity to shine in their task and carry it out to the best of their ability. When delegation is carried out successfully, the victory belongs to the entire team as much as to the individuals who performed the task at hand. When asking others to handle an important responsibility, convey what needs to be accomplished, express your faith in them to handle the job, then step back and let them tackle it. As Theodore Roosevelt said, "The best executive is the one who has sense enough to pick good men to do what he wants done, and self-restraint to keep from meddling with them while they do it."

Develop Communication

Communication is, and always has been, one of the most critical aspects of daily living for any intelligent species. The animal kingdom has ways to communicate in very direct terms, and each species has its own methods. A blowfish says "back off" by inflating his body to a round, spiked protuberance sure to intimidate any would-be predator. Whales can communicate across vast expanses of ocean through their song. Bees give directions to their hive mates by dancing. We humans, of course, have spoken language as well as nonverbal, physical cues with which to communicate. The trouble is, even with the tools of intelligence, vocal cords, and expressive features, we still manage to communicate poorly at times.

Misunderstandings occur because we go wrong with either *what* needs to be conveyed, or *how* it's conveyed. In considering what we're trying to get across, we need to consider how much information is enough, and how much is too much. Is the information we're giving relevant to the subject we're addressing? We must consider how to get our point across as well: Is our timing appropriate? Do our words, expression, and tone match our meaning? Is detail more important, or brevity? We learn to communicate at the most basic level as infants (cry if something's wrong, smile if all's well). We learn what to say as toddlers, and what *not* to say as adolescence approaches. By the time we reach adulthood, we've begun to master nonverbal communication, employing subtle cues like winks, nods, head tilts, and gestures. And still, we get it wrong sometimes. The more important the situation, the more attention must be given to *what* is being communicated and *how* it's being communicated, so we can have a clue as to how the message will be received. Misunderstandings through written media occur all the time, as a sentence written with intended emphasis on one word ("What are you doing *there*?") can be misinterpreted by the reader by perceiving emphasis on a different word ("What are *you* doing there?"). While the sender in this example may be simply asking why his friend is so far away, the recipient may mistakenly think that the sender means to imply that he doesn't belong there.

Leaders of sailing teams or of any other organization are always faced with the challenge of fostering effective communication. The principles used in streamlining the sharing of information on a racing yacht can apply aptly to any group that needs the ability to make decisions quickly.

Assign Roles

Before embarking on an important endeavor, it's important to determine which team members will be responsible for finding and conveying different kinds of information, as well as how it will be passed along. Teams on larger racing yachts have to have a very efficient method of communicating with each other. On the most advanced racers, some crew members may be equipped with microphones so that they can communicate with the helmsman and tactician from anywhere on the boat, including up on the bow or at the top of the mast. A more traditional method of communicating from a distance on board is the use of hand signals.

Another critical component of communication to be determined before going into action is who will be the ultimate decision maker. There is no room for argument between the higher-ups in the group when a decision needs to be made quickly. Often a recommendation will come to the skipper of a racing yacht that he doesn't follow. Sometimes he's right and sometimes he's wrong, but it's his decision and he's the one who stands by it. When vocal disagreement among the afterguard members breaks out, it's a distraction to the entire team that can lead to a chaotic atmosphere onboard throughout the race. Many a group on and off the water has suffered from having "too many chefs in the kitchen."

Filter Information

Sailing on a racing yacht requires filtering of information to the rest of the crew. When the wind is blowing strong, it becomes harder to hear one another, and for those within earshot, there can't be too many wasted words. It is possible to have too much information: that which isn't immediately relevant and therefore distracts from the essentials. Since trimming and tactical decisions must be made quickly based on information being given, seconds count in conveying the info.

To listen to the crew of a top-notch racing yacht is to hear an exercise in lingual efficiency. A number of crew members can go about their jobs silently, but others are given the job of feeding specific information to the helm from their position. Here's an example of some of the communication that might occur during a race:

Tactician: "Equal height and equal speed on the closest boats right now."

Spotter on Rail: "Set of bad waves coming on the bow in two boat lengths."

Helm: "Let's come down five … give me some power."

Jib Trimmer: "Easing jib."

Main Trimmer: "Dropping traveler."

Spotter on Rail: "Smooth spot just beyond these. Waves in three … two … one."

Tactician: "Good speed through these … up to nine-point-five. The guys on our hip will get it in about ten seconds."

Helm: "Coming back up on the wind."

Jib Trimmer: "Grind."

Grinder: "Coming on."

Main Trimmer: "Traveler back up."

Jib Trimmer: "Hold."

Tactician: "Same speed, more height."

It may sound like everything is in code, but these are the kinds of specific and concise phrases that go back and forth between crew members on a boat. There's not a lot of emotion in the air and no extra chitchat. It's just the facts for now, since there'll be plenty of time for conversation after the race. There are a number of jobs where communication needs to be done in a very specific way. Whether it's driving a truck, flying a jet, or requesting a price check on paper towels, there is a right way and a wrong way to get your point across when you're on the job.

Use Secret Codes Where Needed

In team racing, sailors must call tactical moves to each other in order to maneuver their team into a winning combination. However, simply shouting out plays is just a way to tip off the other team and prompt them to go right into an appropriate defense. There have been some unusual (and often humorous) codes shouted over the water for team racing that had nothing to do with sailing, but they had meaning to the team members for strategic purposes.

Sometimes, communicating with specific parties requires having an established secret code that only those involved will understand. It can be as subtle as a husband catching eyes with his wife across the room at a party and adjusting his tie to say "I love you" (or maybe "I'm ready to go home now"). Carol Burnett was known for giving her ear a tug at the beginning of each show she did to say "hello" to her grandmother. Sometimes, what we want to say can't be blurted out at the time, so we need to cook up another way to convey our meaning.

Codes can be helpful in a business situation as well. If you're going into a negotiation with a colleague on your side, the two of you can stay in sync by agreeing on a keyword or phrase to indicate whether an offer should be higher or lower. If you need an escape plan at a function or meeting, you can assign a particular word or topic as a code for your friend to call you away. Whether it's for strategy or subtlety, a secret code can come in very handy at times, on the water or on land.

Listen to Differing Opinions

It's easy to become set in one's ways when at the helm of a boat or an organization. It can be self-destructive, however, to consistently enforce the "my way or the highway" approach when faced with disagreement. Besides discouraging the other members of the team who have come forward with their own convictions, it can rob the entire group of ideas that may indeed be more successful.

It is important, however, for anyone who wishes to offer dissention, to do so in the proper way. When disagreement is offered too forcefully, a battle of egos can begin that could threaten to deteriorate from constructive idea sharing into bitter argument. When presented as a helpful suggestion, disagreement can be easier to accept. For example, starting with "What do you think about …" or "You've got a point, but I was just thinking …" can convey respect for the other person's opinions, thus making the other side more receptive to your own viewpoint. Just as decision makers need to be open-minded, info providers need to make sure that their recommendations don't turn from fresh ideas into challenges of authority.

Every team leader should encourage new ideas and solutions from their team. It keeps the group sharp and connected to the mission, as well as benefiting performance over the long run. However, it should be understood by the team, and clarified and/or demonstrated by the team leader, how and when to provide ideas.

Keep Spirits Up When the Team Is Feeling Down

Whether you're facing tough times on a boat, at the office, or even at home, there are a few ways to kill morale and keep a dark situation from getting any brighter. Here are some of the ways that discouragement and frustration can manifest to hold us back:

Silence: Sometimes in sailing, when the boat starts falling behind, the team's communication starts to taper off until you hear nothing but whistling wind and the waves against the hull. When the crew starts feeling discouraged and stops actively feeding information, it's up to the skipper to keep them alert by asking questions, and better yet, adding some encouragement: "What's the compass heading here? I'll bet we can make up some ground by playing the shifts on this leg." You may find yourself in a situation where it's up to you to break the stony silence when the mood gets gloomy, so be sure that you're in tune with what the appropriate tone and choice of words will be. Sometimes breaking the silence will help elevate the mood back to where it should be, but be sure to allow times for reverence or concentration through silence when it's called for.

Sarcasm: In the aftermath of a bad tactical call, an aggravated teammate may thunder, "Oh, THAT was a GREAT idea, Jim!" The chances are good that Jim knows his idea hasn't worked out for the best in this case, and doesn't need salt in the wound. In the best-case scenario, Jim's response will be a witty enough comeback to lighten the mood. In the worst-case scenario, an argument could break out, or you just might not see Jim on the boat again in the future. Sarcasm stings on land or on the water, and it doesn't do anything except vent anger in an especially salty way. The best thing to do when you feel a sarcastic comment coming on is to bite your tongue until you can think of a more productive way to express yourself.

Screaming: Despite the onset of adulthood, many sailors are still subject to temper tantrums when the chips are down. It's amazing how the pleasant guy from the dock can sometimes become a raving tyrant at the helm. This is probably the most destructive of reactions to adversity. Some think of themselves as a drill sergeant, just putting some fire in the bellies of their troops. Most others simply have cracked under pressure and are venting their frustrations at their own teammates. Either way, screaming generally isn't very motivational, except to inspire mutiny. Often, when the emotional storm passes and the angry skipper calms down, he'll be back to his old pleasant self and ready to explain how he didn't really mean it when he called the main trimmer a "#$@&!%." Nobody drives, works, or sails well when they're having a fit, and acting out in anger only puts it out there how difficult you are to be around. It's up to us to know how to manage our frustrations so they don't go spilling out all over the people who are there to help us. You may see the occasional tantrum on a boat in the back of the fleet, but it's often just as much the cause of their poor performance as the result.

A rough patch in interpersonal communication doesn't have to spell ultimate doom for a team. By addressing the issue, people can prevent a downward spiral and find their way to get back on track. In the first race at the 2009 Star World Championship, George Szabo and Rick Peters had to get through some stress on board the boat. Working their way up one side of the course, the opposite side suddenly became more favorable and they found themselves far back in the pack. As frustration took hold, it didn't take long for the team's communication to break down to the point of silence. At the end of the day's race, they finished fifty-fourth. On the long trip back to the dock, the two got to talking about the causes for the communication breakdown and what they needed from each other on the course. With the air cleared, they came back out to win the race the next day, and keeping that momentum through the series, they won the Star Worlds.

Effective communication with teammates through adversity in any enterprise includes the ability to lift the team up when disappointment threatens the group's ability to perform. A darkened mood among an organization's members can have real, tangible effects on its execution of important initiatives, so it falls to the leadership of the team to provide a mental boost from time to time to keep chins up and minds sharp.

Don't Kill the Messenger

Taking bad news can be difficult for anyone. When we become frustrated in an uphill battle, emotion can sometimes flare up when more bad news comes our way. The old stories of tyrants lashing out at the unfortunate youths who had the task of delivering word of a battlefield defeat are still occasionally relived today in some form or another. Anyone heading a team and expecting reports of relevant information must expect that not all of it will paint a rosy picture. Positive or negative, information is essential to keep any effort underway, so there must be no reason for info providers to feel hesitation at delivering news that the decision maker needs. If you're driving on a road trip, wouldn't you prefer to be informed sooner rather than later that you'd missed a turn? Make sure that any frustration at bad news isn't directed at the one delivering it, or it may threaten the kind of candor that is needed when gathering all the facts for better decision making.

Don't Spare the Compliments

A kind word goes a long way to motivate teammates, whether it's at the office or on the racecourse. There's no need to lay it on too thick, or your compliments will come off as disingenuous. Rather, give credit where it is due. Being acknowledged for a job well done can be highly motivating to anyone looking to do their best. Furthermore, instant positive feedback when something has gone right seems to stick in people's minds most effectively in helping them learn. Skippers that offer the occasional, "Nice tack" or some similar comment not only help to keep the crew motivated, but also help their crews learn right away what is working.

It isn't necessary or expected for a leader to be cheerful and positive a hundred percent of the time, but team members do expect and need some balance to the positives and the negatives that they hear. Families occasionally find moods darkening around the house when people begin spending more time saying, "I hate it when you ____" than saying, "I like it when you ____." Constructive criticism about what is wrong is best delivered when coupled with some mention of what is right. Some managers favor a "compliment sandwich," in which the issue needing improvement is addressed between two comments of a complimentary nature. A little positive remark once in a while, even about the most innocuous thing, can go a long way for another person. It isn't coddling or currying favor to dish out compliments to those around you; it is simply a better way to encourage learning and to help invigorate their efforts.

SUPPORTERS

Just about anyone who accomplishes anything worthwhile will have someone to thank at the end of their effort. We often hear sayings like, "No man is an island" or "Behind every successful man is a supportive woman (and vice versa)." Whether we need to depend on others for moral, financial, emotional, or logistical support, everyone needs assistance at some point along the way. It therefore bears mentioning the importance of recognizing the value of a strong support group. Even if your endeavor is an individual one, it is possible to build a support team—a group of peers that you respect with whom you can carry on a dialogue that will be to mutual benefit. A wise approach is to surround yourself with the best and brightest you can find and benefit from their insight, even if you feel that you may be outshone from time to time.

We've seen some of the important roles that people play in a sailing campaign or a business, but there are also many who are not directly involved in the effort that can keep you going when times get tough. They are not crew on your boat, employees in your business, or singers in the chorus. They are the outsiders that you turn to for advice when life starts throwing new challenges at you. It could be teachers, coaches, or any mentor you may have, or it could be friends and family.

Stephen King has often credited his wife Tabitha for standing by him through some tough times in the beginning of their relationship. They didn't have much money when they were first married, and he didn't even own a typewriter. Through the stress to keep the bills paid and the frustrations of writing his first novel, King continued to receive Tabitha's encouragement; she even rescued the draft for *Carrie* from the trash when he was about to quit. Thanks to the faith and support of his wife, King continued on in his writing career to become one of the most prolific and popular writers of the industry. An accomplished writer in her own right, Tabitha's support for her husband has been rewarded in kind over the years. As the Kings can surely attest, the emotional support that a loved one can provide through times of struggle and frustration can make all the difference in the world.

MENTORS

Mentors are a wonderful resource because they help provide insight through experience, perspective in a crisis, and support through understanding. History, as well as literature and cinema, is full of stories of heroes who could not have won the day without the help of their mentors. Sometimes you have to seek them out and sometimes they fall into your lap, but anyone with their eyes to the future will find themselves on a path that brings them into contact with a potentially valuable role model in their field. Your environment is the biggest determining factor in your success in meeting a great mentor. Where are successful people in your chosen field getting their "education"?

For a young sailor, yacht clubs and racing clinics can be full of opportunities to meet and learn from great sailors. Mark Reynolds, a two-time world champion and three-time Olympic medalist in the Star class, benefited greatly from the wisdom of members of the San Diego sailing community in his youth. "I'm sure I didn't realize it at the time but I had a lot of support when I was starting out," said Reynolds. "First my parents, who gave me the tools I needed (my first boat at age eight for Christmas!), my dad's sailing knowledge, sailing lessons, and the encouragement to stay the course but never really pushing me in any way. I also was fortunate to grow up at the San Diego Yacht Club where they not only had one of the top junior sailing programs, but also plenty of mentors I could learn from like Ash Bown, Malin Burnham, Lowell North and particularly Dennis Conner, who was often coming by our house when I was a kid. I later worked for Dennis at his business and on his boats—what better teacher could one have? I also hung out a lot at the North Sail loft, which at the time was right next to our club where I learned from many of the best sailors and sailmakers who were working there at the time. They would often give me new Sabot sails to test out which gave me a big head start on learning about sail shape. It does 'take a village' but at the end of the day I got the most help from my family who were always there, not only to get me started but (also) teaching me to be self-sufficient."

Many Olympians, world champions, America's Cup winners, and other giants of the sport have succeeded through their club or local sailing community's ability to build upon itself through the helpful sharing of knowledge. This principle is how universities gain prestige and corporations expand and thrive over time. As demonstrated by the philosophers of ancient Greece, each new generation learns from the greats of the previous generation: Socrates taught Plato, who taught Aristotle, who taught Alexander the Great. People with their eyes on success in their chosen field know where they need to be to meet and learn from the experts in that field.

PRACTICE & PREPARATION

Striving and struggle precede success, even in the dictionary.

—Sarah Ban Breathnach

A devotion to practice and preparation is a key element of planning for success. You can't control how lucky you may get in life, but you can control how well prepared you are for challenges that lay ahead; to some degree, you can make your own luck. With a dedication to constant improvement, athletes and professionals from all walks of life can set a tone of commitment to their own growth. With each step taken on that ladder of progress, it becomes easier to take the next one. Much of success comes from not only putting in plenty of time, but deriving the greatest benefit possible per hour devoted. It isn't just about working harder, but about working smarter. By applying some foresight into the planning process, one can allocate their efforts efficiently to get the most out of their time and prevent redundancies, lapses, or burnout. Put your heart and your head into your commitment to preparation—if you make the most of the time you have available, your performance will be significantly sharper when the time comes.

GET PLENTY OF PRACTICE

A motivating thought that may run through any competitor's mind as they prepare for an upcoming event is the dreadful mental image of their rival off somewhere, preparing even harder. It might not be someone they've even met yet, but they're out there, sweating and straining to their absolute limit so that when the two strangers eventually do cross paths, they will have prepared themselves to make the contest as difficult as possible for each other. A boxer straining for just a little more motivation to get even one more rep into his workout may find himself snarling his opponent's name as he pushes himself, as a reminder of the tough competition he will soon face.

Sailors reach a point where they can't do much more to prepare their boat, but what they can do is get more time on the water. Intercollegiate sailors in particular know the value of time spent in practice, as they are not only racing in boats that are all nearly identical, but also often rotating in a round-robin format so they don't sail the same boat twice. When the condition of the boat you're racing is that far out of your hands, experience is your best asset.

Everyone knows the value of practice. A pianist needs to put in plenty of practice to be ready for a big recital. A student preparing for college entrance exams will need to put in quality study time to get the best possible grade. A baseball player will want to spend some time in the batting cage to be prepared for the upcoming season. A champion debater will always have talking points prepared for the next meet. A comic will need to rehearse her routine for weeks before ever going on stage. We have all seen someone perform a difficult task and make it look easy, but the majority of achievers are not at the top of their field because it was easy for them, but because they put in the time and work to master their craft.

Practice can feel like a difficult chore, and improvement isn't always immediately apparent. However, with time devoted to practice, a keener instinct is automatically planted within us that can take over when the time to perform has arrived. Sailors reach the point where they can reach for a line without looking, instinctively knowing exactly where it is. Musicians' fingers swiftly fly over their instruments to create beautiful music without much conscious thought, thanks to hours upon hours of rehearsal. A golfer is able to repeat her perfect swing through muscle memory gained by repetition of the swing in practice. In dedicating time and effort to the fine tuning of your craft, you build the all-important advantage of experience, which tends to prove most valuable when you're under pressure.

DEDICATION TO PREPARATION

The tougher the journey, competition, or obstacle ahead, the more dedication to preparation is needed to achieve the goal. The most difficult challenges are mercilessly unforgiving to a half-hearted effort, and tend to punish those lacking a strong commitment with, at least, a disappointing loss. Just making a commitment to succeed at something difficult requires strong belief in oneself as well as extensive focus and discipline to keep up the practice and preparation required. Putting in the hours necessary can seem grueling or tedious along the way. When it's all said and done, however, the results of those hours spent in preparation show in the success attained by those who put them in.

In sailing, the factor that often separates the leaders from the rest of the pack is time in the boat. The sailors who have devoted the most time to practice will be in better shape and have sharper instincts than those less prepared. Lasse Hjortnæs, a four-time Olympian from Denmark, got his start in the Laser class before moving into Finns. Dissatisfied with his finish at the 1977 Laser World Championship in Brazil, Hjortnæs decided to step up his game by practicing every day until the next world championship. This honed his skill in the Laser so well that he came back to win the Laser Worlds in Australia in 1979. All the time and training that he put in during that period to achieve this win was a jumping-off point that elevated him to the next level in his sailing.

This kind of extraordinary commitment is often seen among sailing's top performers. Such devotion to practice expands the sailor's knowledge as well as hones his instincts; it transforms the boat into an extension of the sailor himself, rather than a mere vehicle to be controlled. Paul Elvstrom was highly disciplined in his practice schedule as he advanced to the top of the Finn class. His almost daily practice sessions in all conditions heightened his physical ability in the boat to a level higher than any other competitor on the Finn circuit. When Elvstrom couldn't be out sailing, he would work out at home on a bench that simulated the cockpit of his Finn, making the best use of his time that he could while on dry land. The *Freedom* syndicate won the 1980 America's Cup by taking its preparation to the next level as well. The team practiced for over five hundred hours in 1979 and over fifteen hundred hours in 1980, more preparation than any Cup defender had ever devoted before.

Time spent in preparation helped NHL Hall of Famer Wayne Gretzky to stand out as a hockey player as a youth. Gretzky not only had what he called "a serious addiction to hockey," but a great deal of personal discipline that guided his training regimen. He would devote hours to practice as a boy, rising early to skate before school, and then returning to the ice after school to skate until dinnertime, often after dark. Gretzky also kept up his practice schedule year-round, hitting pucks off metal sheets in the summer to mimic ice, and often staying home to practice when friends invited him to go to the movies. Gretzky's time devoted to practice helped him to build an uncanny instinct for "seeing" plays in his mind just before they happened, allowing him to anticipate where the puck would be going and position himself to meet it. This skill, developed through long hours of practice, helped set Gretzky apart from other players.

Successful teams are often built on a shared commitment to training for the main event. It's vital that the dedication to preparation is shared equally when embarking on a team endeavor and that there is no disparity in the level of effort that each member is willing to put in. Compatibility among team members in terms of attitude as well as ability and personality makes a big difference in the team's ability to take full advantage of the opportunity to prepare for the challenge ahead. Unless everyone shares the same expectations of the commitment needed, there is potential for a loss of momentum through dissention or disinterest.

At the outset, the development of an approach to practice and preparation should include a frank assessment of the dedication of time and of physical and mental effort to be committed to the endeavor:

What will success require?

Am I/Are we willing to make the necessary sacrifices?

Can I/we accept the risks inherent in the attempt?

It takes some degree of bravery to stare down a rough road to the goal and to march forward decisively. An honest look at that road could reveal some real obstacles ahead that can only be overcome through time and effort; so much so, that it could mean missing out on other important things. Sacrifice has often been the price paid for great success, and it's an issue to be considered seriously before moving ahead. As the old saying goes, "No one ever said on his death bed, 'If only I'd spent more time at the office.'" Some sacrifices can be recovered, and others can't, so it's crucial to recognize them early. There are risks in making a bold commitment to a cause; not only the risk associated with sacrifices to be made, but the risk of losing. It's possible that despite all the dedication that went into the preparation of the effort, it might not work out anyway. See the commitment to the journey, the dedication to the pursuit of mastery, as part of the goal itself. When the truest effort has been set forth in any difficult endeavor, even unsuccessfully, it is a victory in another form: as a building block to higher ground.

GET YOUR HOMEWORK DONE

Students often lament the homework piled upon them every night. Homework is just another form of practice, though. Students that shine in pop quizzes and in class discussions may not necessarily be intellectually superior; often it is simply a matter of having put the time in to review the material. With the previous night's assignment fresh in their minds, they naturally are able to perform better in class than their peers who lack the same familiarity with the subject matter.

Homework doesn't go away when school's out. Everyone with an important task ahead of them still needs to devote time to preparation for it. Sailors need to devote time to research before heading off to a regatta, so that they can avoid any hang-ups down the line. They need to know what the wind and water conditions will be, what equipment to bring, what the format of the racing will be, how far the hotel is from the regatta site, where to find food, and so on. Without reviewing these little details ahead of time, there is too much that can go wrong in trying to improvise on the fly. If a lawyer devoted no time to preparing his argument before the jury, his client could be in some trouble. As often as we'd like to be doing something else, there comes a time when we have to do our homework and go into situations better prepared.

SCHEDULING

Racing sailors taking the long view put a great deal of advance planning into their campaigns. These campaigns can be conceptualized in the form of a timeline to an ultimate objective (e.g., a major championship) that includes many steps leading up to it. The optimization of the boat and the team's performance for the best possible result is the project being undertaken. The championship is the final deadline and the numerous regattas and tuning sessions leading up to it are "production steps" with deadlines of their own. The logistics required of a successful sailing campaign necessitate thoughtful planning ahead of time to allow all the needs of the campaign to be met without mishap, and such is the case with any undertaking which requires long-term planning.

Any busy person can find time management to be a challenge; there is the process of meeting daily needs as well as preparation for big events down the line. For a marketing professional, that event could be a big sales presentation or trade show. For a movie producer, it could be the launch date of their next film. For a happy couple, it could be their wedding date. The big event might even be a family dinner over the holidays. Whatever the occasion on the horizon is, there are some techniques to organizing an approach to any "campaign" that can help logistics come together within the required time frame.

See the Big Picture

First and foremost, determine the final deadline for the project. An uncertain deadline can be a ticking time bomb to anyone struggling to organize a complex project. A sailor could not effectively plan for a world championship that was scheduled for "midsummer," for instance; there are too many logistics to manage. The more elements the preparation of your project will require, the sooner you'll need a rock-solid date to work with. Some forward thinking is required to determine how realistic the time frame is: Keeping in mind all that needs to be done before the final date, is there adequate time to complete each task beforehand to meet the deadline? If the answer is yes, you can keep moving forward in the planning process.

Having looked forward to the end, try looking back from the future to fill in the blanks from the present time to the ultimate deadline. Pick up a calendar that gives a "year at a glance," and pencil in the final date first, working back through the calendar and writing in the smaller steps along the way. It's a good idea to also include outside commitments on this calendar in order to avoid being expected in two places at once later on.

Plan the Production Steps

Each step of the planning process will have a time frame of its own that will need to be considered. The steps to a major sailing championship will include practice days as well as various "warm-up" regattas and a travel schedule for each. There are numerous points to consider, such as transporting the boat, getting air and hotel reservations, getting around the regatta locale, and allowing sufficient time to prepare beforehand and pack up afterward. A busy racing schedule can become crowded and sometimes some improvisation is required when there is a short time frame between points on the calendar. For instance, if a sailor has a major regatta in Florida, followed by another in Sydney a week later, there isn't a realistic chance of using ocean transport to get his boat to Australia in time. This sailor would have to consider other options, such as flying the boat over on a cargo jet or chartering a boat at one of the events (a much cheaper option). Consider how much time each step along the way requires and block them out on the calendar, overlapping them as necessary and practical. Recognize early on where the time crunches will be, and plan early how to deal with them.

Consider the way each step of the process influences the others; for instance, "A needs to be done before starting B, C can be started at the same time as B, and D can be started after B is completed." To make the best use of the time available, it is helpful to know exactly how each step is reliant upon another one. This makes it possible to get started concurrently on those steps that function independently, holding off on those that rely on the final details of others. A vacation to the South Pacific has a number of logistical challenges, for example. You can't book a hotel until you know on what island you'll be staying, and the dates you want to travel, but as long as the plan is definite, you can still buy a swimsuit in the meantime. Whether planning a vacation, a regatta, or a moving day, we often face situations in which we have to juggle a number of details in a small time period.

Work with Reliable People

Overlapping priorities on the project timeline will often require the help of others on whom you can thoroughly rely. Since your time is valuable, it is best spent on the tasks that require your personal attention, freeing you to delegate projects that your support group can handle. A complex project will often demand the simultaneous efforts of multiple people, and having the right people in place to perform these jobs is crucial to keep the project running on schedule. Reliability, mostly meaning punctuality, dependability, and trustworthiness, is even more important than skill. A manager can give guidance in a large number of tasks that are simple enough for even the most inexperienced novice to pick up quickly and with zeal.

Racing sailors traditionally had, and occasionally still have, junior sailors assigned by their yacht club as "boat boys (or girls)" to help gather sails, move the trailer, get the hull cleaned up, or launch the boat. These juniors are given fairly easy but time-consuming tasks to help out the sailors preparing for the race, and are given in turn a chance to converse with and learn from some of the top guns of the fleet. When any effort with concurrent production steps is underway, the ability to count on the various members handling these steps is critical to staying on schedule.

Plan Daily Activities

Once the timing details of the project have been broken down from months to weeks, the daily activities can be addressed to keep things on schedule. Not every project will need to be worked on every day, but on the days when there is work to be done, have a plan for how to make the best use of time and stick with it as closely as possible. For a sailor planning a practice day, it can be summed up as a few simple times to go by, such as, "We'll meet at the boat at noon, leave the dock by one, and return to the dock by five." It's not always possible to know the exact timing of a day's activities, but a reasonable estimate can keep you on track for the project and help keep your other commitments in balance as well.

Leave More Time Available Than You First Think Is Necessary

Plenty of people plan their daily schedules diligently but still find themselves running behind, perhaps not leaving enough time to account for traffic between appointments or just getting hung up in conversations with people who need their time. This can expand into a long-term plan as well, with steps to the process getting delayed because of a holdup somewhere else. Sometimes we can't help it if our schedule becomes more hectic, but whenever possible, it's good to leave more time available for our plans than seems necessary. For a lot of people, it can be stressful and exhausting to be constantly hurried, and important details can be missed when in a rush. Not only could there be some forgotten factor in the schedule that could eat up more time, but there may be hang-ups along the way that need to be allowed for on the calendar.

Any creative project with a lot of moving parts is susceptible to disruptions in the schedule. Developing a product catalog, for instance, can be a complex task in preparing a production schedule. The company may know the deadline for its catalog's release, how many products will be featured, and how long the graphic design team will take to complete a single page, but even this isn't quite enough to determine a realistic timetable. Staff may be out for days or weeks for sick leave or holidays; there could be computer crashes and glitches in the system; management could decide to add another product, requiring photographers, copywriters, designers and marketers to scramble through interior redesign.

It can be tempting to set start and finish dates according to the minimum requirements for task completion, but overly ambitious timetables will usually backfire. Without a generous time cushion in the production plan, you can end up with overworked people making more mistakes as they rush to make the deadline, or you could miss the deadline entirely. When many people are coordinating a project with many moving parts, they need to allow time for changes, mistakes and corrections, and breaks. Even when we go into a project with a well-organized schedule and thorough attention to detail, we need to allow some room to maneuver when life throws in some complications.

A campaigning sailor can relate to this kind of scenario. As much as the sailor tries to eliminate unknowns that could cause delays, a surprise is always a danger on the campaign trail; the boat might get held up in customs, bad weather could delay the flight, or the luggage might get lost by the airline. It would be foolhardy to plan for the regatta under the assumption that factors outside of his control such as these will always go smoothly. The tighter the time crunch, the more ambitious and optimistic many people tend to be with scheduling forecasts. If it's necessary to work within an extremely challenging time frame, allow extra time wherever possible and try to eliminate unknowns that could sabotage what precious time there is.

For the sake of body and mind, strive to allow time to rest and recover both during and after a big effort. Nobody can be at their best when they are exhausted, and time to recharge helps to keep energy and enthusiasm up over the long haul. Everyone has their own preference as far as the pace they operate at and the recovery time they need after a tackling a challenge. Breaks shouldn't be so long or so much of a diversion that they cause you to take your eye off the ball or to fall behind, but they are an essential part of the pacing of a long effort. When scheduling your campaign, be sure to add in a little bit of free time to keep yourself going at a manageable pace.

Update Plans Regularly

Throughout the planning process, it is a good idea to look at the task calendar or timeline and evaluate whether the tasks for the project are ahead of, behind, or right on schedule. It is not uncommon for a project to need some revision to the schedule to accommodate new developments that either help or hinder progress. Progress evaluations may be done daily, weekly, or monthly, depending on the chronological scope of the undertaking, but they should be made as often as possible to keep an awareness of existing conditions and allow quick response to make any due accommodations. It's also vital when making any refinements to the schedule to make sure that each member of the team has been updated with the most current version, in order to avoid preventable delays. Rein in delays as quickly as possible when detected, or they will likely expand from a few days' delay to a few weeks', and so on. With sensible foresight, conscientious planning, consistent performance, and responsible management, a reliable schedule can be crafted to help any project run more smoothly.

MAKE THE MOST OF PRACTICE TIME

What sailors and experts in other walks of life know about practice is that *how* you practice is as important as *how much* you practice. A sailor in training will try to match as many variables as possible to the expected conditions of their future competition. They will seek out similar wind and water conditions, practice with people they expect to be racing against (or who are of comparable skill), tune their boat's rig accordingly, and spend as much time in the boat with their regular crew as possible. The notion is to excel in practice that imitates expected conditions so that under those conditions performance under pressure is a habit. Sometimes, sailors must go out of their way to practice in conditions that will adequately prepare them for the big event. It's hard to do well in an ocean race when you've only spent time on a flat-water lake, for instance.

As you consider how you want to spend your time practicing for your endeavor, the following principles that are often used in competitive sailing will likely serve as a helpful guideline to your own preparations.

Find a Practice Partner

Sailors often use tuning partners to gauge experimental changes in rig setup. By communicating what is being tested and how, and then reviewing the results afterward, both can benefit from the experience. Practice partners in any field can be an excellent way to build skills; JFK helped his brother Ted to prepare for his first political debate, for instance. Likewise, students have study partners to quiz them on the material, and boxers have sparring partners. A good practice partner is someone that is strong where you are weak, who can expose your vulnerabilities so that you can target what needs to be worked on. Practice partners are also a motivating force, pushing you to keep up the hard work. As exercise buddies know, it's easier to keep up the pace when you've got someone else working hard alongside you.

Go Where You Can Match Expected Conditions

Preparing to sail in a new venue should include practicing in similar wind and sea conditions. Likewise, if you're going to be giving a speech before a large audience, practice in front of a group. If you'll be taking a big exam, take a practice test in a quiet room with no outside resources at your disposal. Most of the time, you'll be able to get an idea of the environment that you'll be expected to perform in. By finding a similar environment (or better yet, the actual location), your preparation time will be much better spent.

Introduce Expected Challenges

Thinking ahead of potential speed bumps can help keep you cool under pressure. A sailor can benefit by practicing with a group in order to be able to easily maneuver through a crowded fleet. Debaters must not only anticipate their opponent's points, but respond coolly under a time constraint. As you build a better understanding of any challenge you undertake, you should be able to spot many possible issues that could come up. Think about what sort of potential issues you can be sure to face in the future and work responses into your preparation routine.

Throw Yourself Some Unusual Curveballs

Sailors often practice emergency sail changes and man-overboard drills. Security teams and public safety services have a knack for drills that foresee bizarre and far-fetched potential catastrophes and test their response to them. You can throw yourself some curveballs to keep yourself sharp for any unforeseen circumstances as well. This is where practice partners come in handy, because they can surprise you in practice to keep you on your toes. Think of anything that could potentially go wrong and consider how you'd be able to respond to the situation. Planning for even the weirdest turn of events may serve you well someday—you never know what might come up.

SHOW UP

As Woody Allen once said, "Eighty percent of success is showing up." Commitment to success in any effort depends greatly on one's ability to show up, not only for the ultimate occasion, but for the little events leading up to that point. A popular form of competition in sailing is the High Point series. It earns its name because it is typically an inversion of the usual scoring; your final finish at the end of the day earns you more points the higher you placed and the larger the fleet. These series are often run over weeks or months, with each participating sailor's score added up over all of the events to arrive at a final score. It should be noted that there are some ways that a registered sailor can actually score worse than last place: He can be disqualified, fail to finish, or fail to start the race. Missing a race in a regatta or a series does terrible damage to a sailor's score, because it penalizes him on points even further than if he slowly went around the course in last place. Often in a long High Point series, which could last all year, the winner of the whole series is one of a small percentage of sailors who has competed in every single race.

Participation is how ambitious people climb their way through the ranks. An unknown politician will attend every public function possible to get his name and face into the public consciousness, for example. He must attend numerous events if he wants his name and his message to be well-known on Election Day. A sales representative will want to attend as many trade events as possible in order to meet and talk to potential customers, as well as to keep aware of the latest products and services in her industry. For a sailor, a racing season will consist not just of drilling and practicing before the big championship, but attending small regattas leading up to the final event. Even the most casual club race gives valuable time on the water to keep the sailor's instincts sharp. When making your plans for a long road to your goal, be sure that you are participating in as many educational, social, or competitive events as possible to build on your expertise and involvement in your chosen field.

MIND THE TIME

Timing is everything in sailing; if you're late, you're in trouble. Nowhere on the course is this better illustrated than on the starting line. When boats crowd together, the resulting disturbed air slows down the whole pack. As boats line up to start a race, they are jockeying to be moving at full speed at the starting gun. The boats that get it just right will be at a significant advantage; the boats that are a little late will be caught in the disturbed air of the boats just ahead off the line. When a boat falls behind just a little on a crowded start line, that small disadvantage quickly turns into a big one, giving the straggler a long uphill climb to fight back through the ranks.

Besides the issue of etiquette, punctuality works to anyone's advantage on or off the water. First of all, people aren't usually as mentally sharp when they are running late. We leave things behind, forget important details, and miss mistakes to be corrected when we're rushing. Also, when we're behind schedule, we miss an opportunity to better prepare for the situation at hand, both logistically and mentally. For the sailor, this could mean a chance to double-check the boat for any sharp corners that could tear a sail or any fittings that look a little loose. That extra minute or two spent on being thorough could avert a problem down the line. Getting out to a racecourse early lets the sailor take wind readings, trim the sails to the conditions, and get to know the course. Without that opportunity to plan a little better by being late, the sailor could be handing the advantage over to her more punctual competitors.

Anyone who has ever been locked out of a performance or a class due to their late arrival can attest to the importance of punctuality. There are more situations one is likely to encounter in which it is to their benefit to be on time or early than there are in which it is acceptable to arrive late. So much of success in any area is derived from the ability to plan responsibly, and thorough preparation depends greatly on timing. Even if you need to set your watch a little bit fast to arrive where you need to go, it will be to your benefit to make punctuality a habit.

STRATEGY

Ignoranti quem portum petat nullus suus ventus est.
(If a man does not know to which port
he is sailing, no wind is favorable.)

—Seneca the Younger

Strategy for life, as for sailing, business, or war, is the foundation of sound decision making when the occasion calls for it. Strategy is based on the big picture, challenging the strategy maker to answer crucial self-evaluative questions:

- What is your objective, and what direction will take you there?
- What strengths do you have that will be of benefit in your cause, and what weaknesses will you need to overcome?
- What obstacles will you encounter along the way, and how will you be equipped to handle them?
- What information can you gather that others may not possess?
- How will you deal with competitors that seek to block your path, and how are they likely to respond to your actions?

The tactics that a sailor may employ all around the racecourse are derivative of a sound overall strategy; without the ability to keep the big picture in mind, it is too easy to lose one's way in minutiae and momentary crises. Strategy can be amended when conditions and circumstances change, but this should only be done with thoughtful consideration, and not impulsively. Develop a wise strategy for your efforts, and you will be able to stay on course to success over the long run.

PLAY TO YOUR STRENGTHS

Whether in the face of competition or for the sake of personal growth, a great advantage can be gained by conscientiously playing to one's inherent strengths. Sailing's various formats provide different areas in which a competitor might find an advantage. In one-design sailing, where all the boats are very closely matched, nearly to the point of being identical, a sailor's advantage generally lies in his own techniques more than in his equipment. In more open events such as on the Maxi circuit, the America's Cup, or offshore racing, parameters for the yachts are set that allow for certain advantages in a boat's design: designers may need to choose between better performance in light air vs. heavy air, smooth water vs. choppy water, sailing close to the wind vs. sailing lower and faster, or better maneuverability vs. better straight-line speed. Creating and executing a better game plan in sailing or in life can be best accomplished by exploiting one's strengths, whether they are to be nurtured from the ground up or developed into a stronger advantage.

Making the most of one's strengths in competition also means being aware of and minimizing one's vulnerabilities. The 1988 America's Cup was more a study of contrasts than a conventional contest. The two yachts competing were extremely different, and each had strengths to play and vulnerabilities to guard against. At some point in the course of the contest, both sides felt that they had been dealt with unfairly. In the summer of 1987, Michael Fay of New Zealand surprised the San Diego Yacht Club with a challenge for the America's Cup, in a proposed matchup of 90-foot yachts of a new design. Fay's unconventional challenge was ultimately met with an unconventional defender: a 60-foot catamaran, to be skippered by Dennis Conner.

While Fay's 90-foot monohull *New Zealand* was large and powerful, the *Stars & Stripes* catamaran was smaller but much quicker, to the point that the match would not even be close in a side-by-side contest. As long as *Stars & Stripes* had clear air and clear water, there was little chance that *New Zealand* could win through anything short of gear failure on the catamaran. However, the Kiwis' potential advantages had to be considered. *New Zealand* with its towering mast could cast an enormous wind shadow, possibly blocking the breeze of the cat. If the winds on a designated race day were particularly strong, *Stars & Stripes* would be vulnerable to capsize or breakdown, as there was no way to reef its wing sail. Furthermore, catamarans can be vulnerable to stalling during maneuvers; if *New Zealand* could gain control with right-of-way, she could potentially force the catamaran into a foul.

After much acrimony ashore, the two boats met on the water for a best two-of-three series. Conner, understanding the strengths and weaknesses of both boats, avoided close maneuvering before the races, and thus the potential for a stall or a foul. Only once on the racecourse did *New Zealand*'s potential advantages become relevant. On the first leg of the second race, *Stars & Stripes* held the lead, conservatively tacking to cover *New Zealand* with each maneuver. When *New Zealand* began to tack away, *Stars & Stripes* began a tack to cover, but stalled out when *New Zealand* bore away again. *New Zealand*'s momentum carried her forward, coming up to leeward of *Stars & Stripes* with the right-of-way. *Stars & Stripes* had to tack away at low speed to avoid a foul, and for a moment, *New Zealand* took the lead. The catamaran got away with clear air, however, and was able to speed back into the lead. The Americans won both races by large margins, but without the defender's understanding of its possibilities and limitations in answering New Zealand's challenge, the outcome of this unusual Cup match may have been different.

In the late sixteenth century, Queen Elizabeth I also faced a foreign threat that forced her to weigh her strengths and weaknesses in preparing a defense. The Spanish Empire had grown to the height of its powers under King Philip II, who sought to spread Catholicism throughout Europe. By the 1580s, only England stood against Spain, under the Protestant rule of Elizabeth. While Spain had great wealth, England's economy had been struggling for years, and Elizabeth's priorities were soon split between buying time by maintaining diplomatic relations with the hostile Spanish and developing her fragile economy. In order for England to survive the imminent war with Spain, Elizabeth would have to find Spain's Achilles' heel.

Her opportunity to mitigate Spain's advantage lay in cutting off Spain's money supply, which was funding the expansion of the Spanish Empire as well as the construction of a massive invasion armada. She dispatched Sir Francis Drake to attack Spanish ships bringing in gold and silver from Mexico and Peru, while shrugging off Drake's actions as piracy. Although delayed by Drake's raids, in 1588 the massive Spanish Armada set sail for the invasion of

England. On the water, the English found another Spanish vulnerability to exploit. While the Spanish ships were large and powerful, the English ships were fast and maneuverable. With these advantages, the English ships could get close enough to the Spanish ships to do some damage and still maneuver out of harm's way before being bombarded or boarded.

Using clever tactics in combat off the coast of Calais, the English led a bold assault that broke the Spanish formation and forced the Armada to retreat. Blocked by English ships to the south, the Spanish set sail the long way home northward around the coast of Ireland, only to run into more rough weather which would claim dozens of their ships. With the invasion of England a dismal failure and the Armada defeated, Philip's holy war came to naught and the Spanish Empire was financially ruined.

Elizabeth's evaluation of her strengths and weaknesses in planning to meet the Spanish threat allowed her nation to survive. While England was limited in financial resources, Elizabeth was able to cleverly manage this weakness while creating an advantage, creating an agile navy to meet the large and overbuilt Spanish ships. In addition, by employing Drake's aid in raiding Spanish ships, she had reduced the Spanish Empire's advantage by striking where it could be hurt most: its finances.

Muggsy Bogues, who played as point guard for the Charlotte Hornets from 1988 to 1997, faced what would seem to be an insurmountable challenge as the shortest player in the NBA, standing at only five feet, three inches. Height is one of the most valuable physical attributes in basketball, with most players standing well over six, sometimes seven, feet tall. Bogues used his smaller stature to his advantage, however. He was able to dribble so close to the ground that bigger players found it difficult to get the ball away from him. This, combined with his foot speed, helped him to set records for steals, even from much taller players, during his years with the Hornets. Not unlike the English navy or the *Stars & Stripes* catamaran, Bogues was able to handle much larger opponents by being clever and quick.

Competition and conflict aren't the only forums in which strengths and weaknesses should be evaluated. Personal and professional growth can be based upon finding one's natural abilities and building upon them in order to thrive. For a business looking to build a more effective workforce, its understanding of its employees' strengths and weaknesses can be just as important as understanding its competitors'.

There are skills that can be learned and talents that seem innate; some people have an ear for music, for instance, and others take years of training to develop it. Not everyone working in a particular field needs to share the same abilities to be effective. Team efforts can be improved by creating complimentary alliances, putting together combinations of people who are strong where their counterparts are weaker, just as an intuitive sailor can sometimes benefit from having a naturally analytical teammate aboard to interpret compass bearings and wind readings.

Competence in one area does not always translate well to other efforts. It's common for employees who excel in their jobs to find themselves boosted into management positions when they have no gift for managing people. One of the reluctant promotions of history was William Howard Taft's ascendency to the presidency after serving in Theodore Roosevelt's cabinet. He easily won election on the coattails of Roosevelt as a close friend of the former president's, but was unhappy in the post. Uncomfortable with the political realm, Taft found that his new job made weaknesses of his usual strengths; he had none of the critical bluster nor tactical savvy of more successful politicians, and his good-natured personality did him little justice as president. He did not miss the White House after leaving office four years later, and devoted himself to his real dream of being chief justice of the Supreme Court, much happier in robes than in the Oval Office.

Augie Diaz found that one of his great strengths, his ability to maintain a sharp focus, could serve him well in his family business, as it had in his sailing. "In my professional life, I'm not that good at multitasking and overseeing a lot of people and a lot of projects, but when it was crunch time and we had to go get a deal, I've been very good at focusing on that deal, and figuring out what we needed to do to get the business. Fortunately, I was partnered with my brother, who could take care of the stuff I was not as good at," he said. With an understanding of where his inherent strengths lie, Diaz has been able to emphasize his stronger capabilities, while working around any weaknesses. "I'm a big believer in leveraging your strengths. I worry about my weaknesses and I have to recognize them, but I don't dwell on them. I try to improve, but I don't put as much time into managing my weaknesses as I do leveraging my strengths."

Understanding your strengths and weaknesses is a critical step in developing a strategy for success. It helps set direction, allocate resources, and promote growth. Nobody is without weaknesses, but not everybody is particularly effective at managing those weaknesses' influence on their lives. By gaining awareness of our weaknesses, we can take steps to eliminate, reduce, or compensate for them, as long as they are seen through honest and rational evaluation. A sailor driving a boat with a small rudder will know that he is far better off racing in a straight line than trying to outmaneuver a more agile opponent. Likewise, his competitor will try to force him into maneuvering in order to gain the upper hand by exposing that vulnerability. Such is the nature of competition: not all abilities are similar or equal, but the contest can still go either way, based on the actions of its contestants. Make it a habit to make the most of your strengths, and your weaknesses will lose significance in the long run.

CRAFT A WINNING STRATEGY

Any organized effort requires forethought into a strategic approach. Strategy, loosely defined, is a big-picture plan through which an individual or group determines the path to be taken to the ultimate goal, incorporating various tactics and contingencies along the way. A sailboat race introduces so many competitive and environmental variables to the sailor that it would be impractical to improvise one's way around the racecourse without some strategy in place. Likewise, life itself often demands a strategic approach in the biggest and most complex plans, both personal and professional, that we as individuals undergo. Without a necessary gathering of information and thoughtful interpretation of conditions past, present, and presumable, it becomes more difficult to find direction in one's efforts and therefore more difficult to respond to changing conditions. Strategy is made all the more effective when productively created, communicated, and executed by a competent team. When a team is able to look at existing conditions and communicate the facts to their decision maker(s), as well as to be prepared to contribute suggestions without being concerned whether they receive the credit, then some essential elements of a successful team effort are in place.

Effective strategy is a complex undertaking in any field, but a sailor's principles of crafting a plan of attack before a race can provide some valuable maxims that apply aptly to a number of efforts, from business and investing to politics to planning a family vacation. The key steps to developing strategy discussed here are to: 1) interpret trends through clues in your environment, 2) separate facts from opinions, 3) discuss the plan with your team, and 4) for every "What if" have a "Plan B."

INTERPRET TRENDS THROUGH CLUES IN YOUR ENVIRONMENT

Every sailor must at times function as an amateur meteorologist. Even before leaving the dock, the sailor must decide how to approach the conditions she is likely to face on the racecourse: What is the right clothing? What sails will be the most suitable? How should the rig be tuned? Much of this is determined by looking at the type of forecast just about everyone sees and hears from the news—detailing water and air temperature, likely wind strengths, movement of high- or low-pressure systems, etc. Arriving on the racecourse, however, there is a whole new forecast that the sailor must craft for herself to allow her to make better strategy for the upcoming race. Tide and current behavior, patterns of wind strength and direction, and the behavior of the fleet all must be considered when creating a prerace strategy.

For example, a sailor may know from her tide chart that high tide will be an hour before the racing begins. Assuming the racecourse is in a bay or harbor, the sailor could determine that the tide will be going out for much of the racing that day, and the geography of the bay will tell her which way the water will drain toward the open ocean. Further, she will need to know the depth of the water in particular areas around his racecourse, as the current flows faster in deep water than it does in shallow water. A deep shipping lane, for instance, could provide a valuable boost at times during the race. Using a compass and taking regular readings on both tacks, the sailor can determine what angles she is sailing upwind and look for a pattern of wind shifts. Depending on the location, the wind could have a persistent shift in one direction as the day goes on, or it could oscillate back and forth. Each locale tends to have a pattern (or lack thereof) which will help the sailor to decide how to position her boat up the racecourse. There may be geographical factors that affect the wind as well: a tall building to windward of the course may block the breeze, or a small peninsula off to the side may bend the wind close to shore. The sailor may also be aware that the fleet has certain behavior patterns that make them relatively predictable. For instance, a fleet that tends to get into position late for the start can open an opportunity to be the first one in the front row at the favored side. Also, the aggressiveness of a particular fleet may make a crowd particularly unattractive, due to the disturbed wind, lack of maneuverability, and danger of possible rules infractions.

As the sailor's mind races through each of these details (and many more), the factors under consideration paint a picture of the future. She knows what the past has shown, and is looking at the conditions of the present. Armed with all this data, she can create a fair projection, or at least an educated guess, of what the future will present either in the big picture or in moment-to-moment situations. Understanding trends not only helps craft a big-picture strategy at the outset, but keeps the sailor from reacting to momentary changes against the trends along the way. A sudden heading wind shift may create a temptation for a sailor to tack right away, but whether that's a wise decision or not depends on where the sailor is on the course, where the other boats in the fleet are, and whether the wind is likely to shift right back, stay as it is, or keep shifting in the direction it's going. The top sailors don't react to change nearly as much as they anticipate it, which is why an understanding of trends on the course is so important. Just as Wayne Gretzky would skate toward where he expected the puck to go, a sailor sets their course based on the next expected puff or shift.

The business world functions on the same principle of gathering data to interpret trends in order to develop better strategy. Investors need to know past and present market conditions as well as the history and current financial health of their target. Entrepreneurs need to know the patterns of changing consumer preferences and behaviors to know whether they are getting into the right business, and whether they will be able to compete if they're going into an industry already populated with well-entrenched competitors. Marketing is a field that depends greatly on the understanding of trends. Whether it is in fashion, movies, literature, or any consumer-driven industry, marketers must be keenly aware both instinctively and analytically of changing conditions in their marketplace. For instance, the 1970s saw a growth in the number of gyms in the US, particularly in urban areas. While the fitness craze was taken as a fad at first, it was really the spark of a larger trend toward the pursuit of better health.

At the movies, fads drive a slew of similar releases within weeks of each other, but they reveal trends in the general mood of the audience. In the tough times of the early '70s, themes tended toward disasters, urban decay, and personal struggle. By the late '70s and early '80s, the most popular films were those of a more fantastic nature, almost as if it were a jump to the polar opposite of recent fare (perhaps the audience was ready for some cheering up after the gloomier films of the Watergate era). The entertainment and toy industries not only create fads, but spend much money and effort reacting to them. The more competition companies in these industries face, however, the faster they must jump on a new fad. When it comes to the hottest new thing in these fields, you have to be an early mover if you want to have a chance at competing. Like wind shifts to a sailor, marketing opportunities must be seized and acted upon if they can be exploited quickly and effectively, and only if it will serve the purpose of positioning the product in a competitively advantageous way looking ahead. After all, if you don't know where you want to go, you can't have any idea of how to steer.

SEPARATE FACTS FROM OPINIONS

Major decisions in life are generally made on the basis of an informed opinion. When creating a new strategy, sailors generally either seek information for themselves or obtain it through teammates or coaches. It's important in this process to recognize that there is a distinct difference between facts and opinions that come their way. A person making a statement about conditions on the racecourse may consider their opinion to be a fact, but actually their conclusions have been arrived at by gathering facts and forming an opinion from them.

For example, a statement such as, "The left side of the course is favored" can sound factual, especially if it does indeed turn out to be true. However, this statement is simply an opinion because matters such as the conditions of the waves and current, the placement of the next turning mark, the strength of the wind in particular areas, and the general pattern of wind shifts are all *facts* that must be taken into consideration before the *opinion* as to the favored side of the course can be formed. The more advanced the sailor, the more they will rely on accurate facts in order to form opinions of their own.

The business world also functions at a rapid pace, and information is the most valuable asset there is. A decision maker must have a great deal of information at his or her fingertips, but there is seldom time for them to go out and gather it all on their own. A corporate executive may rely on managers within the firm to provide certain forms of information. However, those who bring information to the decision maker must be aware of how they present their findings—are they stating the facts or their opinions? Bringing information to the CEO that is not only pertinent but factually reliable makes for a valuable contribution. The boss also needs to make clear when he is seeking facts and when he is looking for an opinion, so that conjecture from his team doesn't interfere with his own decision making. Likewise, he must be able to recognize whether he is listening to a fact or an opinion before basing his decisions on the information he receives.

Separating facts from opinions can be important in social settings as well. We all can be guilty of mixing the two up from time to time, since there's a thin line between what we know and what we believe. When topics like politics or religion come up, the corralling of fact and opinion can be difficult. Many an argument has broken out when two parties started stating opinions as facts. A productive discussion needs the two to be combined, rather than confused. Opinions without facts are unsupportable, and facts without opinion are simply data, which leaves little to discuss. The next time someone seems to be presenting opinion as fact, see if you can get them to support their position. You'll either shed new light the issue, or they'll manage to deconstruct their argument on their own.

DISCUSS THE PLAN WITH THE TEAM

In sailing, aboard any boat from a two-man dinghy to an 80-footer, the skipper must communicate the plan to the crew before the race begins. This may include a discussion of race strategy as well as a review of what each person's responsibilities will be. Addressing the specifics of crew tasks in the race ahead allows smoother execution, but also keeps motivation up as each member takes a moment to focus on their contribution around the course. The meeting can stir the crew to racing concentration as they devote their energies toward active race planning. Prerace meetings also instill confidence in the skipper, showing that not only has the skipper come prepared, but also that he recognizes the vital roles of each crew member. The crew also can have the opportunity to contribute to the strategy being laid out, which allows voices to be heard and ideas to be flushed out ahead of time, rather than discussing lots of "if only's" after the race is over.

In the middle of a race, the skipper must often give the crew a quick and concise update to the plan, so they know what to expect through maneuvers. The most experienced crews become so attuned to each other's movements and reactions to various situations that they actually speak less in the course of a race than a group sailing together for the first time. However, the essential maneuvers around the racecourse are always called clearly by the skipper with enough notice for the crew to execute their movements smoothly.

For instance, a skipper approaching the leeward mark on starboard tack may call out, "Start getting ready to drop the chute on the port side—Be ready for an early tack around the mark—Ready to drop in three two…one…drop!" Not much information is conveyed, but just enough to let the crew know what to expect as they go around the buoy and how to time their actions. This skipper doesn't need to tell the bowman how to drop the pole, the pitman how to ease the halyard, the sewerman how to gather and pack the chute, or the trimmers how to ease the sheets—everybody already knows their tasks, but his concise directive got the message across to everyone so they can function as a unit. He's not telling the crew how to do their jobs, but he is guiding them through the essentials they need to know.

Meetings at the end of a race offer the opportunity to both review the team's performance and to plan ahead for the next race. This is a chance to reinforce what is working, and to identify and correct what isn't. Sailors in a crowded and competitive fleet find themselves busy from start to finish, and need this time between races to contemplate areas that need attention and prepare accordingly in order to be ready for the next start.

Meetings are a part of life off the water, too, whether you sit through several every day or just one a year. Office meetings can be tougher to run than crew meetings on the water, and not only because it's a captive audience aboard a boat. Office meetings can wander off task and turn into opportunities to complain or kid around. Office meetings also tend to be held at a regular time of the week to cover a laundry list of business to be handled, rather than immediate actions to be tackled in the next hour such as in a race. Office meetings are often long, with much of the discussion about subjects that only apply to a minority of people in the room at a time. Some office meetings can also turn into opportunities for finger-pointing and criticism, which is destructive to morale. However, meetings can be tamed to be a force for motivation and progress. Here are some of the ways in which the principles of success in communicating strategy with your team can apply off the water as well as on:

- Keep it short, direct, and positive
- Remind the group of the big picture
- Don't spend too much time talking to the group about business applying only to individuals
- Cover the essentials and don't micromanage
- Allow contributions, but stay on task
- If you need to critique someone, do it privately

For Every "What If," Have a "Plan B"

It takes imagination and foresight to stay one step ahead of adversity. Prerace strategizing on any race boat often includes some consideration of reaction to possible changes, be it in regards to equipment or tactics, should they occur. This should generally be communicated as an "If … then" scenario.

For example: "If the wind gets above 15 knots, then we'll change to the heavier jib"; "If the fleet crowds up at the windward end, then we'll start about 1/3 down the line." When conditions could require a change of plan, the sailor will have already determined what his reaction will be. Thinking ahead in this way can also help a sailor to proactively prepare a solution to a potential problem. For instance: "If the spinnaker bursts, then we'll already have the backup ready to go"; "If that boom vang breaks again, then we've got the parts and tools here to fix it."

Anyone can find themselves in a situation that could feasibly change and require a quick response. We often consider what we would do in case of an emergency like a natural disaster: What would we save if we could only take what we can carry? Politicians in a tough campaign must consider how they will respond to their opponent's tactics: If he puts out a negative ad, how should I respond? Stores must consider how to adapt to the changing competitive environment: If our competitor drops their price, do we drop ours?

It's often necessary to think through decisions to their effects and the necessary responses down the line. The game of chess is one of the most universally appreciated games of strategy the world over. For every move made, there is a countermove. Whenever we watch a game being played, we can see the tremendous concentration each player puts into their decision as to their next maneuver. They don't need to just respond to their opponent's last move; they must think several moves ahead as to how their immediate response will trigger their opponent's next move, their own response to that, and the opponent's response in kind. Chess players, like sailors, know the value of thinking many steps ahead in order to make the best decision facing them at the time.

Generals at war must often plan for every contingency, as well. As general in chief of all US armies during the Civil War, Ulysses S. Grant devised a plan to support General William "Tecumseh" Sherman's army on their march into the Carolinas after the capture of Savannah in December of 1864. By preemptively positioning supplies in strategic locations that Sherman may need to reroute to in the face of the opposition he was likely to encounter, Grant ensured that Sherman's troops would not be left empty-handed in the event of a change in plans. This anticipation paid off: Sherman successfully captured Columbia, South Carolina on February 17, 1865, bringing the Civil War significantly closer to its conclusion two months later.

The strategies of the Kennedy administration in handling the Cuban missile crisis of 1962 demonstrate the importance of anticipating an opponent's reaction to a potential move. When Soviet nuclear missile sites were photographed on the island of Cuba by a U-2 spy plane, the crisis began to unfold. This new incursion of Soviet military strength into Cuba would provide the USSR with the potential to strike against virtually any target in the western hemisphere. The White House weighed two primary options: to bomb the sites before their construction could be completed, or to set up a blockade outside of Cuba to deny them resources to complete them. In considering these two options, the Kennedy administration had to consider what the Soviets' reaction would be to either course of action, and the offensive strike option carried particularly grave potential consequences.

Contrary to some of his advisors, Kennedy was convinced a bombing of the missile sites would lead to retaliation, if not in Cuba, than certainly elsewhere. US bases in Turkey were of great concern to Kennedy, and factored heavily into the potential consequences of military action during the crisis. Had the Cuban missile sites been bombed, the Soviets could very well have attacked American sites in Turkey. Under the NATO treaty, this would demand an attack response from US bases in Europe against the Soviet sites that had launched against Turkey. This, in turn, could lead to an attack from the Soviet Union directly on the United States from either the USSR or Cuba, which would require an immediate response against the Soviet Union by the US. Other potential targets for Soviet retaliation existed all over the map, including Korea, Iran, Pakistan, Scandinavia and Italy. In essence, a lack of restraint by either side would quickly escalate into a nuclear war.

The blockade option carried the day, largely because it left more doors open for a way out of war. However, Kennedy ordered readiness for potential military responses not only from US bases, but around the world, particularly in Berlin, where it was assumed that the Soviet Union may respond with a blockade of its own. A US attack response was still a possibility to be prepared for, but was to be pursued only as a last resort to diplomatic efforts concurrent with the implementation of the blockade. The process of stopping a ship in the water still carried dangers of armed conflict. If a ship refused to stop at the blockade, the option of disabling her rudders had to be considered. This, in turn, would lead to boarding the ship and taking it by force. Each "What if?" that was brought up seemed to carry dangerous implications, but the preparation for any and all eventualities was still carried out.

In the end, both sides pulled back from the brink. The Soviet ships stopped at the blockade and then turned back, and the missile sites were dismantled. In turn, the US agreed to remove the quarantine and pledged publicly never to invade Cuba in the future. By understanding the opposition's position and motivations, and therefore its potential responses, the US and the Soviet Union were able to avoid a nuclear war, even if just barely.

Effective strategy means having a game plan that is not only sound, but adaptable. Robert Burns said, "The best-laid plans of mice and men often go awry," meaning that whoever you are, however well prepared you may be, you may be thrown a curveball along the way. Having a "Plan B" or even Plans "C," "D," and "E," for that matter, can help ensure that you are better prepared for any eventuality on the road ahead.

PART THREE

PERFORMING

If happiness is activity in accordance with excellence,
it is reasonable that it should be in accordance with the highest excellence.

—ARISTOTLE

PERIODS OF PERFORMANCE ARE GENERALLY SEEN as the markers along the highway of our lives and careers. These are the moments when planning gives way to action, the results of which will provide a measure of success. For this reason, it is natural and instinctive to place the highest level of significance on this period, yet it may only make up a minor fraction of the achievement cycle in terms of the time it consumes. Three minutes in the spotlight may be the accumulation of a decade's preparation. While the moment of actual performance may be the most significant in the short run, it is only a stop along the road in the long run. At the moment that the time to perform ends, the learning process begins. Every challenge that we face, whether we succeed or not, is a step toward the preparation for the next one. Success may be measured in part by our ability to meet these challenges, but in a larger sense, it is also measured by the growth that occurs between these periods. The time to perform is that which generates the most interest, provokes the most anxiety, and is rewarded the most richly. Kept in perspective, however, it is a chance to measure our own mettle and pursue excellence for its own sake. By giving your all when it is time to perform, you will not only increase your likelihood of winning the day, free of regrets or excuses, but you will also be able to learn from the experience for next time.

GAME TIME

Don't flinch, don't foul—hit the line hard!
—THEODORE ROOSEVELT

AFTER ALL THE PLANNING AND PREPARATION, the constant flow of time eventually brings us to the moment of the contest. For the sailor, the morning of a regatta is often one of great excitement tinged with a hint of nervousness. The well-prepared sailor is significantly less likely to worry, but not necessarily free of nerves. Rather, he is focused on the job at hand and mindful of necessary details. There is a checklist to go down, making sure that the boat is ready to race and that all possible contingencies have been prepared for. There is a constant awareness of timing, making sure that the day's activity is running according to schedule in order to avoid last-minute panic. There is a thorough and well-considered strategy to be developed, evaluated, and executed when the race begins. There will be constant activity all around, so the sailor must maintain focus in order to make decisions quickly and efficiently. It is this kind of focus that is the key to managing the lead-up to, and execution of, a winning performance, whether in sailing or any other challenge. When game time arrives, you will want to have your best game face on. Draw comfort and confidence from the preparation that you have already devoted to your efforts, and concentrate on the task at hand. The past is past, but the race is now.

MIND YOUR MOOD

It's amazing how much of a role music can play in the life and career of an athlete, or anyone for that matter. Morning radio is generally peppy and upbeat to lift people's moods as they face the morning traffic, while music at a big stadium game is loud and exciting to fire up the crowd. It's clear how different kinds of music may affect us; rock may pump up our energy level, while reggae or classical music may bring it down. Many sailors have a few "game time" tunes that help them to psyche up for a first race or rally into a comeback. Some classics have come in handy for America's Cup teams: Ted Turner would play the theme from *Rocky* on the way out to the racecourse, and Dennis Conner's crew would leave the dock to the theme from *Chariots of Fire.*

While it's common to see a pro ball player or golfer listening to headphones before going into action, many of us have a sort of "internal soundtrack" going to manage our nerves. How many times have you seen someone whistling softly or humming to themselves in a nervous situation? You might occasionally see young people drumming on their notepads and humming softly as they wait outside an office for an interview. You don't have to share your music out loud, but if there's a song or tune that comes to mind that will bring you up or down to where you feel your energy needs to be, just let it play in your head and take your mood where you need it to go.

Nerves are common, even to be expected when you're embarking on something important to you. Don't let nerves knock you off your game, though. You can be secure in the knowledge that you've done your homework and prepared thoroughly. You know that you're capable of great things and you're ready for the challenge ahead. You know that the other guy is likely more scared of you than you are of him. And, you know that whatever happens, you'll be doing your best the whole time, no holding back and no regrets. With all that in mind, smile and enjoy the music.

ASSERTIVE OR AGGRESSIVE?

Sailing offers a wide variety of racing formats. There's fleet racing, in which all competitors start together and race around the course, each working to be first across the line. There's match racing, a one-on-one contest in which the tactics are a bit more aggressive. And there's team racing, which generally consists of two teams of three, with each team seeking to finish the race in a winning combination by delivering the lowest combined points relative to individual finish positions. Team racing often requires sacrificing one's own position in order to help bring your teammate up in the standings; the good of the group outweighs the individual's placing. Each of these formats requires the sailors to behave in different ways, sometimes more aggressively than others.

There is a difference between being assertive and being aggressive. Being assertive is generally acting in a strong, decisive way, while being aggressive tends to be more intimidating, with a greater emphasis on dominating the other party. Assertive action is more measured and intellectual than aggressive action, which is more forceful, and often motivated by emotion. Sailboat racing always has times to be assertive, such as when calling for room to round a mark, or fighting for space on a crowded start line. More aggressive maneuvers in sailing are those you might see in match or team racing, such as forcing an opponent away from the mark or maneuvering to block his wind to maximum effect (and often both at once). Assertive moves can be made as if no other boats were around, while aggressive moves are meant generally as an attack on another boat. Being assertive means staying focused and resolute in the face of opposition and moving steadily toward your objective. Being aggressive means going on the offensive with an expectation of a spirited back-and-forth contest.

A fleet-racing sailor needs to be careful not to be more aggressive than is necessary. For example, he may fight so hard for position on the start line that he pushes the whole fleet over the line early. The race committee generally starts imposing stiffer penalties for premature starters when they continually have to recall the fleet. He may find himself quickly disqualified in the next start if he continues to push so hard. Another overly aggressive move might be to engage another boat in a tacking duel, continually tacking to block his wind. It angers the other boat and slows both boats down while the rest of the fleet continues sailing along at full speed. In the big picture, the overly aggressive sailor can lose more than he gains by pushing so hard. He gains a reputation for being a bully (and more colorful names), and sacrifices a better performance for himself by focusing too hard on dominating the guy next to him. In situations like match racing, where you only have to beat the other boat, or team racing, where you have to do all you can to keep your team in a winning combination, aggressive maneuvers are necessary and expected. In fleet racing, however, when you've just got to do your best and keep the big picture in mind, an assertive, rather than aggressive, approach is often preferable. Sometimes, too much aggression doesn't get you what you want; it just antagonizes others and holds you back in the process.

Life on land requires different approaches between assertion and aggression as well. In negotiations, for example, it is necessary and proper for each party to know what their limitations are and to be assertive enough to draw the line in the sand where it needs to be drawn. A simple and polite, "I'm sorry, but that's the best I can do" is assertive enough. It means you've got a spine, but you're reasonable enough to maintain a relationship with. Whatever your career, you will eventually meet someone who favors in-your-face, fist-pounding, coronary-inducing aggression to get their point across. Unless the person is putting on an act to intimidate you, this generally comes from one of two places: 1) an overwhelming desire to be listened to and the feeling that volume is the only way to be heard, or 2) an emotional reaction to whatever difficult situation they're in. Either way, calm and attentive listening and understanding can go a long way when you're facing someone who's breathing fire at you. Acknowledging that you understand their perspective will help address the problem, while a calm demeanor can provide some soothing reassurance to them.

You can be assertive in your daily life, much as a sailor can be assertive on any racecourse. You can see plenty of assertive conviction day to day in something as commonplace as a person ordering coffee. After all, with so many options available, many coffee customers have come to know exactly what they want and are prepared with a detailed (and occasionally long-winded) order. There's no anger or bossiness to it, it's just decisive and clear, and generally pleasant. Polite assertion is a sign of leadership potential, while aggression is simply off-putting when misused. Pick your battles and save your more aggressive responses for the appropriate situations and you'll have less stress and fewer adversaries.

CLAIM YOUR POSITION

Even before the race has begun, the sailor must have a positioning strategy in mind. The strategies of positioning in sailing are numerous and complex, and dependent upon a number of factors, such as the course layout and expected wind and water conditions up the course, the positioning of the competition, and the sailor's tolerance for risk. Considering each of these factors, the sailor can put together a plan for navigating up the course that begins with initial positioning on the start line. Such strategy is often of great value through other challenges as well. Positioning is a commonly used term in marketing circles; It is the place that a product or brand holds in the mind of the consumer, or perhaps that of a candidate for office in the mind of voters. A company launching a new product or a campaigning office seeker would need to consider similar issues to those of a sailor on a start line.

What do trends in the environment indicate will be a good position to occupy in the near future?

Sailors looking to move into the lead in a tough fleet must be attuned to the conditions of wind and water. In addition to being at the favorable end of the start line, they must know whether the current will be favorable on one end of the course or another, where the wind velocity is stronger up the course, whether large waves will be a factor in certain spots, and what trends the shifts in wind direction are showing. Only by taking the long view up the course will the sailor be able to have the full picture in mind when crafting a strategy.

Marketing strategist Al Ries notes the importance of long-term vision when it comes to successful positioning in business. "Changing the direction of a large company is like trying to turn an aircraft carrier," says Ries. "It takes a mile before anything happens. And if it was a wrong turn, getting back on course takes even longer. To play the game successfully, you must make decisions on what your company will be doing not next month or next year, but in 5 years, 10 years ... instead of turning the wheel to meet each fresh wave, a company must point itself in the right direction." One of the pitfalls for a company in setting strategy is the danger of committing strongly to a particular product line or service, but neglecting to determine whether those are the right products or services to offer over the long run. Many a sailor has fought tooth and nail to move to the front of the pack on his side of the course, only to discover as the fleet crosses near the next mark that he's chosen the wrong side of the course to fight for.

Successful positioning in politics can often entail the fine-tuning of the message. Presidential candidates often must "hug the corners" of their party with a more liberal or more conservative message (depending on the party), to win its nomination. To win the general election, the same candidate will often need to appeal to independent and undecided voters with a more "middle-of-the-road" approach. To get too far off to one side of the political spectrum in a national election is to risk alienating a large group of voters, leaving them open to be won by the opposition. By determining the details of their platform first, the candidate can chart a course through the campaign, allowing for minor adjustments down the road while maintaining consistency in the message. Candidates may also shift their campaign schedules to concede certain areas on the map as a waste of time, moving instead to campaign in areas where the margin is much tighter. Whether in a geographical or a conceptual sense, positioning becomes increasingly important in the face of an increasingly competitive environment.

How will you stand out against the competition?

Sailors on a crowded start line place a high priority on the ability to break away from the pack right away. The best possible option is to have a space all to themselves, free from the effects of the other boats. They may also find an opportunity to break away by starting next to an opponent that is not as fast off the line. Positioning themselves next to a slower boat, they are able to leap out ahead of the group sooner, as their slower neighbors continue to affect the rest of the nearby starters with disturbed air. By finding a spot in the crowd that will present an opportunity to shine, the competent sailor reduces their chance of being left behind in the wake of the fleet.

We often see a lot of side-by-side comparisons in the auto industry, as consumers seek out the best possible value for a major purchase. As such, automakers must often stake out a competitive brand position in order to compete in a crowded market. Subaru struggled against competitors like Toyota and Honda in the early 1990s, advertising its cars as "Inexpensive and built to stay that way." Subaru was able to increase sales by repositioning itself through selling only all-wheel drive in its passenger cars, increasing its price, and upgrading its luxury image. Rather than continuing to struggle as a look-alike to its competition, the Subaru brand was revitalized by carving out a unique niche for itself as a safe car appealing to the weekend warrior.

Candidates seeking political office must also play a constant positioning and repositioning game in able to connect to a particular group of voters. In bad times when the public tends to become disillusioned with current office holders, the advantage goes to candidates who can position themselves as political outsiders. Conversely, when times are good, the voting public tends to stick to the names they know. Jimmy Carter both benefited from and suffered for this phenomenon. Carter was elected to the presidency in 1976 in a close election with Gerald Ford, who carried the burden of Richard Nixon's pardon on his shoulders, and was struggling to keep inflation under control. Carter positioned himself as a Washington outsider, emphasizing his rural Georgia background and reputation for honesty. Additionally, he had made reference in his campaign to the "misery index," the sum of the rates of inflation and unemployment, being brought over thirteen percent under the Ford administration. Unfortunately for Carter, his own tenure saw the misery index brought near twenty-two percent, and his inability to quickly resolve the Iran hostage crisis or to keep a solid connection to the voting public led to his defeat in the 1980 election. The struggles of Carter's presidency resulted in the concession of the role of Washington outsider from Carter to his successor, Ronald Reagan.

How far should you go in the pursuit of an advantage?

Sailors may find themselves having to decide how risky or conservative an initial approach to take in their race. If one end of the start line is positioned further into the wind than the other, the fleet will recognize the advantage of starting at that end and a crowd will develop. Crowds on a start line are risky places to be, due to the increase in disturbed wind by more boats as well as the possibility of being pushed over the line early by aggressive competitors. To win the favored end of the start line puts the sailor at a significant advantage, but the risks can outweigh the potential benefits at times. Sometimes sailors can temper this risk by starting about a quarter of the way down the line from the favored end and out of the biggest crowd, taking some advantage of better overall position while keeping clear air. Taking a risk in positioning can pay off at times, but must generally be managed prudently in order to avoid going outside the ideal realm of opportunity.

The positioning of a brand can include some risky marketing strategies, sometimes in terms of financial outlays, and other times in terms of unusual promotional gimmicks. Television advertisements during the Super Bowl, for example, are some of the most expensive ad spots available. The phenomenal exposure of such ads can offer great rewards, but the financial investment in buying time on the air creates a large amount of risk. The 2000 Super Bowl saw many advertisements for dot-com's, several of which went out of business shortly afterward, regardless of the exposure gained from the ads. Positioning in the consumer's mind can also be misdirected with the wrong advertising approach. For instance, while some companies such as Victoria's Secret may benefit from risqué advertising, other companies can draw criticism and controversy rather than customers by taking too steamy an approach. Virgin Mobile drew complaints in Canada over a billboard ad campaign showing couples embracing passionately over the caption "Hook Up Fearlessly," resulting in many of these expensive ads being removed.

Barry Goldwater paid a price for going to extremes in his uphill battle against Lyndon Johnson in the 1964 presidential election. When LBJ metaphorically picked up the fallen president's sword with the salvo, "Let us continue," he positioned himself as the keeper of JFK's legacy. To distance himself from the popular Democratic incumbent, Goldwater went in the other direction, making the statement at the Republican National Convention, "I would remind you that extremism in the defense of liberty is no vice! And let me remind you also that moderation in the pursuit of justice is no virtue!" As the Cold War continued to ramp up, both candidates emphasized how high the stakes of the election were, but Goldwater was quickly branded as a radical who was all too ready to jump into nuclear conflict. Trying to calm criticism of his far-right platform, Goldwater's campaign put out a new slogan, "In your heart, you know he's right." Wags retorted, "In your guts, you know he's nuts." In any number of situations, whether political, athletic, commercial, or personal, it is important to factor in limitations in order to avoid going to risky extremes in positioning.

In a crowded and competitive environment, being able to stand out from the crowd often means not only being able to perform at your best when the time comes, but putting yourself in the right place at the right time. Positioning yourself to take advantage of environmental factors and to respond to competitors, be sure to recognize the risk of going too far in one direction or another. Just as a sailor stuck on the outside corners of the course has lost the option to play shifts, a company or candidate on the outer fringes of the competitive field faces a hard road to reposition themselves. Positioning is a vital, dynamic process that keeps any competitor better equipped to take advantage of future opportunities and to reduce and handle potential threats. It is also a valuable opportunity to define yourself and to build a solid and positive reputation among your peers and the people you want to influence. Determine what your ideal position will be early on, and make it your own.

STARTING STRONG

The beginning is the most important part of the work.

—PLATO

GETTING OFF ON THE RIGHT FOOT is beneficial to any effort, in life or in sailing. Just as a sailor who is well positioned and moving well off the start line carries an advantage over the majority of the pack, so does anyone who can begin their endeavor with direction, energy, and competence. A good start sets a positive tone, opens opportunities, and helps to build momentum. While starting from a disadvantage doesn't rule out ultimate success, it does create an uphill climb and hinder your odds of victory. This principle can be seen in as commonplace a situation as meeting someone new; to get off on the wrong foot with a bad first impression makes it extraordinarily difficult to change the other person's perception of you. With time, you may be able to bring them around, but how much time and energy goes to waste in undoing the damage of a bad start! The beginning stages of any social, professional, or athletic endeavor tend to be the most critical to get right because of the implications that they carry for the future. Just as a rocket must blast off with maximum thrust to be able to reach the upper atmosphere, so must we all make a powerful start in our efforts in order to reach the greatest heights.

GO FOR IT

Getting a good start in sailing comes not only from being properly positioned, but in charging off the line at full speed. By hitting the line with good speed, the sailor will have the ability to leap into an advantageous position earlier in the race, thus improving the chances of a better finish. He must have the boldness on the start line to really go for it and overcome his anxieties, focusing instead on making the charge off the line with faith and courage.

The more difficult the challenge ahead, the more difficult it can be to overcome the self-doubt that prevents you from leaping into action. Business entrepreneurs often struggle with hesitation born of anxiety. They may dwell on concerns over the financial risks involved, whether they'll find a market for their product, or how to deal with the threat of tough competition. For an entrepreneur, it can be tempting to think through the business plan indefinitely, waiting for the perfect opportunity to arrive to actually get started. Without jumping into action, though, the business might never be born. If you can bravely take those first steps, your new venture can take shape like a snowball that gains size and momentum with each push you give it.

Launching at full speed not only gives your effort greater momentum from the start, but it energizes those around you, whether you're starting a business or just arriving at the office to go about your usual routine. How you launch into your day not only affects your own pace from the start of the day until the end, but also has an effect on the energy levels of your coworkers. If someone charges into a room with energy and enthusiasm, it tends to wake up the people who are still struggling to keep their eyes open. Energy can expand among individuals, whether on a boat, in an office, at a party, or in a new business venture. Whether you are getting off to a start for a typical day or for a long-term effort, follow the example that sailors draw from racehorses: Don't just step out of the gate, but launch.

KNOW WHEN TO HOLD BACK

There are times when the sailor needs to hold back a bit, such as when the current is running into the wind and threatens to push the fleet over the line prematurely. Boats that cross the start line early and don't return behind the line to start properly are disqualified from the race. In a particularly aggressive fleet, this can mean that many of the leaders that jumped out in front right away have actually already taken themselves out of the game. Often, sailors may find some surprises upon seeing the day's race results, once all the premature starters have been accounted for. Whether it's good news or not depends on whether they started correctly, and how many of those who finished ahead of them did not. A conservative start that didn't seem good enough at first may turn out in the end to be far more beneficial than it initially seemed.

There might be situations off the water when it is more prudent to ease conservatively into new territory as well. You might be coming in to a new job to take over a popular former employee's position, for instance. In this case, it can be better to tread a little softer in the early days while the other employees get to know you and your style. There's often a danger of pushing too hard, too fast in a number of situations, such as in management, sales, casual conversation, or relationships. Try to be aware of what the limitations of your speed of progress are or could be perceived to be, and work within those boundaries. It may feel frustrating to hold back at times when your gut tells you to go full speed ahead, but let your head keep you in check with your situation; hanging back at first could pay off in the end. As any sailor who has been penalized for a premature start knows, if you come on too strong, you can get yourself disqualified.

TAKE AN EARLY LEAD

For sailors, a crucial element of staying out in front, in addition to getting a good start, is getting to the first shift in as favorable a position as possible. The advantage of an excellent start can be wiped out by being on the wrong side of a big shift early in the race, when everyone is still relatively close together; and breaking away from the pack on the first leg will have much to do with how the first one or two wind shifts affect the fleet. If a sailor has had a superior or at least an even start and played the first wind shifts correctly, they should at least be in the top few boats at the first mark. In sailing, it is generally easier to protect a lead than to regain one, so there is a great benefit to taking the lead early. Standing out from the crowd early in the game can be beneficial off the water, too.

History best remembers those who led the way as pioneers in their fields: Men like Neil Armstrong, Charles Lindbergh, and Edmund Hillary are well remembered for their accomplishments as the first to walk on the moon, fly solo across the Atlantic, and summit Mount Everest, respectively. Being the first mover in any new field can have its advantages; you can take advantage of opportunities before others join in, and you can establish early credibility as someone with special knowledge and expertise.

There are some disadvantages to being the first to lead the way, however.

In a sailboat race, the fleet is able to watch how the wind affects the leaders to be better prepared for approaching shifts. On the shiftiest days, the leaders could find themselves suddenly trapped in a windless hole, which the rest of the fleet can spot and sail around in order to catch up. Likewise in business, the first movers may find themselves plagued by imitators. Tech companies that are first to market may find their designs leapfrogged to the next generation by competitors that follow them. As much as being the first to launch in a competitive arena can be an advantage, it isn't always enough to establish early or long-lasting leadership in the field.

Just as the first boat to the windward mark isn't always the same boat that won the start, taking an early lead in the business world doesn't always come from being the first to market. In the race for customer mind share, marketers strive to establish their brand's leadership early on. Leaders in an industry may not be the first on the scene, but rather the first to claim the best position in the consumer's mind. Although two brothers in Massachusetts, Charles and Frank Duryea, produced America's first gasoline-powered automobiles, many people today might assume that Henry Ford was the country's first automaker, thanks in part to Ford's ability to penetrate the public's consciousness. The difference between the first to move and the first to gain mastery is a matter of how a competitor takes advantage of opportunities early in the game.

For sailors, both a good start and good positioning at the first wind shift make the formula for taking an early lead. One can still make their way to the front of the pack without one or the other, but not both (assuming near-equal speed versus the other boats and winds that aren't wildly unsteady). Passing a competitor that has established an early lead is a tough challenge in sailing, particularly in match racing where the boat to the first mark usually goes on to win the race. Companies that are late starters face an uphill battle, too, rarely gaining an advantage from waiting for the first movers to make a mistake, and instead struggling to keep up with the competitors they follow. For anyone seeking to establish a leadership position in their field of expertise, there's an advantage to taking the lead early, be it in sailing, business, art, engineering, or any number of areas. Make the most of early opportunities, and you won't have to play catch-up with the rest of the pack.

DECISION MAKING

*Some problems are so complex that
you have to be highly intelligent and well informed
just to be undecided about them.*

—LAWRENCE J. PETER

A SAILBOAT RACE IS AN ONGOING exercise in decision making. It takes a prepared and informed mind to be able to constantly weigh the big- and small-picture implications of the decisions being made on the racecourse, but unfortunately there is seldom time to employ these qualities to their fullest potential. The faster the boat, the faster the decisions must be made. It therefore takes no small degree of courage and commitment to make such decisions, particularly in the face of uncertainty. Even the most seemingly obvious choices on a racecourse can result in turnabout, which leaves the ever-present specter of risk hanging over the sailor's head, leaving her to wonder in the deepest regions of her mind, "What if?" When faced with an important and urgent decision, our capacity to take the right course lies in our ability to trust our own judgment, having gathered as much information as possible, weighed the alternatives, and considered their implications for our objectives.

When the different angles of a situation have been evaluated, the determining factor to making the ultimate decision may lie in our intuition. Following a gut feeling when it's time to make a difficult call is often what determines the final outcome for both sailors and non-sailors. It can be intimidating to have to make tough decisions under fire, but generally the people that find themselves entrusted to make important decisions are those who have been brave enough to repeatedly make them with conviction, see them through, and own the results.

MAKE THE CALL: TACK OR STAY THE COURSE?

Sailing often presents the racing sailor with situations in which they only have a couple of seconds to decide whether to change course or to continue, be it spurred on by the presence of a close competitor, or by a change in the wind direction. In the case of a change in the wind direction, the decision rests largely on what the trends in the wind's behavior are indicating, and what will allow the boat to sail the best course to the next mark. This is a strategic decision, determined by the skipper's expectation of how the current wind direction and subsequent wind shifts will affect his boat's course upwind. In the case of the presence of competitors, the skipper is either forced to alter course to avoid a collision with another boat holding the right-of-way, or respond to his competitor's positioning in either a defensive or offensive maneuver. Tactical decisions like these are ongoing, particularly in a large fleet. Since sailing is a game of intangibles, strategic and tactical maneuvering under fire is a skill best demonstrated by teams with plenty of experience and keen instincts.

The decision whether to tack or stay the course can pressure anyone off the water as well. How often have you sat in a traffic jam at rush hour and started mentally calculating alternate routes? How many people have come to the realization that they would like to change jobs, but hesitate to quit for any number of reasons? How many people have been in a relationship that had lost a certain spark and wondered whether to try to rekindle the romance or to move on? Military leaders certainly face tough decisions at times, whether to stay the course with a course of action in the field or to change tactics.

The business world in particular offers up a constant stream of forks in the road to be faced. The more competitive a field in which we operate, the more factors influence our decision and the more possible outcomes there are to consider. Boats that are closely competitive around the course affect each other's tactics with each move that they throw at one another, as do closely competitive businesses. When Pepsi started gaining market share in the cola industry in the 1970s and '80s, Coke decided to "tack" with the radical move of changing its flagship product. New Coke was soundly rejected, though, so Coke had to tack back and bring back their original formula as "Coca-Cola Classic." The cola wars would go on, but Coke's drastic change of course served as a lesson in competition that would set its marketing strategy for years to come.

A successful change of course in response to changing environmental conditions can be illustrated by the rebranding of Banana Republic in the late 80s and early 90s. The Banana Republic image was originally one of adventure; the stores resembled large thatched huts with jeeps and wild animals serving as the décor. By the late 80s, however, the brand began to lose its appeal with consumers and sales began to slide. New management was brought in, and the safari motif was phased out. A brighter, more sophisticated look was adopted for the clothing line and same-store sales growth began to climb. The adventure clothing of the original catalog had been replaced by more traditional fare, with advertising catering to young urban professionals. By transitioning to an "accessible luxury" brand, Banana Republic was able to evolve and avoid obsolescence in the face of changing consumer tastes.

Change can come quickly, whether you're navigating through a competitive fleet of sailboats or a field of hungry business competitors. Either the actions of the competition will prompt a response, as in the cola wars, or a changing environment will require a change of course, as demonstrated by Banana Republic. In some cases, (and perhaps Coke's, in the case given) the best response may be to stay the course. In others, only by moving swiftly and decisively onto a new tack can a more efficient course to one's objective be set. It takes awareness of both the competition and the environment in order to make the decision wisely; Coke's underestimation of its customers' attachment to the company's image, not necessarily the product itself, resulted in a disastrous change that had to be swiftly undone. Further, a decision to take a new tack or not can rely largely on the decision maker's ability to look several steps ahead and anticipate how competitive and environmental influences will affect the outcome of a change or lack thereof. This ability is generally a product of the analysis of all necessary and pertinent information, as well as the instinct inherently gained through experience over time. On or off the water, a change of tack can change the game, and it takes a quick, forward-thinking mind to make the right call.

RECOGNIZE AND MANAGE RISK

Sailors are faced with risk evaluation all over the racecourse, from start to finish. The opportunity for a bold move often presents itself in some form or another, but the sailors who succeed over the long run are those who consciously manage the risks that they take, rather than betting it all on every leg of the course. For sailors, the outer edges of the racecourse tend to be areas of high risk for high reward. Those that get out to a corner on their own may find a shift or a puff that launches them into a big lead, or their own private vacuum that leaves them to wallow alone while the fleet sails away. Picking a corner is not generally the way that long races are won. Rather, a savvy sailor works their way up the side of the course that indicates better wind or water conditions and opportunities to take advantage of likely future wind shifts. The top sailors don't win by gambling; they win by considering what certain moves on the course will have to offer, weighing the risks involved, and executing them successfully.

Mark Reynolds often takes a conservative approach to his racing, which has made him one of the most consistently successful Star sailors in the history of the class. "In the 1988 and 1992 Olympics I'd say we sailed very conservatively all the way through," said Reynolds. "In 1988 we lost the gold by a few points to the British, who won an early race by taking a flyer on the last leg, passing a huge chunk of boats." Reynolds's combination of consistent speed and smart tactics earned him silver and gold medals in '88 and '92, but for his third Olympic appearance, the fickle winds of Savannah made strategy particularly challenging. "At the 1996 Olympics about half way though we were losing contact with the leaders and so took on more risk … it didn't work and we were essentially off the medal stand."

Despite disappointment in '96, Reynolds would return for a fourth Olympic appearance in Sydney. "We struggled for the first half of the regatta," he said. "Our coach (Ed Adams) pointed out that we weren't sailing our normal conservative up-the-middle, fighting-it-out races and needed to get back to that style. We did come back substantially enough to have a shot at the silver or gold going into the last race. We couldn't do worse than a bronze so taking on some risk had a big upside for that last race. We were too aggressive at the start and were OCS, but after immediately returning and going against the grain on the first beat, rounded second and ended up with the gold."

Sailing strategy generally favors more conservative decisions early in a series, in order to avoid taking a poor finish or a disqualification that could limit tactical options down the line. If a sailor has had a relatively strong series coming into the final stretch, and particularly given the option to discard his worst race, it is much more beneficial to preserve the ability to take on some risk in the endgame. "Risk and reward are always in play in sailboat racing—I tend to sail pretty conservative tactically, minimizing risk, but particularly late in a regatta I might need to take on a bit more risk to improve my position," said Reynolds. "I would prefer to let others make high-risk moves early, which tends to thin the field at the top as the regatta progresses."

Risk is a word that can bring out an emotional reaction for many people, because it carries with it the threat of loss. In sport, in war, in finance, or even in relationships, people are faced with decisions that weigh heavily on their hearts and minds, as they struggle to balance the promise of reward against the fear of disaster. Everyone has a certain tolerance for risk at a given time in a given situation. Investors for instance, may be classified as risk seeking, risk tolerant, or risk averse, and these classifications may change for the individual over time. Managing risk for decision making generally comes down to weighing how big the potential reward can be versus how big the potential loss can be, and what your emotional comfort level is in choosing one path over the other.

While many have paved their road to success through more conservative approaches, some embrace the highs and lows of a risk-seeking philosophy, making the most of successes and quickly moving beyond shortfalls. Sir Richard Branson, the founder and CEO of the Virgin Group, is a man who thrives on risk. Branson was barely into his 20s when he founded Virgin as a mail-order music business. He quickly expanded Virgin to a chain of record stores, and then a music studio and a recording label. Virgin would sign such artists as Phil Collins, the Sex Pistols, Boy George, and the Rolling Stones, cementing it as a viable music brand for the long term. Branson was quick to branch the Virgin brand into numerous other areas over the years, including air travel, phone service, car sales, health clubs, financial services, cosmetics, cola, vodka, rail travel, and even space tourism. Not all of these endeavors were particularly successful, but Branson's acceptance of risk has made him willing to push into new areas over time in search of new heights. "For a good slice of the upside," wrote Branson of his approach, "I'll generally accept the greater risk." Branson has also jumped headlong into risky personal efforts in sport.

He has made record-breaking attempts in sailing and hot-air ballooning, both successful and unsuccessful. These efforts were not only costly to mount, but dangerous to life and limb as well. "Every risk is worth taking as long as it's in a good cause, and contributes to a good life," he says. In sport or in business, Branson has remained undaunted in his zeal for new adventures.

Managing risk is more than personality classifications and probable outcome analysis; decision making in a risky endeavor is often based on good instincts gained through experience. Sailors riding a favorable shift sometimes have to force themselves to tack and consolidate their position with the fleet in order to manage risk; they know that the further they get out toward the outer edges of the course, the greater the risk. A less experienced sailor may stay on a lifted tack far too long, neglecting their positioning for the next likely shift. This can also be seen on Wall Street, where an investor needs to know where to draw the line in terms of how great a risk to accept. Joseph P. Kennedy was working on Wall Street in early 1929, when he sensed that something was amiss with the stock market, even as many others continued to invest as stock values rose. He had to make a decision: whether to stay the course and see how high his own stocks could go, or to break ranks and sell. Recognizing the dangerous conditions developing and the enormous risk of staying invested, he sold his shares just months before the market began to spiral down into a crash. Kennedy had sensed when to break away from the pack, and his fortune was preserved through the Great Depression while others went broke.

Experience brings with it not only the knowledge necessary to make a good judgment call when faced with a risky decision, but also the instincts needed to do so. In the end, our assessment of risk and our capacity for making a sound decision needs to come from intuition gained over time as well as calculation. It might put many of us at ease if statistical analysis could account reliably for every possible contingency and give us a quantified answer as to how to handle risk in every situation. However, not every problem can be number crunched to a solution, and we aren't usually given the time to put a lot of advanced analysis into every tough decision. What we can do is to gather all available information, consider the possible outcomes for one move versus the other, evaluate where our priorities lie for expected results, and listen to our gut.

BUILD YOUR DEFENSE

One of the main principles of competitive sailing is covering, or positioning oneself between the opponent and the next mark in order to minimize his chances of finding a passing lane. There is little opportunity in covering for the leader to go off and find their own wind to increase their lead, but through these defensive tactics, they take an active approach in preserving the position that they have already gained. The successful application of a cover on a trailing boat depends on the leader's ability to know certain factors about the nature of the challengers he faces and the tactics they are likely to use to threaten his position:

Who the greatest threat is

The strongest challenger is not always the greatest threat, particularly when it is well into the game. Competitive corporations taking the long view often must consider whether to defend themselves against a close competitor or a distant competitor. For example, Coke spent decades focusing its defensive marketing strategies against a close competitor, Pepsi, only to lose market share over time to a distant competitor, bottled water. In sailing, the boat to stay ahead of may not necessarily be the closest boat or the toughest boat to beat, but rather the one that stands to alter the final score by their placement versus your own at the finish. It may be necessary to sacrifice one's own position and focus on keeping a particular boat out of the top ranks, as Great Britain's Ben Ainslie did to secure his gold medal at the 2000 Olympics (more on this story later), in order to preserve one's place atop the leader board. To employ this tactic may be to lose a battle in order to win the war.

What defensive position to take against the challenger(s)

Sun Tzu wrote, "One does not rely on the enemy not attacking, but on the fact that he himself is unassailable." This is sound advice for anyone that needs to set up a strong defense. Facing opposition requires anticipation of the challenger's most likely course of action and creating a defense ahead of time to reduce the threat posed. For a sailor, this means thinking a few steps ahead and getting his boat into the right place at the right time in order to preemptively block his competition from getting past. By considering environmental conditions as well as the position of the entire fleet, the leader of the pack can maintain his lead by positioning himself in such a way that takes advantage of current conditions and also keeps his rivals in check. If a sailor wishes to protect a position on the right side of the course due to stronger wind or an expected shift, for example, he would position his own boat to the right of the competition and herd his competitors to the left, away from conditions that may prove beneficial to them.

How your actions will affect the challenger

On the racecourse, the leader must consider whether to 1) apply a cover at all, 2) apply a close cover, or 3) apply a loose cover. When crossing ahead of the challenger, the leader could keep going, which will give the challenger incentive to continue going in the other direction for a while. If the leader applies a close cover, he is positioning his boat to block the wind of his challenger, which in most cases will force the challenger to tack away in the other direction. If a loose cover is applied, the trailing boat's wind is not threatened, but the leader comes along with the challenger in the same direction, in order to minimize the effect of any wind shift that may threaten his lead. Each action taken by the leader has a likely reaction from the challenger, which must be considered before being executed.

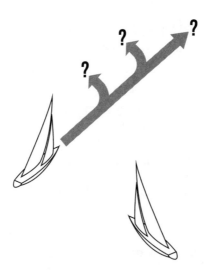

Anyone in a competitive environment will need an understanding of what a new course of action will mean for the opposition. Will he have incentive to retreat, or respond? Is he being tempted with options or threatened by assaults?

Is he likely to engage in mutually destructive behavior in order to prevent a win for you? Whether it's a matter of saving face or cutting losses, a competitor backed into a corner can implement responses that can adversely affect both sides, so it's only prudent for any defender to gain some perspective as to how his tactics will drive his challenger's next move.

How the challenger's actions will affect you

When a trailing boat's wind is blocked, its best response is generally to tack away to seek clear air. When the leader provokes a response from the challenger in this way, it will commit her to make a decision whether to continue a defensive attack through a tacking duel, or to split and regain momentum, having sent her opponent off in the opposite direction. If a trailing boat tacks away for clear air and tacks back again in the same direction as the leader, the decision now rests with the leader whether to tack twice to cover again, or to continue on in search of the next wind shift. The close cover can therefore be a double-edged sword for the leader; it slows the trailing boat temporarily, but forces additional risk onto the leader's shoulders as a result of the inevitable response of the challenger. The leader must expect aggression to be answered, and she, in turn, must have a response in mind. When a trailing boat gets within passing distance, it may initiate a tacking duel with the leader. This becomes a rapid boat handling and positioning contest, in which the leader strives to block the air and the passing lane of the challenger, while the challenger looks to gain the upper hand through better maneuvering.

Close competitors in retail often face a "tacking duel" of their own when price wars are initiated. If one company lowers the price of its product in order to gain the business of its competitor's customers, the competitor must consider whether to lower its price as well. This can result in a race to the bottom, in which both competitors' profit margins are whittled away. So it is on the water as well: when two boats get into a fierce tacking duel with one another, they often lose momentum to the point that other teams that are uninvolved in the conflict are given the chance to catch up.

We may occasionally find ourselves in a back-and-forth duel with people in our personal and professional lives, engaging in retaliatory behavior after some unfortunate incident. Children often get drawn into such efforts to "get the other guy back." These sorts of rivalries can turn self-destructive, as each party tries to best the other, with both sides hurting in the end. When tempted to get drawn into a little war of your own, consider the appropriateness of the acronym for mutually assured destruction (MAD).

How environmental (in)stability could affect your defense

When the winds are steady, covering tactics are fairly straightforward for a sailor. Because the boats are sailing in the same breeze, covering is a more reliable defense against a challenger of relatively equal speed. When the winds become shifty, with large variations in direction and velocity across the course, it becomes much more difficult to make a "textbook" cover stick. Boats in close proximity can be sailing in a very different breeze, greatly reducing the advantage of covering. In a shifting environment, the leader has more incentive to focus on sailing the best course to the next mark over his positioning in comparison to his closest competitor. It becomes a balancing act of responding to the compass and keeping the fleet in check, as the skipper tries to spend as much time on a favorable shift as possible before heading back to stay in phase with the competition.

Volatile conditions can demand a change of strategy off the water as well. Personal tech devices in general evolve quickly, reflective not only of competition within their industry, but also the changing habits, tastes, and expectations of the consumer. Our devices change so quickly that the line can become blurred whether we adapt to our toys or they adapt to us. The video game industry has been through some big changes over the years, having to respond not only to a fiercely competitive and rapidly changing market, but also a customer base that is a constant challenge to satisfy. There was a big environmental shift in the game industry when concern grew that video games encouraged a sedentary lifestyle. Nintendo was losing out to Sony and Microsoft, until Nintendo developed the Wii in 2006. Gamers found the physical activity involved in playing on the Wii console a refreshing change, and sales soared. Like a sailor balancing playing the shifting winds and staying in touch with the competition, Nintendo was able to regain the lead in the industry. When the course becomes too unstable to stick with the herd, it's often better to focus on finding your own direction to the next mark.

KEEP THE BIG PICTURE IN MIND

As the wind is constantly changing, the racing sailor must be constantly attuned to its subtle shifts in direction and strength, positioning his boat in the best possible way to take advantage of these changes. Since the wind itself is difficult to see, its effects on the environment around us provide the best clues as to the wind's actions. The dark ripples caused by the wind over smooth water makes puffs of wind more visible to sailors watching for them. Such patches aren't as obvious when being observed while swimming, or sitting just above the water, when compared to being viewed from higher up. Sailors on the largest racing yachts often hoist a crewman up the rig so that he can communicate to the skipper and the "brain trust" what wind he is seeing from his lofty perch. Seeing the big picture can often open our eyes to the world around us in other ways as well.

There is an ancient eastern parable about a king who gathered six blind men to describe an elephant to him, an animal that none of them knew anything about. The six blind men each approached the elephant and inspected a different body part with their hands. The man who felt the ear said the elephant was like a hand fan; the one who felt the trunk said it was like the branch of a tree; the man who felt the tusk said it was like a pipe; the man who felt the leg said it was like a pillar; the one who felt the belly said it was like a wall; and the man who felt the tail said that the elephant was like a rope. The men disagreed fiercely until the king set them straight and gave them the full picture. Each of these men was right in describing what they could perceive, but each was also wrong because they lacked the viewpoint to understand the elephant as a whole. This fable offers a lesson that one should look at any situation from a new perspective to get to the truth of it. Sometimes we can see much more clearly by broadening our view.

A sailboat race also requires a big-picture view when it comes to the other boats, as well as the wind on the course. As the fleet spreads out across the racecourse, the sailor's strategy must encompass their tactics. Strategy refers to the overall plan of attack, while tactics refers to the maneuvers made between boats to make it happen. For example, if a sailor's strategy is to keep to the left side of the course to take advantage of the best wind, they may aggressively block the wind of other boats heading in that direction in order to force them away in search of clear wind, and thereby keep the left side for themselves. The big picture strategy keeps you moving in the right direction and helps you keep an eye on your competition.

Just as the sailor must always know where he stands on the course in relation to shifts that he can take advantage of, he must also be aware of the position of his closest competitors. Similarly, business strategists must employ clever tactics by way of pricing, advertising, and packaging their products, but they must keep a big-picture strategy in mind in order to maintain their position in the competitive marketplace. When two companies constantly update their promotional efforts with clever ads and occasionally renew the packaging of their well-known products, they also have to be aware of consumer tastes in order to remain viable over the long run in their market. Their promotional tactics may keep each other clawing for position, but their overall strategy must be in line with consumer preferences, or they risk irrelevance. Close competitors undergoing any important endeavor must mind the forest as well as the trees.

Successful investors know the value of keeping the big picture in mind as well. Numerous economic, social, and political factors affect the value of investments the world over every day, so it becomes critical for any savvy investor to widen their gaze in order to make informed and intelligent decisions about their investment strategies. It isn't enough to know what the current condition of a potential investment is; world events, fluctuating market conditions, and potential environmental disruptions are all factors that can influence the future value of an investment, and must therefore be considered in order to make a well-informed decision.

Looking at a problem from a bird's-eye view can be an eye-opening experience. While the task at hand may be pressing, the best decision for handling it may lie in clues seen from a different perspective. The long-term and further-reaching implications of different alternatives, once recognized, can determine the wiser course of action in a given situation. You'll find that getting hypnotized by the close-range details of a situation can distract you from the opportunities that lie from a big-picture perspective. The Age of Exploration followed an era in which a common notion was that the world is flat, and that ships that strayed too far from shore may fall off the edge.

Indeed, from ground level, the world does appear to be flat, so the idea that it may be round would seem absurd to the average person at that time. It was soon enough theorized, then tested, then proved, and finally photographed from outer space, that the world is round. Who knows how different history may have been if sailors and scientists hadn't opened people's eyes to this larger world view?

RECOGNIZE PRIORITIES

When conditions start to get dangerous in sailing, skippers must often change their strategy from contention to preservation. Whether the conditions or the other competitors are the source of the danger at hand, the skipper and the team must keep in mind what is truly important in a crisis. The priorities that make the most sense for a sailor, in order of importance, are:

1. Protect the crew
2. Preserve the boat
3. Pursue the race

If a collision between two large yachts is imminent and unavoidable, the important thing is for the crew to be out of harm's way, not to throw the fenders out to save the paint job. If a decision ever comes down to damaging the boat in order to avoid harm to a sailor, the sailor's well-being takes priority every time. People are irreplaceable; they are the most important asset of any organization, and the safety of others always has to take priority in a crisis. As Confucius said, "He who wishes to secure the good of others has already secured his own."

The boat is the next most important thing to protect, not simply because it is expensive and well loved in its own right, but because it is the support system of the people aboard it. During the Jules Verne or the Volvo Ocean Race, teams have to push their yachts to extremes in order to stay in the race, but they have to know when to throttle back to keep the boat in one piece. If the keel or the hull's integrity were suspect in a cold, windy environment like the Southern Ocean, it would be madness to risk the boat to gain an extra quarter knot of boat speed; if the boat fails, the crew is endangered. The boat also represents a large investment in terms of both time and resources. Nobody wants to see a valued and valuable asset lost when things go wrong, but the safety of an object can't take priority over the safety of people.

The pursuit of the race may be the team's original purpose, but emergencies can put things into a new perspective. To protect the boat, the team may have to leave an excessively dangerous race, just as to protect the crew they should be willing to risk damage to the boat. Races come around again, or can be restarted. Boats, while expensive and treasured, can be repaired or replaced. The people on board are truly the most important thing to be guarded. When all is well and the team is out of danger, the people can push themselves and the boat to pursue the race once again.

In the 1988 Olympics, sailed in the waters off Pusan, South Korea, Canadian Finn sailor Lawrence Lemieux found himself looking at a situation that meant losing a shot at a medal in order to help someone in trouble. Lemieux had worked his way into striking distance of a medal as the winds rose to thirty-five knots in the fifth race. During the race, he sailed past the capsized 470 team from Singapore. They were clearly in distress, as one sailor clung to the overturned hull and the other drifted further away from the boat, too hurt to swim back. Lemieux sailed over to the hurt sailor in the water and picked him up, then went back to help the other, staying with them until they could be picked up by a Korean Navy boat. He managed to return to his race, but finished far enough back in the pack that his hopes for a medal were lost.

Lemieux did not go home empty-handed, however. In addition to winning the respect and admiration of his fellow competitors, he was awarded the Pierre de Coubertin Medal for Fair Play by IOC president Juan Antonio Samaranch, who told Lemieux, "You embody all that is right with the Olympic ideal." Lemieux was in the race of a lifetime, within reach of a career-topping achievement, but he knew that if he sailed away and anything had happened to those other sailors, he'd regret it for the rest of his life. Years later, he would reflect that although he could have won gold that day, if he had to go through that situation again, he would still do the same thing.

A common question that arises for people is, "If your house were on fire, what would you take with you?" Arthur Conan Doyle's story *A Scandal in Bohemia* provides an interesting illustration of this scenario. In this tale, Sherlock Holmes smokes out a blackmailer who is hiding a potentially scandalous photograph. Holmes learned the location of the incriminating photograph by making a false alarm of fire and watching the suspect's reaction;

"When a woman thinks that her house is on fire, her instinct is at once to rush to the thing which she values most," he explained to Dr. Watson. "A married woman grabs at her baby; an unmarried one reaches for her jewel-box." Holmes expected that his suspect would dash to preserve the photo that she was using to blackmail her victim, and she did. As the great detective pointed out, different people have different priorities; since she had no baby or jewel-box to protect, she sought to protect the asset that would further her plan. If an emergency suddenly arose, what, or who, would *you* rush to protect?

It's worth taking the time to consider what is of value in one's life before danger strikes. With a full appreciation of what is most important, protecting it in times of danger is instinctive. A sailor has no wish to sacrifice the race or the boat when a dangerous situation arises, but he must be prepared to do so to protect the safety of the people aboard the boat. Careers, like races, can be renewed. Assets, like boats, can be rebuilt. It's natural to value ambitious objectives and prized possessions, but people are more valuable than gold or glory.

NEGOTIATE INTERFERENCE AND OBSTACLES

Sailboat races in lumpy water and shifty winds tend to spread the fleet out, because there are more environmental challenges that can slow a boat down. Sailors find their racecourses fraught with obstacles and interferences that complicate their strategy. For inshore racers, there could be a shoreline, an island, moored boats, sandbars, reefs, or lobster pots to get around, and those are just some of the obstacles that are standing still. There might be litter or large strands of kelp floating on or beneath the surface to catch on the appendages. Additionally, there is often interference to wind and water consistency by other boaters nearby, such as other racing fleets on the same course, a spectator fleet or recreationalists like jet skiers and cruisers. The factor that determines degrees of success is how each boat responds to various influences, such as waves, windless holes, or adverse wind shifts, which can slow progress to the next mark. When a boat can't get around an obstacle such as a hole or wave, it must go through or over it as fast as possible. Not only does the racing sailor have to plan their tactics according to wind shifts and other competitors, but also allow for the ability to maneuver around or through anything that could hurt their progress. Winning a race doesn't always depend on who went faster so much as it reflects who slowed down the least.

While some obstacles must be steered around, such as solid land, sailors are occasionally faced with less tangible forces that can harm their progress, but can be either steered around or plowed through. This could include disturbed wind from behind buildings, trees, other sails, or waves, either natural or created by other boats. Sailors and non-sailors alike must ask themselves two questions when something gets in their way:

Will going around take us too far off course to be worthwhile?

Will going through be too harmful to justify staying the course?

These questions have faced leaders throughout history. Hannibal of Carthage is best known for his treacherous crossing of the Alps into Italy in 218 BC in an effort to confront Rome's forces and protect his homeland from Rome's expansion. While the Mediterranean coastline would provide an easier and more direct route to Italy from Carthage, Hannibal had to make a course change when Roman forces arrived at what is today the city of Marseilles. Concluding that engaging the Romans at that point would be too risky to the overall mission, he decided to reroute north along the Rhone River toward the mountains. Even though he was criticized for this decision, Hannibal kept the final objective of the invasion of Rome in mind and avoided a conflict that could have ended his campaign early.

Hannibal's decision to go around one obstacle forced him to go through another, however. By traveling so far north into the Alps, Hannibal's army faced bitterly cold conditions, fierce resistance from mountain tribes, and treacherous climbs and descents. After six months of hard travel, Hannibal had lost thousands of his men, but had accomplished an impossible journey with an army still strong enough to battle Rome. An advantage of coming through the Alps was the element of surprise; the Roman army knew that Hannibal was on his way, but couldn't imagine an enemy invading from the mountains and thus amassed their forces in the south, expecting to meet him near Sicily. When Hannibal arrived, the Romans were forced to reroute forces to the north to oppose him. Through wise tactics and dogged persistence, Hannibal led his army to victories at the Trebbia River, Lake Trasimene, and Cannae. Although Rome eventually did overtake Carthage, Hannibal's battle against the Romans on their own turf had successfully kept them tied down in conflict with him and away from his homeland for another fifteen years.

A rough road ahead may be worth enduring if it keeps you on track and doesn't detract too much from your progress toward your goal. A sailor in clear air and on a good course to the next mark will generally choose to drive through some choppy water ahead rather than tack to avoid it. If she can find the path of least resistance through the waves ahead, the sailor can carve through the smoother parts without tacking at all, thus keeping on the favored tack, maintaining speed, and avoiding some extra spray in the face in the process. Disturbed air from other boats also needs to be avoided, but if the other boat is traveling in the opposite direction, the sailor can hold her course and endure it briefly until it passes. The sailor may have to consider tacking away though, if the other boat is traveling in the same direction and could hold its wind shadow over them for more than a few seconds. It's simply a matter of give and take; what is being sacrificed for the sake of making a gain. Decisions such as these in response to obstacles are a fundamental element of strategic thinking in any endeavor.

Golf, like sailing, is a cerebral sport in that it places a premium on strategic thinking. Golf courses are designed to challenge players' ability to make decisions that will allow them to navigate a variety of obstacles along the way: water hazards, sand traps, tall grasses, and sometimes even sheer cliffs lie in wait for the ball that soars off course. Using his judgment of his own swing and the potential distance to be covered by the choice of a particular club, a golfer must constantly decide whether to go for a longer drive toward the pin or to take shorter shots to allow better accuracy through the hazards that lie ahead. Often, a golfer may find his ball in a difficult lie, perhaps behind some trees. The question of whether to try to shoot through the trees on a straighter course to the pin or around them for an easier shot from the fairway must now be considered. A bold golfer may decide to take the difficult shot through the trees, but runs the risk of adding even more strokes to his score if the shot is less than perfect. The more conservative player would take a shot away from the trees, even though off course from the most direct line to the pin, in order to line up a clearer shot to the green. The nature of the game sets up numerous challenges like these that test the player's judgment of risk and reward.

Obstacles appear before us regularly in the course of our daily lives in a variety of forms. A business may find that factors outside its own control have suddenly and drastically reduced demand for its products, for instance. The question whether to go through this obstacle (shift marketing strategy to rebuild customer loyalty) or to go around it (change the product line to match shifts in preferences) stands before the company for management's decision. Or, in a more universal context, the obstacle facing us could be a traffic jam along our preferred freeway route; do we tough it out through the traffic and drive less distance, or escape to a longer alternate route along surface streets? The obstacle facing us could be another person with an opposing stance on an important issue to our own; do we ignore their criticism and stick to our guns, or try to win them over to our cause?

Whether it is better to go around or through an obstacle depends entirely upon the situation as you find it; the best decision under the circumstances depends on the potential gain and loss of either move. Ask yourself whether a temporary change of course will help or hurt your ultimate progress to the objective, and make the call to the best of your ability.

THE BEST PATH ISN'T ALWAYS A STRAIGHT LINE

There's an axiom in mathematics that states that the shortest distance between two points is a straight line. This may be true in geometric terms, but when applied to the human experience, the shortest distance from point A to point B isn't always the most effective for us. There are times in sailing or in life when we need to go a bit off course in order to make the gains we need to truly shine.

On the off-wind legs of a yacht racing course, boats have more freedom of movement in choosing their course to the next mark with the wind astern. The presence of waves on the course can create surfing conditions which add a new element to downwind sailing: the ability to steer and trim the sails in order to catch and surf the waves. Multiple world champion and Olympic medalist Torben Grael of Brazil gained a reputation for excelling at surfing waves early in his sailing career. The technique he would exploit to make massive gains on the downwind legs of a racecourse meant sailing fifty percent extra distance, but going one hundred percent faster. Rather than pointing the bow of his boat directly at the next mark and starting and stopping through short rides while going straight downwind, Grael would sail a higher and faster course first, reaching across the face of a wave, and then bearing away sharply as soon as the wave lifted the boat's stern. This would launch his boat down the wave's face at double speed. When his boat would catch up to the next wave ahead, he would sail high and fast again to stay on the wave for a longer ride. This is a technique that top sailors demonstrate with exceptional skill when conditions permit. Surfing this way means curving and snaking through the waves all the way to the next mark, but the extra distance is worth the payoff for the added speed. You don't have to be always aimed directly at your objective to get there successfully.

Former Vice President Al Gore has had a career full of twists and turns. Gore entered Harvard intending to pursue an English major and to write a book. The assassination of Martin Luther King Jr. spurred his interest in political affairs, however, and Gore switched his major to government. After two years serving in the army, Gore embarked on a journalism career and studied law at Vanderbilt. This marked a tipping point in his career, in which multiple options were open to him for the future. When his father's former seat in the House of Representatives was about to become vacant in 1976, Gore ran for Congress and won, kicking off his political career. Gore would hold his seat in the House until 1984, and in the Senate from '84 to '93, serving on the US House Committees on Energy & Commerce and Science & Technology. Becoming Bill Clinton's VP in 1993, Gore continued to promote environmental awareness as well as the development of information technology. After losing a closely contested Presidential election to George W. Bush in 2000, he fed his passion for environmental activism with his production of the documentary *An Inconvenient Truth*, which addressed the topic of climate change and earned him an Oscar in 2007. Gore was also co-awarded the Nobel Peace Prize that same year for "efforts to build up and disseminate greater knowledge about man-made climate change, and to lay the foundations for the measures that are needed to counteract such change." Gore's standing in the political, technological, and environmental fields allowed him to write and publish several books over the course of his career, including the *New York Times* bestselling companion book to *An Inconvenient Truth*.

Gore's rise to prominence took some turns that could have launched him onto a very different course. His journey seemed to come full circle in the aftermath of his political career; the young man who had wanted to be an author and took a new path into politics still wound up the author of a #1 *New York Times* bestseller, apart from, but thanks in part to, his political career. Like the sailor seeming to sail away from the next mark at first, only to come surfing back in a better position than before, Gore found great success in areas that appealed to him before he ever ran for office. Anyone can find their journey through their life and career taking some turns that are seemingly off course, but as long as the new course keeps you growing and moving forward, you can still get to your destination in better shape than you could have imagined.

WATCH FOR OPPORTUNITIES

Opportunities in life, as in sailing, are not obvious to everyone, nor does everyone know what to look for in search of one. They do appear for everyone at some time, in some form or another, and it is those individuals who can recognize an opportunity and seize it that open up new possibilities for themselves. An opportunity can come and go quickly in sailing; it may appear in the form of a small puff of wind just forming on the corner of the course; it may be a brief moment in which to tack and cross the bow of a competitor; it may be a chance to gain an inside overlap at a crowded mark rounding; it may be a wave just big enough to surf past the nearest opponent. The craftiest sailors are those who see opportunities forming and can make a fast decision in order to take advantage of them. At the conclusion of a race, the top finishers can recount each opportunity they took advantage of, the middle finishers can remember some they took advantage of and others they wish they had, and those at the bottom of the pack often didn't see any opportunities at all.

Ray Kroc was a man who saw an opportunity late in his career and took full advantage of it. At the age of fifty-two, Kroc was working near Chicago as a milk-shake mixer salesman in 1954. One of his biggest customers was a drive-in restaurant in San Bernardino, California that was owned by two brothers, Dick and Mac McDonald. The McDonald brothers had purchased eight of Kroc's machines, each of which could blend five shakes at a time. Kroc was interested to see what kind of restaurant might need to make forty shakes at once, so he went out to see the McDonald brothers in California. He was impressed when he saw their restaurant's efficient operations: the menu was simple and competitively priced, the food was prepared within a minute by assembly line, and there was no need for cleanup thanks to paper plates and plastic utensils. Kroc had a lot of experience in the food industry, which gave him good instincts about the business. He also had seen many of his customers struggling to keep their businesses running smoothly due to disorganized operations and management. Seeing the possibilities for the McDonald brothers' restaurant, he brokered a deal with them to expand the business by selling McDonald's franchises.

Kroc quickly expanded the business as a chain, starting back in his own hometown in Illinois. He implemented standards for each restaurant to follow, such as standardized ingredients for each menu item, employee training, and restaurant upkeep. To keep the restaurants operating consistently, he needed to have them all operating beneath one umbrella of management, so he decided to buy out the McDonald brothers. In order to keep control of the restaurants and pay off the loan used to buy out the McDonalds, Kroc would purchase the land for a McDonald's franchise to be built upon, earning rent from the franchisee and maintaining control over the use of the property. This allowed McDonald's to expand not only nationwide, but around the world. Kroc's ability to take the initiative and build up McDonald's restaurants created a fast-food empire and a giant of American industry.

When Kroc happened upon the McDonald brothers' restaurant, it was in a time when families were moving to the suburbs, the automobile was becoming a major part of daily life, and people were embracing convenience in their lives. Recognizing that America would surely embrace the McDonald's formula, Kroc took advantage of an opportunity and worked relentlessly to make it succeed and grow. Kroc's sales career was winding down at the time, and he knew that such an opportunity would not likely come along for him again. Rather than ease into retirement, he found and nurtured a new enterprise for which he would hold a passion for the rest of his life. A sailor knows that his surroundings are constantly changing, and golden opportunities will only appear once in a while. If he doesn't seize the opportunity, someone else will, or it will go away. Use your instincts to spot opportunities as they present themselves, as they eventually do, and grab hold of them. Like they say in baseball, you'll never hit a home run if you never swing the bat.

DEVELOP AND USE YOUR INTUITION

Intuition is a valuable skill in sailing or any other area. Everyone has some degree of natural intuition, evidenced by a general "feeling" about a situation that may weigh on our minds from time to time. This inner voice is there to keep us on our toes to make decisions that will serve to our benefit, even when little information is available to drive those decisions. Hiring managers often have to listen to their intuition when considering various candidates for a job; there may be several qualified prospects, but there may be one about whom the manager has a better "feeling" than the others, and that is generally the one who gets the job in an otherwise dead heat. While we all have natural intuition, not unlike animals able to sense an approaching earthquake before instruments detect it, intuition is also the result of experiences long filed away in the information stores of the mind.

Buddy Melges gained a reputation in his sailing career for being a "seat of the pants" sailor. He had all the necessary training in the scientific side of sailing, but his time on the water sharpened his instincts as well. Many top sailing teams use advanced instruments to provide constant data feedback about their boat's performance. Melges didn't deny himself any of the tools and instruments for developing better boat speed, but he also learned to use all of his senses to drive a boat more efficiently.

Sensitivity to one's surroundings can give a sailor an advantage over the competition. He may be able to sense a wind shift coming by the smell of a barn on shore, for instance, or he might feel a subtle change in the helm indicating a change of the current. Some skippers cut their hair extra short just before a regatta to allow themselves to feel the breeze on the back of their neck. Experience in a particular boat will attune the sailors to the sounds the boat makes, and what they indicate. By actively tuning in to what's happening around him, a sailor can develop his sixth sense to give him an edge over the competition. The sixth sense is a heightened awareness of and intuition about the situation that demands focus. When it is working well, little clues pop up which indicate what's happening and what could happen next.

Intuition can be a defining advantage in athletic, personal, or professional decisions, not based solely on a gut feeling, but on a sense of direction deduced by influential factors like knowledge, experience, and rationality. Intuition in practice is quite different from impulse; impulse is a quick and emotional reaction, such as screaming or running away when frightened. In most important decisions, it is not an impulsive gut reaction that steers us on the better course, but a reasoned and well-considered conclusion in concert with an intuitive feel of the situation. Intuition also demands action through its provision of insight into opportunity. It takes follow-through on intuitive decisions to take advantage of them. Without action, intuition can ring hollow. Sailors often face situations in which something in the wind or water suddenly changes and the feel of the boat is all wrong. A less experienced sailor may act impulsively, tacking out of phase with the wind or fiddling with sail trim, but the more experienced racer will think about what the issue could be and trust his instincts as to how to deal with the new conditions.

A sense of urgency can often cloud our ability to use our instincts in a reasoned and constructive way. It takes a presence of conscious mind in combination with ingrained intuition and instinct to act in our own best interests. A diver must keep constant watch on their air supply in order to avoid having to rush to the surface for oxygen. If they run short of air while diving deep, the body's impulse will be one of survival; to return to the surface as fast as possible. To give in to that impulse would give the diver a case of decompression sickness, also known as the "bends," which would result in a quick trip to the hospital. When pressed to make a decision, your intuition can be your best asset, but it must be employed in concert with reason to avoid doing anything rash. Whatever your field, keep your antennae tuned to your environment as much as possible to develop your intuition over time; the instincts you gain will serve you well when they are called upon.

BE PATIENT

Difficult undertakings frequently challenge our patience. Whether we're trying to win a race, earn a profit, learn a skill, plant a garden, or get into shape, we don't always see results as fast as we'd like. There might be temptation to quit, but only through patience and persistence will the time spent prove to have been worthwhile. Aristotle knew this when he said, "Patience is bitter, but its fruit is sweet." There may also be a temptation to change course in the hopes of making a big leap forward when things aren't going as expected. We may even find things going our way and, with great rewards in sight, act to hasten their attainment. This impatience—the desire to speed up the moment of ultimate success—can often be to the detriment of an otherwise well-planned effort. A cool and patient approach to one's efforts means being able to choose the right opportunities to take and to manage the emotions which tend to flow from the undertaking of a difficult challenge: the fear of loss, the frustrations of slow progress, and the thirst for greater success.

Don't Panic When Things Are Looking Bad

Patience is a virtue, but it can be elusive. It is a state of mind that requires calmness to the core, a difficult state to reach when pressure is on. Pressure can be borne of high expectations and the frustration of not having met them. Pressure can also result in a panic response, leading rational individuals to make irrational decisions to salvage some small degree of success.

Investing is a constant exercise in patience, particularly when the investor begins to see a loss. Those intending to buy low and sell high often find themselves buying high and selling low instead, in a panicked response to a downturn in their shares' value. Unwilling to wait out the latest fluctuation, they sell their investment to "cut their losses," sometimes to find that the asset recovers its value down the line. Warren Buffett has said, "If you can't control your emotions, you can't control your money." Two emotions that can drive investors' decisions are greed and fear of loss, which lead to frustration and impatience. When they do not see the results that they wish for and expect, they may irrationally respond in a self-defeating manner. Such knee-jerk reactions to anxious situations can get us into trouble in any number of commonplace scenarios. How many of us have gotten impatient and bailed out of our current situation to no avail at the grocery store? It can be tempting to jump out of a long line to the register and move into a shorter one, but we often find that our new, shorter line is moving much slower than the one we were just in!

Impatience in sailing, likewise, stems from fear and greed: the fear of losing and the greed for gains in position. Falling behind can set off the panic response for a sailor watching his lead evaporate, due to an unfavorable wind shift, for instance. When a confident sailor has high expectations of himself, and the skills to back up those expectations, but not the patience to keep cool when things get tough, panic sets in and he may take a big risk in an attempt to regain the advantage. A threatened and panicked person can quickly go from rationally playing the odds to gambling on risky moves and hoping for a good result. Hope, however, is not a strategy, and emotional reaction under pressure doesn't typically give a successful result.

A sailor struggling to make a gain from an unfavorable position may act against his better judgment, only to suffer all the more for his impatience. When a race begins to go sour, a challenge for the sailor is to avoid panicking and making desperate calls, such as the "Hail Mary" move of sailing out to a corner of the course hoping for a private wind shift in his favor. As hard as it can be to wait for it, the savvy sailor needs a *reason* to change what they're doing, not just the chance to do so. With patience and persistence, the sailor will be able to find and act upon the right opportunity when it presents itself.

DON'T AUTOMATICALLY CHASE EVERY OPPORTUNITY

Shifty winds test sailors' patience regularly. With every change in wind direction that a boat encounters, the boat's course is altered as a result, thus changing the angles that it is able to sail to reach the next mark. When sailing upwind, if the wind shifts toward the bow of the boat (a header), the boat will sail a lower course, away from the next mark. If the wind shifts aft, the boat will sail a higher course to the next mark. Tacking on a header puts the boat onto the new, lifted tack, therefore reducing the amount of distance needed to sail to the mark. However, every time a boat tacks, it slows down through the maneuver. The prudent tactician will therefore pick their opportunities to tack on wind shifts, keeping up speed and planning their positioning, rather than reacting to every shift in a flurry of tacks up the course. The proactive sailor pays attention to changes coming and looks for the right opportunity to act;

the reactive sailor is at the mercy of the whims of the wind, giving up control of his destiny to the weather and the competition.

Jumping at one opportunity can often mean closing the door on another one not yet revealed. Understanding exactly what you're looking for and being patient enough to wait for the right time to move on it can pay big dividends. By contrast, many people get caught up in a new craze and jump in with both feet without understanding what they are getting into. Investors in particular experience this phenomenon every once in a while. Many investors were swept up in the euphoria of the dot-com boom of the late 1990s and the limitless possibilities that were evident at the time. Not all of these new tech businesses were sustainable, however, and the suddenly rich soon became the suddenly average when the bubble burst. Warren Buffett was among the skeptics during the tech boom, avoiding tech stocks while his contemporaries enthusiastically dove in. Mass enthusiasm for the latest "big thing" can lead to temptation to hop aboard the bandwagon before the opportunity passes by. Chasing opportunities without devoting sufficient forethought to their potential outcomes and the burdens they may carry, however, can create a waste of time, resources, and energy that can leave an investor further frustrated with their outcome.

Although it may generate protest from the most enthusiastic advocates, it is wise to be selective in the pursuit of new opportunities that arise. You may hear that you will miss out and be left behind, and you may even worry that such things could be true. Honestly weigh opportunities for yourself and the demands they are likely to place upon you, whether it's a business deal or an invitation to an evening out (is it really worth going out if you're too tired to have any fun?). Many situations call for seizing the moment, but have the patience to give each opportunity thorough consideration before pouncing.

DON'T BE GREEDY WHEN THINGS ARE GOING WELL

A sailing course can offer promises of tremendous gains at times but can quickly deliver a reversal, much to the dismay of the sailor that has gone to its very ends in search of golden opportunity. Sailors often face a risk of outsmarting themselves in the pursuit of a greater advantage, and there are a number of opportunities for them to get too greedy in their tactics. To name just a few, they may get themselves out of phase with the wind or the competition in pursuit of a puff, stay on one tack too long, hoping for a wind shift that never comes, or recklessly attempt to cross ahead of a boat with the right-of-way because they couldn't bear to duck behind them. A sailor chasing big gains imprudently may relate to Aesop's story of the goose that laid the golden eggs: when the farmer killed the goose expecting to get all of its golden eggs at once instead of one at a time, he found none inside. He didn't get the big payday, and lost his income of gold eggs entirely in the process.

When things are looking up for you, take advantage of the situation, but do not act hastily in the pursuit of bigger gains. A weight lifter may find himself making excellent progress with his routine, but he would risk injury to himself by stepping up his training beyond his capabilities. A storeowner may find initial success selling the hottest new product, but could find herself overstocked if she boosts inventory dramatically to save unit costs and demand goes away. Everyone wants to make the most of their situation, but they should also take the long view and consider possible outcomes if they commit themselves further. Sometimes the pursuit of bigger gains can backfire, leaving us to wonder why we were so impatient for more, when we were doing so well where we were.

The challenge of keeping patience grows with our personal investment in our situation. Whether you've invested your money, your labor, or your heart into something important to you, strive to be patient through the ups and downs of the journey, and your judgment will be better for it.

FOCUS

The longer the road ahead, the more difficult it can be to maintain focus. Focus can be compromised by a number of factors: fatigue, outside distractions, and fear are just a few of the common phenomena that can cause anyone to take their eye off the ball. Anyone acting in the pursuit of anything difficult, whether it's winning a major sailing championship or earning a degree, will at some point encounter these bumps in the road. Part of every challenge is the self-mastery it takes to keep focused on the objective.

FOCUSING OVER THE LONG RUN

Endurance can be tested when there's a long campaign ahead, and the more the bar is raised for the competing parties, the more staying power will be required for success. The America's Cup is an excellent example of an escalating long-term endeavor. Before the 1980s, most America's Cup campaigns could be measured in months rather than years. As the racing became more competitive, however, teams began putting in more time, more money, and more boats than ever before. Today, teams venturing forth in pursuit of the Cup have plans that may stretch out over a decade, and fundraising can begin before the current match is even over.

A high-and-dry counterpart to the America's Cup is a modern US presidential campaign. The nature of campaigning has changed in a variety of ways as technology has played an increasing role in the delivery of a candidate's message. The fast-paced, instant-response campaign environment that has emerged with the introduction of the Internet and twenty-four-hour news coverage has put a new financial burden on candidates to have larger staffs, to travel more, and to buy as much media coverage as possible. In both of these contests, campaigners can run out of money, peak too soon, or make a mistake that dooms their effort with the finish line still far in the distance. However, when a well-thought-out plan can be developed that will guide the campaigner through the long journey ahead, there can be a structure in place that will allow for the pacing needed to last through to the end without running out of steam.

Focusing under Stress

When going into any major regatta, a sailor's ability to concentrate on the racing may be threatened by outside factors not related to sailing. Many a sailor has found that their best efforts in terms of physical preparation and boat preparation have been frustrated by the stressors of life that they have brought out onto the water with them. Troubles at home or at work can preoccupy anyone's mind, and this is particularly detrimental in a sport as cerebral as sailing. Without the ability to live in the moment and to concentrate fully on the task at hand, a sailor is severely handicapped before the race even begins.

Handling stress that threatens our ability to be our best is a challenge for sailor and non-sailor alike. Sometimes our own mistakes can begin a downhill slide in our performance through anxiety and frustration. For instance, many an amateur golfer has hit a bad shot and proceeded to angrily curse himself, his clubs, the game, and cruel fate, only to see his play decline further, as the longer he dwells on it, the more frustrated he becomes. By contrast, the professional golfer tends to develop the mental ability to leave a bad shot behind and move on to the next one, concentrating not on what he has done, but what he needs to do. As frustrating as it can be to make mistakes that harm our chances for success, our recovery from them hinges on our ability to let them go.

We may sometimes be distracted by events unrelated to our performance, but which deeply affect us regardless. Following the terrorist attacks on September 11, 2001, people everywhere found it difficult to focus on their work as they struggled through the shock of a national tragedy and worries for the future. It was by focusing on the positive things in life that the people as a whole and individuals were able to regain their focus. A wave of patriotism surged as American flags appeared on bumper stickers, lapel pins, and billboards everywhere. People focused on what was most important to them in their daily lives and many found a new appreciation for the good things for which they were most thankful. The attacks did not cripple the American spirit, but instead revealed its enduring strength. Whether afloat or ashore, one of the most difficult, yet most important challenges to those under stress from distracting outside factors is to quiet the mind by a constant return to thoughts of what is good and right in our world, rather than what is wrong.

FOCUSING THROUGH CHAOS

The ability to maintain concentration when all around you is chaos will help you to get through sticky situations and to achieve any goal you pursue. Some people live each day of their career up to their neck in emergency situations, and the best of the bunch are those who can filter out the distractions to manage the job at hand. Jet pilots, EMTs, soldiers, and stock traders can all tell you something about distraction. Sailors deal with distraction constantly—at any given mark rounding, it is typical for two or more boats to arrive at the turn simultaneously. In the time that it takes a boat to sail just three boat lengths, the sailors must concentrate on the rules that apply in their situation with the other boats, what the strategy for the next leg of the course will be just after the rounding, how their positioning near the other boats will affect their wind and their ability to maneuver, and how to steer an efficient course and trim the sails to maintain speed without hitting either the turning mark or the other boats. It's a lot to think about in the span of only seconds, but what makes situations such as these a little less jarring each time is experience. A pilot can react to an emergency in the blink of an eye when he's trained for the situation. Hospital staffs can leap into action when a critical patient is wheeled in if everyone knows their jobs. Experience always takes the edge off when you get into hot water. For the neophyte just wading in for the first time, the key is to think ahead of situations that could come up and prepare for them. There are plenty of disasters that emergency workers have never faced, but train for regularly. It is through their training that they will be able to perform when the pressure is really on.

FOCUSING IN THE FACE OF FEAR

Nothing is quite so powerful an X factor in predicting one's performance under fire as fear. Elementary school students often wonder why they seem to go through so many fire drills, but the constant repetition is an obvious necessity. There are enough situations where even adults may completely lose their cool in an emergency, so if a class of schoolchildren doesn't know their jobs in a crisis, things could go from bad to worse very fast. Fear is a natural part of life that can be instinctive, or it can be learned through experience. One may either go through a bad experience or be warned of potential consequences to become afraid of something. Surfing legend Laird Hamilton has ridden some of the most dangerous waves the sport has seen, but has come to live with fear as a natural factor in his surfing. "If you aren't able to be scared," he says, "you either haven't been hurt, or you're completely ignorant."

Bravery is often mistaken for an absence of fear, but it is actually action in the face of fear. For instance, a baby may not fear a warm and beautiful fire, because the child has never been burned nor seen the destruction that fire can cause. A child that reaches for a flame isn't brave, but simply ignorant of potential consequences. Being afraid from time to time doesn't make you a coward—it simply makes you human. Being brave means acknowledging the fear that you are feeling and moving past it to do what is necessary. Sailors are often faced with weather conditions that challenge their ability to keep the boat together and on course, let alone to win a race. Howling winds and rough seas can damage boat and body, so it takes a cool mind to make all the changes needed to handle the boat safely through a storm. If the sailor can look at the situation, recognize what needs to be done, and do it without allowing panic to set in, he will be able to make intelligent choices to ride the situation out. Fear is the mind's way of protecting us from harm, generally to our benefit, but unnecessary fear gets in the way. Caution is prudent, but fear can just slow your reaction time when you need to be sharp and on your game. There's nothing wrong with being afraid—it's what we do in the face of fear that determines the outcome of a situation. Even if we can't completely conquer fear, we can at least tame self-doubt enough to keep our heads by making sure we've covered our bases and trained thoroughly, and by trusting ourselves to be able to handle things.

KEEP YOUR COOL

Everyone finds themselves in an emotional situation sooner or later. For a sailor, the pressure of competition and the stress of managing multiple variables during the race make mishaps harder to handle when they occur. The reactions of anyone, on a boat or on land, to a stressful situation can be a shock, and are not always as constructive as they could be. Benjamin Franklin offered in *Poor Richard's Advice*: "Anger and folly walk cheek by jowl; repentance treads on both their heels." Many can recall an instance when tempers were lost and a seed of destruction was sown, resulting in long hours of reproach and regret. Fortunately, emotions don't have to run away with us when those stressful situations arise, and can be managed to the extent that they don't drag us away from accomplishing our objectives.

Negative emotions and performance exist in an inverse relationship to one another; as one dials up, the other drops. In sailing, there are infinite opportunities for SNAFUs, so if and when something does go wrong, such as a spinnaker dropped in the water, there is a palpable danger of a downward spiral of performance as emotions crank up. The skipper may shout at the crew, unnerving them such that their ability to catch the problem in time is harmed, and distracting them from solving the matter. The problem then gets worse, resulting in more shouting. The race may go on, but a dark cloud then hangs over their heads, taking their focus off the race and on to their bitterness with each other. Unleashing emotions in such a negative manner just exacerbates the problem at hand. Every skipper and every crew wants to do their best and avoid mistakes to the best of their ability.

Anyone striving for excellence is a stern critic of themselves, so unleashing on them for a mistake is only pouring gasoline on a fire that's already burning. The tendency of some people to lose their cool in a tough spot stems not just from a negative situation, but a negative approach. Some put undue pressure on themselves that ramps their emotions up, and others suffer from a total lack of enjoyment in their chosen task. If a person can build up a more positive attitude about their efforts, they will have already done preventative maintenance on their emotions that will make difficult scenarios much easier to face when they arise.

It's important to put sincere effort into understanding one's own emotional tendencies when under the gun. A number of hot-headed individuals on water and on land genuinely have no idea how volcanic their reactions to tough situations actually are. Self-knowledge allows us to recognize whether our decisions are being made in a rational or emotional state. The more important the decision, the more important it is to recognize the difference. Throughout the Cold War era, the nations of the world dreaded the prospect of an emotional decision being made by a nuclear power. The consequences of emotional decision making to an economy can be severe as well. What we now refer to as an "economic downturn" was previously known as a "panic." Historically, when investors have reacted emotionally to market movements rather than rationally, it would create a stampede of buying and selling. When it spins out of control, it can wreck havoc on asset values, and one panic leads to another. No one should ever make an important decision when they are upset if it can be helped. The real challenge is how to handle emotions effectively when you've got to keep moving ahead.

Pay attention to your own response to a stressful situation as soon as it arises, and try to be aware of the emotions at work. If you can recognize that the tension or anger is building within, you will be more capable of releasing it with a few deep, cleansing breaths. British sailing champion Eric Twiname had a visualization technique for releasing anger: imagine yourself throwing it overboard. You might take another approach, perhaps clenching up your fists or other muscles and holding it for a few seconds, then releasing all the physical and mental tension together. For some, the best thing may be to remove themselves from the situation for a few minutes and scream into a pillow.

Many feel that a certain degree of outward intensity gives them an edge. Some athletes and business professionals have no qualms about unleashing their anger on their opposition, taking the tactic of intimidating the other side to gain the upper hand. Taking a calmer approach doesn't reduce your effectiveness as a competitor, though; it directs your energy in a more positive manner and reduces damaging effects on body and mind, and therefore, performance. Allowing emotions to control you rather than you controlling them harms, not helps, your performance. Every human being has human emotions, and will be upset from time to time. Those who are constructive, rather than destructive, in the expression of those emotions, are the ones who find greater success over the long run.

EXECUTION

The great aim of culture is the aim of setting ourselves
to ascertain what perfection is and how to make it prevail.

—MATTHEW ARNOLD

THE ABILITY TO EXECUTE MANEUVERS WITH precision and competence in the heat of action depends in part on the qualities of concentration, tenacity, persistence, and resilience that the contender demonstrates. The difference between those who make common mistakes and those who make significantly fewer is often not a matter of not knowing what to do, but rather of not knowing the best way to do it. The allocation of effort through a long-term commitment is an important consideration in order to avoid burnout as well as to focus with more intensity on critical turning points in the process. Mental discipline, so much a part of the planning process, also comes into play as a factor in the execution stage. Concentration must be kept up to recognize and make the most of opportunities that arise, and distinguish them from mere distractions. Just as sailors must be able to keep up their concentration through the highs and lows of the race, so, too, must those facing the ups and downs of life ashore; without a level head and a clear eye on the situation at hand, decision making can suffer. Another part of the mental aspect of execution is the ability to push on through discouragement. Things may look bleak from time to time, but it is the person who can fight on through the dark times who eventually reaches the warm sunshine.

SET YOUR OWN PACE

Sailing courses vary in length, as do regattas. Dinghy racers in a major championship may sail multiple races a day over the course of a week, each several miles in length. As such, big events can tax a sailor's energy and stamina, putting a premium on smart allocation of effort. We often face tough challenges ashore that will demand a lot of mental and physical effort over a long period of time. During these times, it's important to know our limits and pace ourselves accordingly in able to perform to our potential for a successful final result. There's a joke that asks: How do you eat an elephant? Answer: One bite at a time. We often find ourselves facing a task that looks overwhelming, but by setting the pace and deconstructing it into manageable portions, we can handle even those gargantuan jobs that seem at first to be too much to handle.

MARATHON OR SPRINT?

In any endeavor, it's important to understand how much time is going to be needed (or is available) for an effort that we undertake. It could be a professional conference, a tradeshow, an athletic pursuit, an academic assignment, or some other project. By understanding whether the goal is going to be achieved through a quick, explosive effort or over a longer period of time, it is easier to plan an approach accordingly, allowing for appropriate allocation of resources, including human exertion.

Some efforts can be rushed, and others simply can't. An athlete couldn't possibly bulk up the night before a competition having neglected his fitness regime for months, any more than a farmer could make a crop appear overnight. Such efforts require long-term planning to ultimately bring them to fruition. There are students who swear by the last-minute cram session as their most effective means of academic success, but it isn't a sustainable formula over the long run, even if panic may provide some measure of focus in the short term. Students who keep pace with the material by allocating a little more effort regularly throughout the course tend to find those final hours before exam time a bit less stressful.

Going into any regatta, a sailor will need to know if the racing ahead will be a marathon or a sprint. Olympic sailors have long races that can require them to hike out for miles around the course before reaching the finish. Long "marathon" races like these require preparation that will train sailors to exert their efforts where needed without depleting their reserves. Collegiate sailors, by contrast, approach their racing as a series of sprints, because the races generally happen two at a time between breaks, and only last about fifteen to twenty minutes. A college sailor can give it their all from start to finish and have a chance to catch a breath before rotating back in.

Take Advantage of Breaks

Offshore racing generally incorporates a watch schedule, in which each member of the crew gets a break for a designated time slot. These breaks typically don't allow the usual eight or so hours of sleep that most of us would like; they're usually a series of short naps and maybe a chance to get a bite to eat. These breaks are crucial to keeping everyone rested enough (if barely) to continue to concentrate and perform, even through the middle of the night. Crew members often need to be reminded to take it easy on their designated break, even when they don't feel tired. It can be a challenge to settle down enough to allow ourselves to rest when there's a lot on our minds, but it can pay off later when it's time to jump into action.

Ronald Reagan was able to laugh off being the oldest man ever elected president, commenting in a debate with Walter Mondale, "I will not make age an issue of this campaign—I am not going to exploit, for political purposes, my opponent's youth and inexperience." Reagan was actually aware of his limitations, and often fit naps into his schedule so that he could not only keep up his energy for cabinet meetings, but so that he could always appear vigorous in front of the press. Likewise, college students understand the value of the "power nap" between classes, in which twenty minutes in a comfortable chair is all the rest that's available before pressing on. We may often feel the urge to work during a break, but we all need a chance to recharge our batteries now and then in order to have the energy to be at our best later on.

Know When to Push

Small-boat racing seldom affords the opportunity to truly relax, but there are short periods on the course in which the sailor can "save fuel." It's important to conserve energy to some degree when the pressure eases in order to have the endurance to continue to perform when others have exhausted themselves. The ideal scenario would be to have such strength and stamina that we would never get tired, and that our boundless energy would carry us through even the longest competitions without breaking a sweat. In reality, although we strive to be at our best when race time comes, we can only expect so much. When the race ahead is long and difficult, we will need to hold a little something back here and there in order to still be able to stride, rather than crawl, across the finish line.

Upwind legs tend to be more physically difficult to sail well in most small boats than off-wind legs. Racecourses often tend to include more upwind than off-wind legs, and generally the start and the finish are into the wind. The sailor will know that he will have the most energy coming off the start line, when it is most important to break away from the pack. If he exhausts himself right away, however, he will surely be passed by opponents with better endurance in the course of the race, and there are still at least two upwind legs to go. If a sailor can have an energy reserve that will be available for the final upwind leg, when the rest of the fleet is tired and slowing down, he will be able to tap that reserve for a strong finish in the end.

It's common to see a competitor peak too soon, like a racehorse that bursts out of the gate into a commanding lead, only to fade at the final turn. To avoid falling into that situation ourselves, we need to understand our limits and abilities and manage our exertion accordingly. Everyone needs to prioritize their efforts when there's hard work to be done in order to have the energy to do it well. Even under a rush of adrenaline, there will be the inevitable crash afterward. Be sure that you know what the important moments of your marathon effort will be, and put forward a plan that will allow you to have the energy needed to make the most of those moments.

BUILD MOMENTUM

Momentum is the lifeblood of an ambitious effort. It is the fuel that keeps the fire of success growing. When it is lost, the effort stalls and stagnates. When it is fed, the effort booms and thrives. The most successful efforts over the long run are those that gain and exploit momentum, allowing success to build upon itself. For a sailor looking to win a long regatta, momentum can be the key to unlocking his potential. If he can create an early success and build upon it, he will vastly improve his chances of ultimate victory over his competition.

Momentum is a force of nature. We know that a falling object will pick up speed until it encounters an obstacle or it reaches its terminal velocity. For sailors, it is a force both tangible and conceptual. Sailors can get a burst of speed from surfing waves, and use the momentum gained to catch the next wave. Racing sailors also know that success leads to more success, so when they finish well in one race, they hope to build momentum to win more races, and ultimately the regatta. Likewise, a person who gains confidence from one big win, whether it's in work, sports, or even a social effort like making new friends or getting a date, will carry that confidence forward to succeed further in the future. In the challenges that we face in all walks of life, finding momentum and building upon it will help us find the "fast lane" on the road to success.

Blast Off

Sailors racing in waves seek to take full advantage of them on the off-wind legs by surfing down the face of every wave they can. As in the sport of surfing, sailors need to have a burst of speed to be able to catch a wave; surfers do this by paddling, and sailors do this by steering a faster course and pumping the sails. It is this little burst of speed that allows them to gain momentum, launching down the face of the wave.

It takes a bold move to give yourself momentum on your road to success. An early success can serve as a launch pad from which your efforts blast off. Barack Obama's "blast off" moment came at the 2004 Democratic National Convention. A state senator from Illinois at the time, Obama was largely unknown to the public at that point, but gained national acclaim from his stirring convention speech. Taking office as a US senator the following year, he was quickly touted as a viable presidential candidate. Obama's momentum from his convention speech was so great that he won the presidency only four years after introducing himself to the American people on that stage.

Pick the Moment and Seize It

Going for a wave is a total commitment of effort for both surfers and sailors. If they hesitate or don't give it their all, the wave could pass them by. Sailors looking to catch a wave must pick their moment wisely, since they are often limited under the rules in the number of pumps that they can give a sail to gain that little acceleration needed to get going down the wave's face. Some smaller waves may roll past before a large enough wave will come along that can offer a surfing opportunity. Just as the stern lifts, the sailor gives the sail a mighty pump; if he's done it just right, the boat will blast forward down the face of the wave with a burst of acceleration. To get the timing wrong, however, results in a wasted effort with no discernible benefit gained.

John F. Kennedy saw an opportunity to run for the presidency in the late 1950s, after he had lost the nomination for the vice presidency in 1956. Kennedy's popularity was growing enough that he was soon considered a favorite for the presidential nomination in 1960. Although some of his contemporaries tried to talk him out of it, saying he was too young and that he should wait for his time to come, Kennedy decided to go for it. He'd become the front-runner more than a year before the election, and he didn't believe such an opportunity would come again. Seizing upon that small window of opportunity, JFK campaigned hard through a very close election to become the youngest man ever elected president.

Stay Focused

Distractions can sabotage the opportunity to find momentum. Sailors have many distractions thrown at them at all times on the racecourse, so they have to know what to look for to gain an advantage, and focus on it. Surfing waves requires great attention to the water conditions, which isn't easy when the sailor also has to mind the trim of the sails, the steering of the boat, and the positioning of the competition. Momentum over a series of races can come from building up a lead over the toughest opposition. This means paying close attention to the position of one's competitors and the point spread on the scoreboard. If a sailor is able to build up enough of a lead on those who are likely to be the fastest contenders, it takes some pressure off at the end of the event and makes a lead easier to maintain.

The discipline to stay focused in any challenge can feel elusive. Distractions and temptations seem to crop up everywhere when there's something important to be done. A diet can be so easily sabotaged by walking by a bakery. A study session can suddenly collapse when friends drop in. A personal budget can take a hit from an impulse purchase when we happen upon a sale. The ability to remember a goal and tell ourselves "no" when those temptations arise is hard to master at first, but ultimately more rewarding when we've succeeded in staying focused. Exercising discipline and focus can be like exercising our bodies: you struggle at first, but it gets easier the more you practice it. The more we are able to make that kind of focus a habit, the more momentum we build toward a long-term goal. Whether you're looking to build momentum for the moment or for the long run, stay focused on what will give you a boost, and take full advantage of it.

Build on What's Working

A racing sailor knows to use every opportunity to its maximum advantage; to stick to what is working and try to build upon it. If he knows that the breeze is stronger on the right side of the course, he will want to be the first one into the puff. If he finds that straight-line sailing is working out better for him than a lot of maneuvering, he will adapt his tactical approach to take advantage of that. If he finds that moving crew weight to leeward in light air is helping performance, he will do so as soon as the wind drops. Through practice and experience, you will learn what methods and techniques work well for you, and which ones don't. Find what gives you a boost, and make it a habit.

The road to success may start on a different path than you first expect. Sometimes, it's not obvious in the beginning where our advantages lie. For instance, an up-and-coming actor may long to play the hero in the movies, but finds acclaim instead when he plays the villain; an artist may seek her fortune painting abstract masterpieces, and find it instead writing daily comic strips. When you've been able to identify your strengths or adapt a style that is working for you, use that as the basis for your improvement.

Mind Your Thoughts

There is often pressure to succeed, both internal and external, in sailing or in other walks of life. An early win can be the first building block to gaining momentum toward ultimate success, but the wrong mind-set can also derail the effort. In trying to build up momentum, we can't allow ourselves to get too excited, overconfident, or worried about the results. Early in the game, too much excitement can distract a contender from keeping up the effort, and overconfidence can backfire. Worry tends to create such self-doubt and anxiety that negative thoughts have a tendency to come true.

Don't get too excited with success, or too upset by a setback. Instead, look at the results objectively. If all went well, talk about what's working (or think about it if you're on your own), and give out a little "good job" or pat on the back. If things didn't turn out as well as you hoped, look back on what didn't work and think of how you'll correct it. Also remember what you did do well, and give yourself credit. Whether racing sailboats, working toward a degree, or making deals, awareness of one's thoughts helps keep the mental discipline to build on success rather than distract from it. Stay positive, focused, and confident, and you'll be in a better state of mind to make a habit of winning.

GET BACK ON TRACK

Momentum comes from staying on an upward curve, but doesn't have to be lost in the case of a misstep. Even the most impressive efforts stumble from time to time, but it doesn't indicate that their performance has peaked. Rather, a little stumble can indicate some weaknesses that need to be shored up or some limitations to the scope of one's effort. In the 1995 America's Cup trials, Team New Zealand had gone undefeated throughout all the early rounds, only to be handed a narrow loss to *oneAustralia* in the challenger finals, after the Australians handily won the start and aggressively protected their lead right up to the finish. Rather than dwell on the loss and allow it to halt their momentum, the Kiwis refocused on getting better starts and improving performance, using the experience as an instructive wake-up call. Team New Zealand went on to win all the rest of their races, winning the Louis Vuitton Cup and the America's Cup.

GLANCE BACK, BUT FOCUS FORWARD

Sailing downwind presents an interesting dilemma, particularly for the single-handed sailor. It's a common axiom that looking back too much when racing downwind tends to break one's concentration and disrupt steering and sail trim. However, with the wind coming from behind, the skipper needs to be able to see puffs of wind and waves coming up, as well as the position of the other boats. The key to getting necessary information without losing focus or control is to glance back quickly and take in as much detail as possible without being hypnotized by the view astern. An experienced sailor will have the feel and instincts to both maintain a steady hand on the helm and reduce the instances needed to look back. Looking back can be instructive, but distracting.

If you're trying to build momentum, the focus needs to be on growing and improving. This means looking ahead to the future, preparing for the challenges that lie in wait, and continually raising the bar in performance.

Perspective from the past can be useful, however. Looking back can teach us what we need to work on, where the opposition has shown vulnerabilities, and what trends may be developing. The danger in reviewing past performance is in dwelling upon it. Focusing on past failures or reliving former glories at the expense of the task at hand kills momentum and is counterproductive. Look back with a rational eye to gain knowledge and perspective, but be quick to return your focus to the challenges ahead.

KEEP CONTROL

A boat surfing down the face of a wave is more stable than a boat struggling to catch one, but it takes control to keep momentum without being knocked over by it. Momentum can be exhilarating, but it can lead to a wipeout. Without careful handling, a boat surfing at top speed can kill its own momentum, plowing into the next wave or stalling the rudder by heeling too much. A fast ride can quickly turn into disaster if not expertly managed.

It's common to see movie sequels drop in quality because the studio overreached in trying to outdo the previous installments. Celebrities riding a wave of popularity in one industry may get into a new business they know nothing about and have a complete flop. A business may have a great product that's selling well, and meander into making other products it has no capacity to produce or market properly. Campaigning politicians appreciate the need for momentum, but a campaign can unravel quickly when momentum is disrupted. Presidential hopeful Howard Dean's campaign was off to a strong start in 2004, but his campaign derailed at the Iowa Democratic caucuses. Dean had been a front-runner in the Democratic field, but finished third in the field in Iowa. At a rally of his supporters, Dean addressed the crowd, hoping to keep spirits high. When he let loose with a rallying cry, his voice cracked and his cheer appeared on television to be more manic than enthusiastic. The "Dean Scream" was replayed over and over in the media and garnered a generally negative response. The scream wasn't the first setback for his campaign, but the coverage of the incident seriously hampered his efforts to regain momentum. Despite his early advantages, Dean's campaign folded a month later.

The thrill of picking up speed and seeing momentum build shouldn't detract from one's focus and vigilance in managing the effort. Nobody wants to wipe out just as things are looking up. Take heart in the fact that you are seeing progress, but continue to concentrate on the task at hand and don't let the euphoria of growing success distract you.

Momentum, once gained, can separate the leaders from the rest of the pack. If momentum is lost, it must be regained quickly or it may not be regained at all. Growing success not only lays the groundwork for further improvement, but motivates us to keep up the good work. The early stage of a challenge may be the toughest, but it's easier to keep momentum than to establish it; it takes a powerful blast to put a satellite into orbit, but once free of the earth's gravity, it circles the earth on its own.

STAY CONSISTENT

A challenge for any competitive sailor is to maintain consistency throughout a series. The fleet-racing format most often seen in the sport tends to reward the sailors that are able to consistently perform in the top ten or so more richly than those who win a race or two but spend the rest of the time in the middle of the pack. At the beginning of a regatta, the sailor with their eyes on a top finish will be focused not on big wins or on beating a particular competitor, but on staying in the top group. This approach helped Anna Tunnicliffe to win the gold medal in the Laser Radial division at the 2008 Olympics.

Over the ten-race series, Tunnicliffe focused on consistency, even off the water: getting up at the same time, eating the same breakfast, and arriving at the boat park at about the same time. She held the overall lead up through the fifth race with all top-six finishes, but with a drop race factored in, each competitor was allowed to discard their worst score, which helped others more than it did Tunnicliffe. Her coaches reassured her that if she stuck to her formula and didn't change the way she was sailing, things would work out. She kept up her consistent scores, finishing out of the top three only once in the next four races, and worked back into the overall lead. In the final race, Tunnicliffe fought back from a bad start and finished in second place, winning the gold medal. Her final scores were: 4-5-6-5-6-3-15-2-2-4 (points counted double for the final race). The silver medalist, Gintare Volungeviciute of Lithuania, won three races in the series, but didn't have the consistency of Tunnicliffe. There were others that had first-place finishes in the series, but finished as deep as thirteenth overall. The phenomenon of consistency paying off for the ultimate victory is common in sailing, and was evidenced in other divisions at the same Olympics: the gold medalists in the Yngling fleet, the Men's 470 fleet, and the 49er fleet all won without a single first-place finish in their scores, but their consistency paid off to earn them the overall win.

Consistency is another form of reliability. When you can perform consistently in your field, you are viewed as reliable. It doesn't do wonders for a person's professional reputation to have a hit-or-miss reputation in their work any more than it does for a sailor's results to consist of a first along with some much deeper finishes. Consistency can be developed, however, and it stems from finding your zone—a calm sense of control over your situation. Finding it depends on experience, mental preparation, and environmental factors.

Anyone tackling a difficult task that doesn't have a lot of experience will be more rattled than an old veteran; the more experienced a person becomes, the more competent and the more comfortable they will be. Mental preparation for a challenge includes visualization and development of self-confidence; if a person can see things working out, they can make them work out. Environmental factors are outside influences that may be either soothing or distracting. The ability to concentrate on the task at hand without being pulled into other concerns is crucial, and one's environment can be controlled to some degree to shut out distractions. Tunnicliffe settled into a routine each day before racing, thus avoiding the potential hassles of rushing in the morning or dealing with an upset stomach from an unfamiliar meal. When a person finds their zone, consistency is easier to attain over the long haul; foolish mistakes, oversights, nasty surprises, and nervous jitters are minimized to help deliver a strong result more reliably.

Consistency is an expectation of customers everywhere; everyone wants to know what they're getting and to be able to have a product or service live up to their expectations. McDonald's rose to the top of the fast-food business by delivering a product that is consistent at every location, the world over. So well known is McDonalds's consistency that its leading product is the basis of an economic indicator of exchange rates. Under the assumption that the value of a Big Mac is the same in any country, the "Big Mac Index" is often used to indicate the strength of a foreign currency against the US dollar. The golden arches of McDonald's have also boosted the morale of many a traveling business executive, seeking a familiar meal in an unfamiliar locale. The great joy that many business travelers derive from finding a McDonald's in a foreign city is not necessarily the food itself, but their familiarity with it. In many products, consistency is not just a nice surprise, but an essential element of the product itself; without consistency in the quality of gasoline, prescription medications, or tires, there could be big problems for the customer.

It's hard to draw conclusions from any scenario that's rife with inconsistency. This is especially true when trying to train a pet, for instance. The pet will only learn from us being consistent in our responses to their actions. If you only scold your dog some of the time for eating your shoes, it will take much longer for him to make the connection between chewing up the shoe and getting a negative reaction. People need consistency in their relationships as well, but people are much more observant of discrepancies in behavior, and are often more willing to challenge them. If we are too inconsistent in our demands and expectations of the people around us, we can slowly lose credibility over the long run.

Consistency in our words and actions is what determines the foundation of our relationships with others. The reputation that we build for ourselves is not generally based on one mistake we made or one comment, but rather how we do over time. Major regattas often consist of a long series of races in order to give each sailor more opportunities to perform to their full potential. As a result, the top sailors generally rise to the top of the scoreboard, even with some occasional low finishes. Likewise, look for consistency in the performance of others in building an opinion of them, and try to be consistent in your own performance each day as well. After all, nobody who's ever had an embarrassing moment would want it to define them.

There are, after all, some cases in life in which you have to get it right every time to consider your effort a win. A brain surgeon, for instance, could not call an operation a success if he performed *most* of the procedure correctly. Such cases demand consistency in the strongest sense—they just provide less room for error than other situations. For most people facing everyday situations however, the human condition itself permits little lapses now and then. People can endure through minor mistakes and still be exceptional in their efforts through development of regularly good performances rather than occasionally brilliant ones. A student with four Bs on a report card will have a higher GPA than a student with two As and two Ds, for instance. Many a young athlete has been consoled after a loss with the phrase, "Well, you can't win them all." Not that we shouldn't try, but not only can't you win them all, but you don't have to. There's no need to lose heart if you're not perfect every time in your efforts, particularly if there's more road ahead to travel; you don't have to win them all to win *overall*.

BANISH WORRY

Although we need to prepare for potential problems when we are able to foresee them, it's a bad use of our mental energy to spend time worrying. Napoleon Bonaparte said, "He who fears being conquered is sure of defeat." To worry about things that haven't happened is to pull ourselves away from the task ahead and create the wrong mental image of the outcome ahead. Just as positive thinking can bring about success, negative thinking can bring about failure. Anticipation of potential roadblocks in any endeavor is wise, but thinking of problems must be partnered with finding solutions before they can materialize. Once those solutions are put into place, the matter needs to be discarded; placed into our mental "shredder" to be removed from the equation, no longer a distraction from the plan for success.

Just about every sailor will get seasick at some point in their career. It's a common fear of landlubbers and an unfortunate scenario that experienced sailors prefer not to dwell on. Once, before an ocean race, I asked a fellow sailor how he keeps from getting seasick, and he replied that he never lets it cross his mind. Skippers in tight races can go through the worst of conditions for hours on end without feeling any affect whatsoever because their minds are occupied with so many details: tactics, sail trim, steering, point spreads ... any number of factors will race through their minds during a close contest. The notion of sickness never occurs to them because they're just too busy. In contrast, many people have had their only boating experience as an idle passenger, in which case the main thing on their mind is the motion of the ocean. A sailor in rough seas who thinks to himself "I hope I don't get sick" usually won't get his wish.

It's interesting to note that the brain never seems to hear the word "don't" when we give ourselves a command. Focusing on what you don't want to have happen seems to only hasten its outcome. The single thought, "Don't choke" has proven to be one of the least helpful thoughts to cross anyone's mind. Ask the batter at the plate, the singer at the audition, or the young man asking a girl out on a date whether his body heeded the thought "Don't choke" successfully, and the answer will be resoundingly negative.

We say to ourselves:	Our subconscious hears:
"Don't choke!"	"Choke!"
"I don't want to lose."	"Lose!"
"I don't have a problem."	"Problem!"

The word "don't" is in itself of a negative nature, which is not particularly helpful to a winning mind-set. The mind doesn't want to hear what you *don't* want; it's much more interested in what you *do* want. We can reframe our thoughts into a positive nature that will have a much more positive effect on our actions and the desired outcome.

Instead of:	Try:
"Don't fail!"	"Succeed at this!"
"Don't slow down!"	"Keep up the speed!"
"Don't forget!"	"Remember this!"
"Don't drop it!"	"Hold on tight!"

It's a simple game of opposites, but the reframing of negative into positive when it comes to self talk can make a tremendous difference when it comes to execution under pressure. All the "don'ts" that come into our minds stem from the natural tendency of human beings to worry. What we all struggle with day in, day out are worries about the things that are important to us, like careers, family, relationships, and even our hobbies. Worry leads to stress and too much stress doesn't do the mind or the body any good. We may not be able to keep ourselves from ever worrying about anything, but we can take the approach of looking at our world in the sense of how we'd like it to be. By thinking positively and visualizing situations as we'd like to see them, we help bring about a positive outcome. The mind is a powerful tool with which to shape your life. A mind focused on a positive outlook will shape a life of positive outcomes. A mind focused on the negative (what is wrong, what could go wrong, etc.) will prove its worldview correct in the long run.

Sailors often find themselves in high-stress situations where the smallest mistake will change the outcome of the race. Windsurfers, for example, have an enormously physical task in pumping their rig all around the course to get little bursts of acceleration from the fanning motion of the sail. After sailing for about an hour, they can get pretty tired. At the top levels, however (e.g., the Olympics), everyone's in great shape and everyone is a smart sailor. So, after an hour of sailing, the racing can still be tight, even though everyone's aching. In a last sprint to the finish line, they have to keep working the rig with just the right rhythm and motion to keep the board moving fast across the line. Under pressure like that, one sailor may think to himself, "Don't lose it now!" By entertaining that thought, his chances of winning just went down. The sailor right next to him telling himself, "Keep it up! Just a little further—you can do it!" has a great chance of pulling off a big win.

You can write your own ending by training your brain to focus on the results you desire and put out of your mind any thoughts of disaster or failure. As Norman Vincent Peale said, "Change your thoughts, and you change your world." Our lives often consist of a long string of self-fulfilling prophesies, and it's our job to make sure that the outcomes we craft for ourselves are positive and successful.

BE PERSISTENT

There comes a time every once in a while for sailors, particularly those in small boats such as the Laser or the Finn, when muscles really start to hurt and a voice in the back of one's head starts to whisper ideas about quitting, or at least easing off a bit. When it's been an hour of flat-out physical and mental exertion, particularly in challenging conditions, that familiar burn in the legs and torso starts to take hold, and the body begins to distract the mind, screaming for relief. Recalling his experience sailing at the 2009 Laser Masters World Championship in Halifax, Nova Scotia, Bill Symes wrote that one of the qualities of champion sailors is that they absolutely never let up. "They just keep coming, whether they are in 1st or 51st," he said. "These championship races are long and it's difficult to maintain 100% physical and mental intensity around the course. I often found myself running out of gas and letting two or three boats slip by in the final stretch. The champions go flat out from start to finish, always in relentless pursuit of one more boat. Take your foot off the pedal for a nanosecond and they blow by. And you never see them again."

Persistence through struggle and frustration made all the difference in the career of Howard Schultz, the CEO of Starbucks. Schultz first got his start in the coffee business as manager of US operations for Hammarplast. On a trip to Seattle in 1981, Schultz was impressed by a small coffee-bean retailer called Starbucks. At first rejected for a job with Starbucks, Schultz kept at it and was later hired, eventually becoming director of marketing and operations. On a trip to Italy in 1982, Schultz was inspired by the many coffee bars that drew customers to sit and chat, functioning as meeting places and social hubs. He enthusiastically pitched Starbucks on the concept of moving from coffee-bean sales to a restaurant model based on the Italian coffee bars, but the company rejected his idea. Not to be deterred from pursuing this concept, Schultz started a coffee-bar chain of his own, called Il Giornale. After his own business took off, he allied himself with a number of outside investors (including Bill Gates Jr., father of the Microsoft founder) and raised $3.8 million to buy Starbucks in the fall of 1987. Starbucks boomed under Schultz's leadership to over one hundred twenty locations when it went public in 1992, up from eleven when he'd purchased the company five years earlier. Starbucks has expanded to an international brand over the years, and its products and distribution venues continue to grow.

Abraham Lincoln is another example of triumph through persistence. Lincoln stands as a paragon of the American spirit today, not despite, but perhaps because of, the agonizing defeats and trials that he endured throughout his life. Before being elected president of the United States in 1860, he had already suffered great heartache in business, politics, and even love. When he was still a young man in 1835, his girlfriend died suddenly and he had a crippling nervous breakdown the following year. In his later adult life, Lincoln would face further tragedy: one young son would die before he was president, and another died while he was in the White House. He also failed in business twice, and lost eight elections in the years between 1832 and 1856. With the outbreak of the Civil War following his election, Lincoln inherited stewardship over the most chaotic period of American history. Under constant threat from conspirators and enemy forces, harsh criticism from the press and political opponents, and terrible emotional strain from the burdens of high office in wartime, Lincoln still performed superbly in his duties through the strength of his character and his ability to endure. He kept at his responsibilities despite all obstacles, once stating, "I expect to maintain this contest until successful, or till I die, or am conquered, or my term expires, or Congress or the country forsakes me." Even though his life and career came to a tragic end, the ending of the Civil War and the reunification of the United States was to be his final victory, a reward for many sleepless nights and many years of toil and frustration.

British Prime Minister Benjamin Disraeli once said, "The secret to success is constancy of purpose." It's impossible to reach the end of a long road to success if you lose resolve and pull off the road. Successful people rarely stumbled into their achievements, but relentlessly pursued them through hardship and disappointment. There have been so many who have failed in their quest for success and kept their efforts up to finally achieve it: Walt Disney, Winston Churchill, Michael Jordan, Henry Ford, Lucille Ball, Mark Twain and J. K. Rowling all suffered through failures of their own before rising to prominence in their respective fields. Anyone can become frustrated or exhausted and consider quitting, but it is through resilience and persistence through the tough times that the road to ultimate success opens up.

MAKE YOUR COMEBACK

Sailing is full of comeback stories. Tales abound of the race that looked absolutely hopeless until a little opportunity presented itself in the shape of a puff, or a wind shift, or a crowded mark rounding, and everything turned around for the better. George Szabo won his third in a series of Snipe National Championships in the summer of 1999, in a remarkable comeback that hinged on the final moments of the final race. Randy Lake, who already had a pair of first-place finishes in the series, led handily around the course for another first, thus needing Szabo to finish fourth or worse in order to win the championship as the point spread stood. At the first mark, Szabo rounded in twenty-second place, and the title looked secure for Lake. Szabo proceeded to chip away at the fleet throughout the race, playing every shift and puff, finally sliding into third place by a few feet at the finish to win the Nationals. "It was not focusing on the end goal," said Szabo, "but focusing on where (and) how we could find wind shifts, pass boats, and move forward to get third in that race and win the regatta by three-quarters of a point." Experienced sailors know that there will always be times when you're down, but there's always a chance to stage a comeback.

Both Apple and its co-founder, Steve Jobs, made significant comebacks. Apple grew rapidly in its early years, having simplified the personal computer in a way that made it accessible to millions of users. In the mid-1980's, under the threat of the growing PC market, which had claimed eighty percent market share, Apple's CEO John Sculley and the board of directors began seeking some changes which put Jobs at odds with the board, and soon resulted in his departure from the company he'd started. Jobs subsequently went on to found Pixar studios, which would turn out such blockbuster films as *Toy Story* and *Finding Nemo*. By the mid-90s, Apple was struggling, so the board of directors brought Jobs back as a consultant in 1996, making him "interim CEO" the following year. Jobs got right to work on a big new project, the iMac, which was elegant in its design and simple to use, in contrast to the utilitarian look and feel of most PCs. This set off a new wave of successful innovation for Apple, including its introduction of retail stores and a game-changing foray into the music business. The simple elegance not only of its products, but of Apple's image through its marketing efforts, made the company even more appealing to consumers, and sales jumped. In 2000, when Jobs regained the title of permanent CEO, Apple was worth about $5 billion. By the end of 2009, the company was valued at about $170 billion, a growth of thirty-three hundred percent in nine years. The reunion of Jobs and Apple was a comeback story for both sides, and it allowed Apple to get back to its roots and focus on the approach that made its products so appealing in the first place. Often when you're down, it's a good idea to get back to basics in order to start the comeback trail.

Winning seldom comes from constant success; more often than not, it comes from a persistent refusal to stay down after being knocked to the floor. Everyone gets knocked down sooner or later, but a key to ultimate success is to see a loss for what it is; a temporary setback and a chance for regeneration. A young Theodore Roosevelt suffered a terrible personal loss when his wife and his mother died on the same night, and he retreated to the Dakota badlands to heal his emotional wounds and reinvent himself. Of course, TR would return to life in the political arena, eventually rising to governor of New York, then vice president and ultimately president of the United States. Recalling TR's trials on the day of his resignation, Richard Nixon spoke of the virtue of struggle through adversity in the climb toward a comeback, saying, "The greatness comes not when things go always good for you, but the greatness comes when you are really tested—when you take some knocks, some disappointments, when sadness comes—because only if you have been in the deepest valley can you ever know how magnificent it is to be on the highest mountain."

COMPETITION

Love your enemies, for they tell you your faults.

—Benjamin Franklin

COMPETITION HAS A ROLE TO PLAY at some point, to some degree, in all our lives. Some embrace the spirit of competition for the inherent challenge in the pursuit of victory, while others may shy away from it. Apprehension in the face of competition is often borne of the "zero-sum" theory that somebody has to win, and somebody has to lose, but competition can be a win-win situation. The contest itself may be for something of minor significance, or even something completely trivial, but the reward lies less in the successful conquest of an opponent than in the actual effort made. Competition is a driving force for excellence. It challenges us to be better tomorrow than we are today, and to put in a little more time and effort than the other guy. Some bristle at the intense animosity that competition can breed in some cases. Such cases are often just demonstrations of a misplaced perspective. Just because your competitor is working against you, it doesn't mean that they are literally your enemy—in fact, your competitor is your teacher. This is the person whose efforts motivate you to go into each day with a passion for improvement. This person serves as the benchmark for your own progress in order to keep you moving forward, and never standing still or drifting back. You should not hate your opponent—instead be grateful just to have them around to keep you on your toes. The principle of competition may be to determine one winner, but its nature creates winners of all who compete.

RIVALRIES

Competition in any area often pits individual players against one another with a great deal more focus than would be cast on the rest of the field. Sailing has always brought out intense rivalries, both on the course and ashore, but by and large it is a friendly sport. All the same, the competition gets heated and it is the nature of the athlete to take particular note of the player who is always on his heels, or always just a hair's width ahead.

Rivalries can get ugly and can threaten a competitor's focus from the task at hand, but there are reasons to be grateful for a tough rival. There is tremendous motivation in the very thought that, somewhere out there, your rival may be working harder than you are. A worthy opponent also tends to be smart enough to be an innovator whose successes and failures you can learn from. Focusing on a rival can be instructive and motivating, but also a major distraction. If one's attentions are directed solely on defeating a rival in the contest at hand, it can sabotage one's own ability to make the best possible decisions as if the rival were never there at all.

There are opportunities to improve one's own performance in working against a tough rival, but it is also not outside the realm of possibility that rivals can team up toward a common goal. This happens in sports, in business, politics, and even in social circles. Rivalries don't necessarily have to be emotional or dramatic. Often they are born out of a mutual respect for one another and a thirst to measure up to, and surpass, a competitor that either holds in high esteem. It is this foundation that leaves the door open to alliances born out of former rivalries, often with great success.

Your Rival as Your Teacher

The year 1962 was a watershed year for retail as we know it today; it was the year that Target, Kmart, Woolco, and Walmart all opened their first stores. When Sam Walton, Walmart's founder, set out to expand his small retail business, he started by learning all he could from his competition. "Most everything I've done, I've copied from someone else," Walton once remarked. Kmart was of particular interest as a retail model to him. He wrote in his autobiography, "I was in their stores constantly because they were the laboratory, and they were better than we were. I spent a heck of a lot of my time wandering through their stores talking to their people and trying to figure out how they did things." Besides noting their merchandising and pricing, Walton would make note of upcoming specials that Kmart would be offering, and advertise similar specials at his own stores. This practice of hands-on research (one might call it "passive espionage"), also gave Walton the inspiration to form Sam's Club by touring Price Club, all the while recording everything he saw. Learning from the competition in this way requires setting aside ego and concentrating on the bigger picture. For any person in a competitive field to take his own efforts to a higher level, it is often necessary to have competitors that will not only be instructive by example, but will also drive them to a higher level of excellence.

Ben Ainslie is one of the most accomplished competitors in the sport of sailing today. Before becoming a dominating force in the Finn class (in the tradition of fellow multiple-gold medalist Paul Elvstrom), Ainslie fought a long battle with multiple world champion Robert Scheidt of Brazil on the Laser circuit. Lasers were introduced to the Olympics in 1996, and Scheidt was already at the top of the field. Ainslie, at the age of eighteen, was the youngest Briton ever to qualify to sail at the Olympics. Through that contest in the waters off Savannah, Scheidt came through in the end for a gold medal with young Ainslie on his heels, earning the silver. This lit a fire in Ainslie's belly to surpass Scheidt, and their rivalry grew intense in the years leading up to the next Olympics. Ainslie's discipline was ratcheted up to the level that, if he went out for a few beers in the evening, he'd be jogging them off that same night. He knew that if he were to have any chance of beating Scheidt, he would have to take his sailing to a level of near perfection.

Scheidt and Ainslie met again and again in the years leading up to the 2000 Olympics in Sydney, both winning two Laser Worlds in that four-year span. As the contest began on Sydney Harbour, however, the two were seen as near-equal favorites for the gold. Ainslie sailed consistently well from the beginning and took an early lead, but Scheidt threatened his chances at victory by taking some top-five finishes in the second half of the regatta. Being able to afford a drop race going into the final contest, Ainslie knew he would come out on top as long as Scheidt finished twenty-first or worse. He attacked Scheidt aggressively before the start, drawing him into a foul and forcing him to execute two penalty turns. With the race underway, the two then raced in a furious battle that dragged them to the back of the pack. Scheidt managed to recover ground, but not enough, finishing twenty-second and giving Ainslie the overall win by a single point.

Scheidt had been widely acknowledged as the powerhouse of the Laser fleet the world over, and intimidated most competitors with his athletic mastery of the boat. It took an enormous amount of focus for Ainslie to catch up to Scheidt's level, let alone to knock him off his throne in one of the most public of sailing forums. While each had their wins and losses over the years to each other, they both benefited. Their rivalry built both men up to a level of performance that has become a new standard in the ever-steepening climb that is competitive sailing, and both would continue to sail at the top of the game. Ainslie moved into the Finn class and took gold medals in the 2004, 2008, and 2012 Olympics. Scheidt continued to win a record-smashing run of Laser World titles and won another Olympic gold medal in Lasers in 2004, as well as silver in the Star class in 2008, and a bronze in Stars in 2012.

The drive that motivates a contentious pair of rivals to outdo one another ultimately benefits not only the rivals themselves, but the game they play. Joe Frazier and Muhammad Ali were fierce rivals in their contention for the heavyweight title in the early 1970s. Ali challenged the legitimacy of Frazier's title, having been stripped of the title himself after opposing induction into the army. Ali also turned the heat up on Frazier by taunting him in the press, which only seemed to drive Frazier to work harder to ensure that he would beat Ali when the met in the ring. The fight in 1971 between Ali and Frazier was called "the Fight of the Century," largely because of the buildup of suspense beforehand due to the escalating war of words. The Ali-Frazier rivalry not only drove both opponents to train themselves, and incidentally each other, to new levels of excellence, but built up tremendous interest in the sport and its personalities for years to come.

It is, of course, possible to misdirect one's focus on a particular opponent while losing sight of the competitive field. This threatens the competitor's chance at winning the war, in the attempt to win a smaller battle. On the off-wind legs of sailing courses, luffing matches between two boats may occasionally occur. Boats behind can attempt to pass an opponent by maneuvering to block their wind. Since the leeward boat has the right-of-way over a windward boat, however, the boat ahead can defend by pushing their attacker into the wind, or "luffing" them. This can send both boats far off track, however, and waste precious distance while the rest of the fleet continues racing a more direct course to the next mark.

Some skippers absolutely refuse to allow a certain other boat to pass them, even at the cost of their own race. Dr. Stuart Walker writes of this phenomenon in his book *Winning: The Psychology of Competition*, "When the same opponent is met again and again in race after race—as occurs when competitors of equal capability race in a local fleet—or when one-on-one situations are protracted, each competitor becomes preoccupied with the other, tending to perceive the race or series of races in terms of beating the particular opponent, and assuming that the opponent perceives the situation in the same way. The result is often a feeling of confrontation and hostility which is at the least distracting and may at the worst force an individual to seek escape, even if it involves surrender."

Obsession with beating a rival can ruin one's focus on the ultimate goal, preventing the sailor from devoting his attention to sailing his best race, and replacing cool, precise execution with sloppy and irrational maneuvers driven by emotion rather than reason. A rival should rather be simply seen as a marker on the road to indicate how you're progressing. Paul Elvstrom advised, "Think of your competitors only as a guide to your own performance." The pressure to succeed against a particular opponent may harm one's ability to perform to their true potential, such as a golfer missing an easy lie after witnessing her opponent make a more difficult shot on the last hole. A healthy respect for a strong competitor is sensible, but do not allow a "pecking order" to establish itself in your mind, even in the face of a rival's success. Even the best and brightest in the world are beatable, and the top performers in any field are those who have taught themselves to be their own toughest competitor.

YOUR RIVAL AS YOUR ALLY

Sometimes, the most beneficial tactic is to team up with a rival in a common pursuit. Olympic medalists in the Star class Iain Percy and Andrew "Bart" Simpson actually had been friendly rivals in the Finn class for years before teaming up. Their friendship goes back to the age of seven, when their parents entered them in a youth regatta in Southampton, England. A decade and a half later, it was Percy who beat out Simpson for the British Finn berth at the Sydney Olympics in 2000. For 2008, Percy and Simpson jumped into a Star together a year and a half before the competition. Percy had been campaigning with crew Steve Mitchell, but knew that for the light winds he expected in China, he'd need to sail with someone who was a strong light-air sailor, and Simpson would be a perfect fit. In their new pairing, Percy and Simpson learned quickly together and not only earned the Olympic berth, but also won the gold in 2008, as well as a silver sailing together again in the 2012 Olympics. As teammates and best friends, they would continue sailing together right up until the tragic accident that claimed Simpson's life while training for the 2013 America's Cup.

The pairing of former competitors is a regular occurrence in the business world, occasionally in the form of friendly mergers (as opposed to hostile takeovers). In 1997, Royal Caribbean International acquired Celebrity Cruise Lines for a purchase price of $515 million in cash and common stock, assuming $800 million in debt in the deal. Celebrity had also been sought after by Carnival Corporation, but was won by Royal Caribbean when its offer was increased by $15 million. Carnival had little company in its objection to the pairing, however. The shareholders of both Celebrity and Royal Caribbean approved the offer, creating a win-win scenario for the two companies; Royal Caribbean gained access to the upscale cruise market, and Celebrity gained competitiveness that it would not have had without the merger.

The world of politics has seen the hatchet buried between rivals for mutual advantage time and again. The electoral process in American politics evolved during the twentieth century to allow nominees for president to select their vice presidential running mate. Occasionally, candidates that fought each other through the primaries later wound up on the same ticket together, such as the Kennedy/Johnson ticket of 1960 and the Reagan/Bush ticket of 1980 and 1984. Entertainment also can see the pairing of rivals for the greater good, such as when movie stars that feud bitterly off screen play a happy couple for the cameras. If there is enough incentive, a pair of rivals can move past their differences (at least temporarily) for the sake of a productive alliance. When facing a challenge that requires advantages that a competitor can offer, don't count them out right away as a potential ally; a solid win-win scenario could make the prospect attractive to both of you.

TAKE A STAND

The goal of any civilized community in creating a set of laws, rules, or standards of conduct is to provide guidelines for handling situations in which the interests of different parties may be at odds. Occasionally in life, we encounter people who pursue their interests outside of such standards. There are those who would take advantage of the passivity of others to further their own aims in spite of the rules that they are expected to follow, taking such forms as the schoolyard bully, corrupt public figure, or illegally "enhanced" athlete. In the business world, we have seen high-ranking corporate executives mired in scandal and ultimately incarcerated because of their pursuit of profit at the expense of their own investors and other stakeholders. Why would someone do something that is illegal or unethical? Generally, it is because they thought that they could get away with it, as they often have been benefiting from little transgressions for some time. We see various scofflaws in the news every day, but the world of sports has its own versions, and sailing's no exception.

Umpires are not often used in sailing, because it has always been a self-policing sport. Generally, it remains so, but occasionally umpires will be called in to be an extra set of eyes on the water and dish out penalties when they see a rules infraction. This is necessary partly because sailors can't always police everything that's going on around them, because they are too focused on making their boat go fast. Without the umpires, a minor incident may occasionally be allowed to slide by due to the generosity of the right-of-way sailor, or simply because the infraction doesn't seem egregious enough to justify the time commitment and courtroom atmosphere of the protest room. Part of the self-policing format is giving the sailors the means to work through such matters themselves.

Sometimes, individuals begin to believe that their practices are acceptable to the group because nobody has called them on it yet. They may feel that they can poke their bow into a crowded mark rounding or give that sail an extra pump because "it's no big deal" or "everyone else is doing it." When that starts happening, it becomes even more vitally important to be aware of any unethical maneuvering going on and do your part to bring things back under control.

A problem facing many competitive dinghy fleets is the use of kinetics, such as rocking the boat or pumping the sails outside of what the rules will allow. When one boat starts to make gains through illegal kinetics, it tempts the boats nearby to follow suit in order to keep up. Eventually, this practice spreads through the group until sailors begin to perceive the situation as a choice of likewise breaking the rules or of being left behind. This is an example of what can happen when nobody speaks up against wrongdoing; it spreads until it becomes the new norm. Sailors can always propose changes to the racing rules to allow for new techniques and innovations, but "everybody does it" is no excuse when nobody should be doing it.

The sailor must be aware of the dangerous precedent being set by the renegade in their fleet. First of all, sailing is a game of feet and inches, and if Mr. X is breaking the rules to gain an advantage, he needs to be called on it, because his unfair advantage can make a difference in the regatta standings, if left free to run rampant. Secondly, even if Mr. X hasn't wronged you in this race, he needs to be set straight soon, or it could be you next time.

History has shown that left unchecked over the long run, wrongdoers inevitably begin to take bigger liberties until their transgressions create problems too big to deny or ignore. One of the most notorious renegades in history was left to push people around for far too long. Adolf Hitler's army invaded the Sudetenland of Czechoslovakia in 1938, and in an attempt to avoid a costly and devastating war, the Munich Agreement was signed by Britain, France, Germany and Italy, recognizing Germany's annexation of the territory in hopes that Hitler would stop at that. British Prime Minister Neville Chamberlain believed that the agreement had brought "peace with honor." However, it would not be long before Hitler had subsequently conquered all of Czechoslovakia. With Germany's invasion of Poland the following year, the Second World War that Europe had hoped to avoid would begin anyway. Upon taking office as Britain's new prime minister, Winston Churchill acknowledged that it was time to fight back:

"You ask, what is our policy? I will say it is to wage war by sea, land, and air, with all our might and with all the strength that God can give us; to wage war against a monstrous tyranny never surpassed in the dark and lamentable catalog of human crime. That is our policy. You ask, what is our aim? I can answer in one word: Victory! Victory at all costs—victory in spite of all terror—victory, however long and hard the road may be, for without victory there is no survival."

With France's surrender to the German army in 1940, England stood alone in the path of Hitler's war machine. Churchill recognized that, until the United States entered the conflict, Great Britain would be democracy's only hope in the face of the Nazi menace. In an address to the House of Commons, Churchill made clear the high stakes of the war, and reinforced the resolve of the British people to endure:

"Hitler knows that he will have to break us in this island or lose the war. If we can stand up to him, all Europe may be free and the life of the world may move forward into broad, sunlit uplands. But if we fail, then the whole world, including the United States, including all that we have known and cared for, will sink into the abyss of a new Dark Age."

Churchill's leadership throughout World War II was a key factor in turning back the threat of the Axis powers. While the European continent fell before the German army, Churchill inspired Great Britain to stand its ground and fight to the end. Even in the face of Germany's relentless air attacks, England held firm and refused to surrender. By never giving up and never giving in, England and the Allies would emerge victorious after a long and costly global struggle. It was due in no small part to Churchill's determination, standing firm against the expansion of fascism, that democracy in the western world was preserved.

It is the responsibility of all to be prepared to put a stop to those who would take advantage of the rules and undermine the order of civilized dealings, whether it's in friendly athletic competition, business, politics, or any setting in which rules and guidelines, written or unwritten, exist to maintain order and harmony. If you're seeing or experiencing a significant wrong being done, you don't have to tackle it alone, but it shows bravery and strength of character to take that first step to correct it. As tedious and tense as it can be, sometimes a sailor needs to protest for more than her own vindication; sometimes, it's a preservation of principle.

FOSTER SPORTSMANSHIP

It's to the benefit of both the individual and their community not only to demonstrate but to encourage the growth of good sportsmanship. Sportsmanship is alive and well in the world, and the sport of sailing appreciates its best displays as well as any other field, often bestowing awards upon those who do an exemplary job of displaying its qualities. Sportsmanship shows itself in many ways, and it is a relatively subjective matter, particularly when applied to differing cultures and situations. From the sailor's perspective, sportsmanship might mean lending a hand where possible, practicing fair play in competition, being a good winner or loser, or just keeping a good attitude in general.

Fair competition is valued the world over in any field, but the definition of "fair" can vary, based on the culture of the competitive field, or the way the rules of the game are written. When parameters are set down, in the form of rules (as in sports), or of laws, there are stricter guidelines in place with which each competitor must comply; to fail to do so results in actions that we define as cheating. Even if someone operating outside the rules is able to get away with it (for the time being), their actions are quickly recognized by others most of the time. When found out, a cheater may be reported and disqualified, and possibly ostracized as well.

Unfair practices in competition don't only hurt the people being cheated, but they also deprive the cheater himself of the satisfaction of success on a level playing field. On the water or off, everyone has rules to live, work, and compete by, and they must not only respect such rules for their own benefit and the benefit of those they deal with, but be able to familiarize themselves with new norms when they present themselves. For instance, business practices vary greatly between different countries, because regulation is stricter in some areas than others. This presents ethical dilemmas for conducting business internationally. For example, when does one cross the line between what one culture considers a business gift, and the other considers a bribe? As another example, outsourcing may provide a strong advantage in terms of cost savings, but raise ethical questions as to the practices of some of the factories performing the work. The corporation may conform to the letter of the law, but face a decision as to how to conform to the spirit of competition in its industry.

For sailors, culture also plays a role in defining one's standards of competition. The environment in which a young sailor receives his training and develops his personal approach to the sport will be a critical factor in shaping the sailor he will become in terms not only of skill, but of ethics as well. Champion sailor Dave Perry, an expert on the racing rules and longtime advocate of fair play in the sport, learned early in his sailing career the value of good sportsmanship. "I grew up and learned to sail at the Pequot Yacht Club in Southport, Connecticut, where the culture was one of pride in one's sailing skill and being nice to the people you race with and against," said Perry. "So it is in my DNA, and that highlights the importance of having a strong backbone of ethics in junior sailing programs and strong adult role models for junior sailors."

While he had a positive learning environment early on, Perry would later see both negative and positive examples of sportsmanship on the water that would stay with him over time. "I experienced a few situations in my post-college sailing where other sailors tried to win by breaking rules (like pumping their Lasers off the starting line in light air) or filing protests over technical violations that had no effect on the outcome of the race, and recognized the disgust I had with that sort of attempt to win a race. And then I had the opportunity to sail with Paul Elvstrom, the greatest sailor of our time in my opinion, and was indelibly impressed with his combination of intense competitiveness but at the same time respect for the sport."

In Perry's book *Winning in One-Designs*, he includes a chapter on sportsmanship titled, "Are We All Playing the Same Game?" which fittingly begins with a quote from Elvstrom: "You haven't won the race if in winning the race you have lost the respect of your competitors." This famous quote has served as a personal mantra not only for Perry, but for sailors everywhere.

Sportsmanship is more than the absence of cheating. It is also the demonstration of genuine decency to the competition. There are times when a gesture of goodwill can make a major difference to someone else and work to mutual benefit over the long run as relationships take root. Most competitive sailors help each other out in little ways at regattas, such as helping to unload boats from trailers or lending tools. Every now and then, a big favor will be granted that any observer can't help but admire. The Danish 49er Olympic team of Jonas Warrer and Martin Kirketerp Ibsen were able to complete their journey to a gold medal in 2008 thanks to a competitor, the Croatian team of Pavle Kostov and Petar Cupac. Going into the final medal race, the Danes were leading the regatta, but broke their mast while practicing in the breezy conditions. Their hopes for the gold seemed dashed, at least until they returned to the dock, when the Croatian team offered the use of their boat to the Danish team. Thanks to this act of generosity, the Danes were just barely able to make it across the start line in time to compete, and finished strongly enough to secure the gold medal. Kostov and Cupac were awarded the Pierre de Coubertin Trophy later that year by the International Committee, to recognize "an act of fair play, which cost or could have cost the victory to a contender who sacrificed or compromised his chances of winning by complying not only with the written rules of the sport, but also the 'unwritten' ones."

Coming away from a tough contest presents an opportunity for the parties to show their sportsmanship, or lack thereof. Again, norms can vary on what defines sportsmanlike behavior; much of the time, the noise made by the winner may just be a show for the cameras to play up an image. When Cassius Clay (Muhammad Ali) won his first heavyweight title over Sonny Liston, he crowed, "I am the greatest!" Cockiness like this made him a more interesting celebrity, and the louder he got before and after his fights, the more interest he was able to generate for the event, and the more tickets were sold. Some sports can be more forgiving of "trash-talking," recognizing it as a form of showmanship. The culture that we live in will determine what the expectations are of us coming away from either a victory or a defeat. A handshake and/or a compliment ("nice job") is generally a fair expectation in most venues following a closely spirited contest.

Being a good winner or loser is born out of respect for one's competitor from the outset. The joy of victory makes the winner much more generous with compliments about his competitors. The challenge for the winner at times may be to rein in his pride at the accomplishment and to be more humble instead. Happiness after a win is natural and expected, but being a good winner comes from how others are made to feel about your victory. Being a good loser is more of an emotional challenge, because of the disappointment of defeat. In reference to the graciousness of his beaten rival Sir Thomas Lipton, triple America's Cup winner Harold Vanderbilt said, "It is easy to be a good winner, but in defeat lays the true test of sportsmanship." Lipton challenged for the America's Cup unsuccessfully five times, but was so well liked and so admired for his display of good sportsmanship in the face of disappointing and expensive defeats, that he was not only enthusiastically invited back time and again for another try, but he also had several sailing trophies named after him in recognition of his gentlemanly ways.

Anyone may occasionally be tempted to sulk or belittle the winner after a painful loss; it's not always easy to be happy for the one who made you unhappy. As such, sportsmanship is easier for everyone when seen as a two-way street. When both parties approach the competition from the very beginning with mutual respect, the loser can come away from the contest genuinely feeling something along the lines of, "Well, if I had to lose, I'm glad it was to him." The winner, in turn, can appreciate the attitude of his vanquished competitor and convey a sense of gratitude for the spirited contest.

Mutual respect can provide mutual benefit in any competitive endeavor. Dave Perry recalled a positive competitive relationship with Dave Curtis, a champion sailor from Marblehead, Massachusetts, while campaigning for the 1984 Olympics in the Soling; "On the water, Dave was the starboard tacker you could cross close in front of, and if he didn't have to change his course to avoid you, all you would hear from him was 'Nice one!' On shore, he was the first to answer a question about how he had set his boat up or how he choreographed the more intricate boat handling maneuvers."

This form of friendly competition turned out to be rewarding for both parties in ways both tangible and intangible. "The reward for us was learning a ton from a great sailor, and having a really fun guy to race against on the water," added Perry. " I don't think [Curtis] was doing it for any sort of reward himself, other than to help others get strong so the racing was more challenging and fun for him, but he was well rewarded both by his numerous National and World championships in several classes, and by his recent induction into the National Sailing Hall of Fame, an honor that recognizes not only sailing skill, but also character and contribution to the sport."

Sportsmanship tends to come naturally when competition is engaged in with a spirit of common values and mutual respect. Sailors compete in a self-policing sport that puts extra responsibility on the individual to follow the rules of the game, and the sport benefits most when each sailor conducts himself or herself accordingly. Sailing, like all sports, also carries the emotional highs and lows of victory and defeat, and places expectations of sportsmanship (what sailors call "the Corinthian spirit") on the sailors that can be an internal challenge at times. These expectations of etiquette and personal conduct, as such, can serve as a valuable model off the water as well. When people are in tune with and respect the written and unwritten rules of conduct in the field that they compete in, the experience of the competition itself is much more positive for all parties, win or lose.

PART FOUR

LEARNING

*Over the long run, superior performance
depends on superior learning.*

—Peter Senge

The learning phase is a unique turning point of our success cycle. It is a growth period that bridges the end of one experience and the beginning of the next. Two approaches to learning will be discussed here: reactive and proactive. Reactive learning is a period of looking back and learning from experience; it comes from gaining a thorough understanding of what contributed to one's success or lack thereof and assimilating the lessons of the experience to benefit from them in the future. Proactive learning is an ongoing process of observing, listening, experimenting, experiencing, recording, and remembering. It is an attitude of constant pursuit; a thirst for more knowledge, greater improvement, and stronger results. It is a belief in unlimited potential and a commitment to a higher level of excellence. Reactive learning is improvement based on lessons of the past, while proactive learning is improvement through research and experimentation as well as curiosity and imagination.

Learning is the cycle that never stops, and must be actively and perpetually pursued. Learning is how we grow, from the moment we're born. There is much that we learn instinctively, and much more that we learn systematically. The world has continued to place increasingly high premiums on the acquisition and dissemination of information; whoever has the information has the power. Further, the speed of change in economic and geopolitical terms has necessitated constant awareness of the changes that happen in the world around us in order to adapt and continue to grow. To thrive in the modern world, learning cannot stop—not after graduation, not even for a day. The advantage in life has always gone to those who expand their knowledge continuously, and this is unlikely to change. Sailing presents vast opportunities to learn, and there will be much to learn far beyond the foreseeable future. It is no different in so much of life; there is always more to know, more to understand, and more to investigate in order to find new ways to raise the bar for your own performance. Learning is the backbone of any great civilization and the foundation of any successful individual's life and career. When you make learning an ongoing habit, whatever your area of expertise, your potential expands to unfathomable heights.

REACTIVE LEARNING

'Why' and 'How' are words so important that they cannot be too often used.
—NAPOLEON BONAPARTE

ONE OF THE CHALLENGES OF REACTIVE learning is keeping an objective eye and looking at past experiences rationally in order to draw valuable lessons from them. The moment of reactive learning comes right on the heels of the challenge to which we devote our efforts. The paradox lies in the fact that, while there is more to be learned from the experience of defeat, such experiences are harder to review objectively because they tend to be clouded by personal bias and disappointment. To learn and grow from any experience, win or lose, we must be able to move forward by reviewing what was done well and what could be improved upon. Often, the contributions of others we trust can make a significant difference in this phase of learning. Coaches and peers can provide a point of view that may open up new trains of thought and inspire new initiatives. While we may compare our performance to others and count on the instruction of experts we trust from time to time, learning is best pursued by acting as our own competitor, setting our own standard of excellence rather than having it dictated to us. Learning in retrospect is largely done using a broad viewpoint, considering a large number of influential factors leading up to and concurrent with our performance, but it must be done with a view inward as well. Mastery over our personal progress doesn't come from satisfying a mentor or outdoing an opponent, but from meeting and exceeding our own expectations. When you set the standard for yourself, you are the one in complete control of your growth and development. When looking back at prior experiences to glean lessons for the future, consider the positives and negatives as if you are your own coach, then reinforce the strengths and tackle the weaknesses with a spirit of focused optimism.

REVIEW

Coming away from any experience, whether it's been very successful or not particularly so, it's tremendously valuable to dedicate some time and effort to reviewing the events that you have been through, in order to better learn from them. It's easy for the harried competitor to come away from one situation and immediately focus on the next task at hand, without thinking over what he did well and what he would have done differently. It's also easy for a competitor to come away from a successful venture assuming that he has done everything right, or from an unsuccessful one believing that he has been the victim of bad luck or foul play. Both of these habits lead to repetition of mistakes and obstruction to improvement. Win or lose, whatever the challenge, it is important to take time periodically to consider honestly where one's performance has been strong and where it still needs improvement.

Self-honesty is crucial to learning from one's own performance. Ego can get in the way of the delivery of accurate feedback, however. Anyone striving for excellence will find it a bitter pill to admit their worst mistakes and take responsibility for them. They are left to consider what the causes of those mistakes were; perhaps it was a lack of commitment to preparation, a poor choice of resources, bad decision making under fire, or even choking under pressure. These are just some of the difficult realities that could have to be faced, but in order to improve, they must be addressed. It can be tempting to actually believe the excuses that we might make when things haven't turned out as we'd hoped, but kidding ourselves doesn't help us to get it right next time. In the excitement of success, it's also easy to miss the opportunities for improvement. We may feel that there is nothing to be learned because we've earned the result we sought, so surely we've done everything right. Whatever the result, everyone gets some things right and some things wrong, but it is rare that anyone gets everything right or everything wrong. There's always a chance for improvement, but the search for it has to start with an honest and realistic assessment of where your performance actually stands. It's easy to see and appreciate our own strengths, but weaknesses are more difficult to pinpoint, often because our inability to understand their roots is what makes them weaknesses. Like a kind of safety inspector, the competitor dedicated to ongoing improvement needs to comb over every detail of their performance, looking for any potential weakness that could lead to disaster.

Sailors going through a long regatta series have some opportunity between races to review their performance. If they've won the race, they'll be thinking about what happened on the course that affected their sailing; where the puffs were, how the wind shifts trended, where the current was strongest, and so on. They'll also be thinking about their own performance, asking questions like: *How was our sail trim? How were our tactics? How was our boat handling? Where can we improve?* The sailor has to recognize what is working and what isn't in order to adapt to the conditions and make improvements wherever possible, however small. The top sailors are constantly evaluating different methods and techniques in order to more quickly adopt the best ones and discard the worst.

Sailors must also understand why something is working in order to continue to benefit from its practice; they may have found that playing the right side of the course in the previous race worked out quite well, but if they do not understand what factors made that side pay off, they may blindly head off in that direction every time, ignorant of impending changes on the course. Successful businesses are similarly susceptible to catastrophe without a real understanding of their strengths and weaknesses. Jim Collins refers to this complacency in *How the Mighty Fall* as "Hubris Born of Success," noting: "When the rhetoric of success ('We're successful because we do these specific things') replaces penetrating understanding and insight ('We're successful because we *understand why* we do these specific things and under what conditions they would no longer work'), decline will very likely follow." Easing into a formula for success without maintaining mastery of the business's processes, a thorough understanding of the business environment, and active pursuit of leadership in the industry makes for a vulnerable organization and turns a onetime formula for success into a formula for obsolescence.

Reviewing past experiences can extend beyond self-evaluation to the competition as well. Others in your field can act as a valuable source of information in the review process. Consider what differentiates your competitors from yourself: What are their strengths? What are their weaknesses? Consider how they will adapt their plans to their advantage, and whether there is a way to nullify their strengths and exploit their weaknesses to your own benefit. Consider whether you can emulate something that they are doing right, or go in the other direction and differentiate from them for an advantage.

During the 1980 America's Cup, the Australian challenger used a radical mast design that allowed them to carry a larger mainsail. The British team had been the first to try the concept out, but was eliminated in the early trials. After *Australia* was named the challenger, they adopted the mast design used by their British rivals. This gave a significant light-air advantage, but less so in windier conditions. With the boat overpowered, the Australians would have to de-power the sail, putting them back on more equal footing with the more conventional defender, *Freedom*. Since both teams were allowed to call "lay days" (days off of racing) when needed, the *Freedom* syndicate could use a day off when light winds were expected. This helped to avoid some of the light wind conditions that favored *Australia*, and *Freedom* proved ultimately successful, winning the series 4–1. In the end, the American defender proved more adept than the Aussies this time at learning from the competition; the Australians had seen great potential in the British team's innovation, but the Americans were ready with a plan to limit that potential.

Whatever your pursuit, whether you're in school or in politics, athletics, business, the arts, or any number of other professional fields, you will find yourself with opportunities to review your own performance. Take advantage of these opportunities to conduct a "SWOT" analysis: honestly assess your strengths, weaknesses, opportunities and threats. Consider what you're doing well, where you can improve, what dangers you'll need to watch out for, and how you can be ready for them. As philosopher George Santanaya said, "Those who do not learn from the mistakes of the past are doomed to repeat them." Take stock of your performance whenever you get the chance in order to keep your growth on an upward curve and leave old mistakes in the past where they belong.

PURSUE IMPROVEMENT

The active pursuit of constant improvement is a vital component of the learning process, in sailing or in any aspect of life. From race to race, regatta to regatta, the most successful sailors are those who can continue to grow through planned improvement in boat speed, technique, and tactics. The process can be long and difficult, but when a program for ongoing performance improvement is implemented with discipline, improved results reflect the lessons learned.

Sailors generally learn how to make their boats go faster by tuning with a partner, using their own form of the scientific method. Two boats, similarly matched, will line up next to each other and race in a straight line. One of these boats will act as the "control" boat, keeping all settings the same, while the other acts as the "variable" boat, making a single alteration at a time for comparison. The changes could be to an appendage such as the rudder or keel, the setting of the mast, or the trim of a sail, for instance. When the variable boat begins to consistently outperform the control boat, the two boats are set up identically again with the new configuration and continue testing something else. This process goes on indefinitely over time, as competitors continue to push the envelope in terms of performance to achieve new levels of excellence.

The methods of improving boat speed can be applied in any number of growth efforts; they drive innovation and make progress a natural habit. Wherever you seek to try something new to improve performance, whether it's in design, business operations, athletics, or any other field, these principles can prove to be a helpful guideline to making progress over the long run.

FIND A GOOD BENCHMARK

Sailors looking for a tuning partner seek out someone who will be an effective benchmark for them. This should not only be a boat that is as similar as possible, but one that is sailed by people of comparable abilities. If the two boats are too dissimilar, then there are extra variables to be considered in the testing process that could make conclusions more difficult to draw. If the sailors are not of similar skill, it cannot be definitely decided, for instance, whether one boat doesn't accelerate well because the configuration isn't fast, or whether it is because that boat is not being sailed well.

It is easier to define goals when working toward improvement when the next level can be clearly defined. Starting on equal footing helps to make improvements more obvious; when the bar is then raised, there is a next step clearly defined that must be reached before the next step after that. If your chosen benchmark is not equal, but already superior, you will be the variable in the process, trying new things until you are able to climb to your benchmark's level. Having a benchmark of lesser quality or performance slows the growth process down, but at least there is still learning going on for both parties as you bring the benchmark up to standards.

MINIMIZE THE VARIABLES

If you are looking to set the bar higher for yourself, you will need to be able to make comparisons directly. The first step is to remove as many unknowns as possible from the two things to be tested, leaving only one clearly identified difference between the two to be observed and evaluated. Tuning two sailboats requires getting everything about them as close to identical as possible. This means thoroughly checking over all the settings to avoid accidentally introducing more variables into the equation. Whatever small differences remain between two boats undergoing a speed trial will influence the result, leading to false conclusions.

In the field of medicine, thoroughness in analyzing a problem with multiple variables can mean the difference between life and death. In 1854, a deadly cholera epidemic struck London, and the cause of the disease was a mystery. Physician John Snow noticed, however, that most of the cases of illness seemed geographically centered around a particular water pump on Broad Street, leading to his hypothesis that the water supply was the cause. Snow's theory was not immediately embraced, however, as chemical tests on the water proved inconclusive, but authorities decided to try removing the pump handle to see if it helped. The outbreak subsided, but doubts remained about Snow's theory, since there had been other people showing symptoms outside the immediate vicinity of the Broad Street pump. Upon further investigation, Snow discovered that the outlying victims had been going out of their way to get water from the Broad Street pump because they usually preferred it to their local water source. The ability to establish this definitive pattern of infection by following up with the outliers helped Snow to prove his hypothesis and advance the field of epidemiology.

Successful experimentation with anything means being able to explain the reason for different results. If you have changed only one thing on one of the test subjects, you can generally conclude that that specific change is responsible for a different outcome in the testing. Sailors can often struggle to reach definitive conclusions while testing due to environmental considerations; little differences in the conditions like current eddies and wind shears can affect an experiment almost imperceptibly. For this reason, big sailing campaigns with an R & D emphasis, such as the Volvo Ocean Race or the America's Cup, make use of controlled environments to test variables, such as wind tunnels, towing tanks, and computer models. When you are trying out something new, try to eliminate any factors that could influence the result of your experiment and your results will be significantly more reliable.

REPEAT FOR RELIABILITY

In any experimentation process, results have to be *repeatable* in order to be *reliable*. Anomalies and outliers do factor into the results of any real-world experiment, but conclusions cannot be drawn from rare occurrences. What most experiments try to establish, whether it's in sailing, market research, or medical trials, is a pattern of results. Trying something once and noting what happens isn't enough to consider the test effective. You must be able to repeat the process and show a pattern of performance in order to draw a reliable conclusion.

Many athletes have a tendency to take things to an extreme in an effort to repeat a good result. After a very good day, they may insist on obsessively repeating every detail of that day for the next contest. Sometimes, that kind of consistency can provide a certain comfort that can keep them focused, but when superstition sets in, it can become a distraction. Suddenly it becomes very upsetting that the buffet menu at the hotel restaurant has changed, or your "lucky underwear" is now in the wash! However, little traditions and superstitions can be harmless and fun if kept in perspective. The crew of *America³* enjoyed a number of lucky charms on board for the 1992 America's Cup, which included a crow's feather, a bag of corn, a pouch of medicine-man tobacco, and a toy airplane.

GAUGE RESULTS HONESTLY

Forming a hypothesis and testing it in an experiment can often lead to expectations that can bias the conclusions drawn. Results that contradict the status quo can influence the experimenters' evaluation of them. Thoughts of, "That's impossible" or "There's no way that can be accurate," whether conscious or unconscious, can take one's focus away from results that may lead to something extraordinary. Unusual outcomes should be retested as standard procedure anyway, but the results must always be reviewed honestly and openly in order to draw valid conclusions from them.

KEEP RAISING THE BAR

In the quest to make constant improvement, it is important to keep raising the bar so that performance moves steadily upward, rather than leveling off or declining. Sailors reconfigure their boats when they are confident that one of them has found a faster setting. By configuring them both to the new "best setting," the bar is raised and the boats continue to look for ways to take another step above and beyond the level they're at. If they've done a good job in this process, the sailors should come to have two boats of equal speed potential. If both boats are not brought up the ladder of performance together, neither can be certain whether any further tests reveal a real improvement or not.

It's important to keep from standing still in any competitive endeavor. Japanese businesses such as Toyota and Canon introduced the practice of *kaizen*. This is a process of learning and problem solving that is driven by the commitment of the entire organization to achieving continuous growth and progress by analyzing every step of its production process, looking for ways to streamline it. Any effective learning organization must be committed to ongoing improvement through the efforts of all its members, and this means gaining and sharing information to keep even the weakest link exceptionally strong.

When new and advanced methods and techniques are determined, be sure to communicate them to your colleagues or teammates to ensure that your collective performance level has been raised. By learning together what makes your boat go faster or your business run smoother, you can improve to the point that what was once considered the performance ceiling has become the new floor.

KEEP A RECORD

Experimentation for improvement can take a long time, and can include many frustrating failures along the way. It's important to make the best possible use of time and effort, so keeping thorough and accurate records of each test is a good way to avoid redundant and irrelevant tests. The most high-tech sailing campaigns have computers and cameras that capture as much data as possible during testing, but small boat sailors often must resort to simpler means, such as writing notes in a book or on the deck. If it's not possible to take notes on the boat, the sailors will need to write the results down upon return to shore, while memory is still fresh. It's important when trying new methods to be able to easily recall what worked and what didn't, and under what circumstances. Relying on memory alone to be responsible for every detail of every test invites the repetition of unsuccessful methods.

Peter Commette started keeping a log as a training tool early in his sailing career. "I crewed in the E-Scow the summer that I was sixteen for a great MIT All-American from the 1930s, an E-Scow National Champ and seven- or eight-time Penguin International champ named Runyon ('Runnie') Colie," says Commette. "The deal was sealed at the end of the summer before, but Runnie said that I could not have the job unless I read three sailing books over the winter. One of the books he assigned was a book by a UK Flying Dutchman world champion named John Oakley, and the book was called *Winning*. Throughout the book, Oakley talked about the value of keeping a log as a means for improving. I copied his log and adapted it to the boats we sailed then on Barnegat Bay... (now) I keep a notebook for each boat I have sailed, a notebook for sailing fast articles, a notebook for sailing smart articles, and I own a ton of dog-eared and underlined sailing books." Commette's organized approach to developing his sailing ability translated well into his college sailing career and far beyond. "My coach at Tufts, the great Joe Duplin, always said, 'Leave no stone unturned'... Since I can't 'leave no stone unturned' by practicing sailing anymore, I try to leave no stone unturned in other areas. That's the great thing about sailing; there are a lot of effective methods for getting to the front of the fleet."

CONSIDER YOURSELF YOUR TOUGHEST COMPETITOR

For the most ambitious people, their own expectations of themselves can greatly exceed those held of them by others. This propensity toward constant self-improvement provides the drive necessary to succeed at higher levels. Sailors at the top levels never are fully satisfied with their performance, even if they win every race they sail. They know that if they are not constantly improving, then all they are doing is standing still while their closest competitor catches up to them. Emphasizing one's own performance rather than making comparisons can also help maintain focus. The top athletes in any sport know that it is more productive to set out to best their own personal standards than to worry about beating a particular competitor, as well as more rewarding in the end. It is one thing to outperform a rival that may not be at their best on the given day, and quite another to set a new personal best.

Businesses taking the long view know the importance of setting the bar high internally. In *Built to Last*, Jim Collins and Jerry Porras wrote, "The critical question asked by a visionary company is not 'How well are we doing?' or 'How can we do well?' or 'How well do we have to perform in order to meet the competition?' For these companies, the critical question is *'How can we do better tomorrow than we did today?'* They institutionalize this question as a way of life—a habit of mind and action. Superb execution and performance naturally come to the visionary companies not so much as an end goal, but as the residual result of a never-ending cycle of self-stimulated improvement and investment for the future."

Concentrating on making improvements based on your own performance can broaden the horizons of potential growth. Your toughest competitor doesn't necessarily represent the best that can be achieved in your field; the only immediate limits to your own performance are those of which your imagination can conceive. You can't know for sure how high you can rise, but you risk setting a limit by concentrating too much on the standards of your competition, rather than the standards you hold for yourself.

KEEP PERSPECTIVE

Coming away from any contest, particularly when there remains more work to be done, poses some mental challenges to any competitor. The winner must overcome the distracting excitement of success in order to keep focused on making further improvement for the future. It is, after all, often more difficult to pinpoint little failures to learn from when the end result was success. One must not succumb to the pressure to be perfect at all times, nor too complacent to continue to improve. The less successful competitor has an easier time of determining what went wrong and a better idea by the performance of others as to how to fix it, but he must overcome the discouragement and frustration of a loss in order to pursue improvement with focus and determination. By keeping either a win or a loss in perspective, the competitor will be able to see the experience objectively and use it as a building block for future success.

WINNING

Winning is a joy, particularly when it's been hard earned, but it also comes with its burdens. Winning can do funny things to your head: a winner may suddenly feel like the king of the world, expecting to win every time, or he may feel unsure of himself and be riddled with fear over losing what he's won. It's natural to take pleasure and pride in one's accomplishment, but each victory needs to be seen as just one step on the road to the next thing. It's more difficult to learn from winning than from losing, because it's easy to feel that because we came out on top that we did everything right. A person can take pleasure and pride in their success, but how they handle a victory's place in their own personal journey can have a major effect on their ability to continue such success.

Pressure for continued success can haunt even the most confident of winners. The more public the stage and the less experienced the competitor, the worse it gets. Many skippers going into a major event with more press coverage will insist that their crews avoid reading or watching the news until the regatta is over. Moving into the lead gains a lot of attention, both from peers and the press, and there is a threat of pressure affecting one's performance. More experienced competitors tend to handle the limelight better because they've been there before and have been hardened over time. When ultimate victory appears within reach, some competitors may find themselves making unusual mistakes as fear begins to tug at them. For many, it is not a fear of losing, but actually a fear of winning—of where winning would put the bar for them in the future, and of how winning would change their whole outlook. An experienced competitor moves ahead expecting to win, while an upstart may be surprised deep down to see a win actually within his grasp. While making the climb through the ranks, don't let either the prospect of winning or the challenge of pursuing the next win intimidate you from performing with the focus and precision that got you to where you are. Likewise, it is important not to let even the biggest or well deserved of victories go to your head and coax you into easing up in your efforts for continued success. You become vulnerable the minute you start believing that you are invulnerable.

Complacency can threaten even the largest lead, in sailing or in business. Coca-Cola has been a leader in the food and beverage industry since its founding in 1886, but has occasionally had its position threatened by competitors. At the outset of the twenty-first century, the attentions of American consumers began to shift toward health concerns, and specifically toward popular food products that contributed to the average American's ever-increasing waistline. The soda industry was targeted as part of the problem, and Coke, being the largest and therefore the easiest target to hit, found its brand suddenly smudged by criticism in the press. The result was a sudden surge in market share for branded water and energy drinks.

Coke had for too long rested on its laurels, relying on the brand's entrenchment in the American consciousness to keep it far ahead of the competition. By neglecting to innovate on pace with changing consumer expectations, Coke soon found that others were controlling the conversation about its products, opening the door for new competition from outside the cola sector. Coke was forced to respond to the sudden competition from alternative beverages by marketing waters and energy drinks of its own. Sometimes, it takes a scare to shake a leader in any competition out of the complacency that can settle in when you're on top. Other times, a leader doesn't realize that they've been outmaneuvered until it's too late.

The 1983 America's Cup was a turning point in the 132-year-old competition. With more challengers showing up than ever before, the undefeated New York Yacht Club would have its hands full against the pool of foreign teams. Only one would face the club's defender in the Cup match itself, but that one challenger would have fought through the toughest field yet seen for the contest. Australian businessman Alan Bond's *Australia II* was the boat that changed the game. Australian teams had been improving through their previous challenges via relatively minor advancements, but Bond had seen how radical design ideas, such as the experimental mast on his previous challenger, could have the potential to change the game. Designer Ben Lexcen came up with a keel design that had never been seen in the America's Cup before. The keel of *Australia II* was narrow at the top and longer at the bottom, with lead wings extending outward from the aft bottom section. By the time the word got out that *Australia II* had an unusual (and unusually fast) keel, the Americans' defense was to challenge its legality. The rulings of the international jury that had measured *Australia II* stood, and she made it to the start line to face the defender *Liberty* in the Cup match, having handily won the challenger trials. Despite the brilliant performance of Dennis Conner and the *Liberty* crew against a markedly faster boat, *Australia II* won the Cup, 4–3.

While *Australia II* was revolutionary, *Liberty* was simply an improvement on previous winners, the differences subtle enough that the average observer couldn't distinguish them. American syndicates had won twenty-four previous Cup matches in a row, resulting in a relatively conservative approach to winning with each respective contest. The defender was always much more risk averse, feeling that the longer the winning streak went on, the more they had to lose. The story goes, a visitor once asked a New York Yacht Club member what would replace the Cup in the trophy room if it were ever lost, the reply to which was, "the head of the man who lost it." The challenger always had the freedom to try something outside the box, because they had less to lose (thankfully, nobody ever lost their head over the America's Cup). It is wise to be conservative to protect a lead, but a winner should not close their eyes to possibilities that can give them an even greater advantage. One of the challenges of being at the top of the pack is to pursue constant improvement—to keep gaining ground, even with a healthy lead. In sailing or in life, conditions can change so fast that no advantage is ever really big enough to be completely safe.

Keeping an edge from a position of leadership is a challenge that constantly faces successful individuals, teams, and businesses. Success tends to paint a target on the back of a leader in any field. Competition sprouts up from every direction, all with a goal of seizing the top spot through new innovations and bold initiatives. Getting to the front of the pack is not necessarily the end of an effort, but simply the next step in a long road of constant improvement. It can be a good feeling to be out in front, but success cannot be allowed to breed complacency, or the competition will quickly displace you from your lofty perch.

To be able to learn from a win, we must be able to see it objectively in hindsight, giving an honest evaluation of the experience: What went right that made the difference? What went wrong that can still be improved upon? What haven't we tried yet that could keep us growing? What are the other guys doing that could be a threat? The euphoria of victory can be a major distraction, and everyone is entitled to take joy in their success. To make winning build upon itself, however, it must be considered as another opportunity for learning and improving as well as a confidence booster.

Losing

Any sailor going into a difficult regatta has to understand the risks of the racing ahead. Between the difficulties of handling the boat and equipment, the challenges of the elements of wind and water, and the spirited chaos of racing in a crowded fleet, plenty can go wrong. There is always risk associated with any challenge, the risk of failure often being paramount on the minds of even the most technically competent people. Indeed, many efforts fall flat, are abandoned, or never started at all because of the fear of failure. Failure is always a possibility at the beginning, but even when it occurs, it isn't always an ending. No sailor has ever gone through their career unbeaten, and every sailor can be grateful for it. Without a loss, there's not as much to learn. We learn much more from losing than from winning, and a crafty competitor that outdoes us from time to time can be more helpful to us than we may realize at first.

There will be times for anyone striving for success when things just don't turn out, despite their best efforts; there's no excuses, but it didn't work out anyway. In the world of finance, there is always a risk of a loss any time there's a chance for a notable reward. The success of an investment tends to involve some degree of unknown variables, so it is up to the investor to make decisions with as much information as possible, still accepting some degree of uncertainty and focusing on those factors that are within their realm of influence, rather than those over which they have no control.

At the end of an unsuccessful effort, the observant competitor can see where things went wrong for him and went right for his opponent. Sometimes, luck plays a factor. How, then, can you make your own luck in the future? Sometimes, the opposition had more help. How, then, can you find better help for next time? Sometimes, your opponent had vaster resources. How can you gather all the tools you need for success? This honest and frank assessment of the results will help open your eyes to find the answers to all the "why's" and build a foundation for a better future effort. As Henry Ford said, "Failure is simply the opportunity to begin again, this time more intelligently."

LEARN FROM MISTAKES

Mistakes are a natural part of the learning process. The ambitious pursuit of perfection can make any minor error terribly frustrating to a competitive person, so it bears keeping in mind that mistakes have their place in everyone's growth. Mistakes are necessary as indicators of the boundaries of new possibilities, as measures of our own performance, and as tests of our resilience. When we have embarked upon a difficult mission of significant importance, we must not only be forgiving to ourselves for our mistakes, but grateful for the ability to learn from them. When we pay attention, we can turn the lessons from mistakes made into an advantage for the future.

In dinghy sailing, it is often said that if you never wipe out, you're not trying hard enough. Fast maneuvering in small boat racing requires using body weight to tip the boat in order to assist in steering, or to propel the boat through a roll tack, in which the boat is rocked vigorously to windward as it passes through the wind from one tack to the other. Roll tacking, well executed, provides much better speed through the turn, but if overdone could result in capsizing. If a dinghy team always returns to the dock from practice bone-dry, it's a good indicator that they aren't pushing the envelope. It's expected that teams find the edge and learn where to back off a bit when they are learning their boat. They may capsize, they may break a mast, or they may have some other accident happen, but without allowing for mistakes while they are trying to learn, how can they expect to avoid them when trying to perform in the future?

The start of a race also presents sailors with an opportunity to find the edge. The objective, as we know, is to cross the start line at full speed in the desired position exactly at the starting signal. This is a judgment of speed and distance that is by and large completely up to the sailors. The chop and disturbed air from the other boats are factors that will adversely affect boat speed, and the skipper must be able to navigate through traffic, accelerating and decelerating as needed. There may also be current pushing the fleet in one direction or the other. With all of this to focus on, a countdown timer is ticking, and the skipper must present the boat in top form at this invisible point at the instant his watch gets to zero. The risk in pushing too hard is that, if any part of the boat crosses the start line too early, the boat must dip completely behind the line again in order to start properly. To continue sailing on when you are called over early disqualifies you from the race. Many skippers hang back too far in the middle of the line, where it is most difficult to judge one's actual position. Others push the line hard every time and get called over early more often. In the short run, the conservative sailors have a better chance to do well because they won't be disqualified by hanging back by that extra little bit. Over the long run, however, the more aggressive starter will benefit because his judgment of time and distance is being corrected with each premature start. He suffers for his mistakes at the time, but comes away having learned how far is too far. A premature start can hurt one's regatta results, but it is still an instructive mistake, and an indicator that a real effort to excel is being made.

We all have our moments through life, even from birth, where we make little mistakes to learn from. Life tends to be a cycle of falling and rising again. When we were learning to walk, we all had to figure out how to stand and then take those first steps. Luckily, diapers provide lots of padding, because we all land on our backsides over and over as we try to get the hang of it. It becomes a process—lean against something and let go, then fall. Stand on our own, then fall. Stand and take a little step, then fall. Stand and take two steps, then fall. Before long, we're running around the house! All those little falls along the way provided the incentive to get up and try again. Our leg muscles get stronger, our balance gets better, and we make a little more progress as we go. We land on our backsides plenty of times as adults, too. Whatever it is that we're chasing, whether it's making a sale, getting a degree, learning a new skill, or any tough new challenge, we're bound to have some flubs along the way. The important thing is being able to stand again after we fall and keep moving forward.

Mistakes can feel all the more significant in close competition. At the conclusion of any true clash of titans, observers naturally look back at what is usually a small margin of victory, seeking where the difference between the competitors truly lay. The 2007 America's Cup was decided in the last moments of the last race. The final 5–2 score of defender *Alinghi* over challenger *Emirates*

Team New Zealand does not do justice to the closeness of the contest; the largest margin of victory over these seven races was just thirty-five seconds. Midway through what would be the final race, New Zealand worked into the lead, looking to gain another win and survive to fight another day. On the way to the last windward mark, *Alinghi* gained enough ground on the right side to gain tactical control at the top of the leg, and prevented *ETNZ* from tacking for the mark. In the process, *Alinghi* drew *ETNZ* into committing a foul, which could only be absolved with a penalty turn before the finish. *Alinghi* regained the lead, but with a huge wind shift to their disadvantage as well as gear failure, *ETNZ* was able to move past her with just meters to go to the finish. However, New Zealand was still required to do a penalty turn, and had barely completed it when *Alinghi* glided over the finish line just one second ahead.

This incredibly close contest resulted in much speculation over every move made by either team over every race, resulting in each win for one or the other. The turning point was at the second half of the last windward leg, when *Alinghi* gained control from the right. The fact that the one-second loss was in the deciding race made the post-race analysis that much more painful for *Emirates Team New Zealand*. The *Alinghi* team did not win this particular America's Cup because it made no mistakes; rather, it was the team's ability to work through its own mistakes and take advantage of its competitor's. Bill Koch remarked after his own winning America's Cup campaign in 1992, "We've made mistakes, but as in anything in life, the boat that makes the least mistakes is the one that wins." While the number of mistakes made in a vital contest must be minimized, their timing and severity make a significant difference as well. Had New Zealand made the same tactical errors in the first Cup race of the series instead of the last one, their ultimate impact would have been far less. It's crucial to look at mistakes objectively, however, and not to dwell on them. What we learn from our mistakes and how we move past them is more significant in the long run.

Making a mistake doesn't necessarily mean that your chances to succeed have been crushed, even though it may seem like it at the time. At the age of twenty-eight, Jack Welch was in the early days of his career at General Electric when a project he was managing blew up, quite literally. "I was sitting in my office in Pittsfield, just across the street from the pilot plant, when the explosion occurred," he wrote. "It was a huge blast that blew the roof off the building and knocked out all the windows on the top floor." His team had been experimenting with a volatile chemical process when a sudden spark created an explosion that destroyed the building, but luckily, caused no injuries. Welch was relieved that no one had been hurt, but was still a nervous wreck when he went to Charlie Reed, the highest-ranking GE executive with hands-on chemical experience, to explain what had happened. Fearing that the accident would end his career just as it was gaining momentum, Welch was struck by Reed's understanding: "He took an almost Socratic approach in dealing with the accident. His concern was what I had learned from the explosion and if I thought I could fix the reactor process. He questioned whether we should continue to move forward on the project. It was all intellect, no emotion or anger. 'It's better that we learned about this problem now rather than later when we had a large-scale operation going,' he said, 'Thank God no one was hurt.'"

Welch went on nearly twenty years later to become the CEO of GE. Although he'd gained a reputation for harsh criticism of underperforming employees, he would strive to temper his candor with the same understanding that he had been given through the plant accident. "When people make mistakes, the last thing they need is discipline," he said. "It's time for encouragement and confidence building … I think 'piling-on' when someone is down is one of the worst things any of us can do … If we're managing good people who are clearly eating themselves up over an error, our job is to help them through it."

Mistakes are most easily forgiven when they are accepted as lessons, whether they are made by us or someone else. Ambitious people tend to be their own harshest critics, and can beat themselves up over their mistakes to no end. When you find that you've made a big mistake (and everyone does), acknowledge it, apologize (if there's someone else affected to apologize to), forgive yourself for it, learn from it, and try not to do it again. Many a sailor has missed a wind shift on the first leg of a race and spent the next hour cursing himself under his breath about it, but dwelling on mistakes made only holds us back. It's much easier to deal with the fallout of an error if we've mentally allowed ourselves to move on in order to handle the challenges we still face.

TIME-OUTS

The pursuit of excellence often puts an enormous amount of pressure on anyone striving for the ultimate prize in their field. Stress in small, manageable amounts can keep a person motivated and alert, but when it has built up to a large enough degree that a person's mental and physical health begins to suffer, the time arrives to reconsider one's priorities. There's something to be said for hard work, but nobody should drive themselves so hard in the pursuit of a goal that they do irreparable harm to themselves and their family life. Anyone who has achieved something incredible can relate to the need to make a sacrifice. However, when the sacrifices for the sake of success have gone beyond the degree that allows an ambitious person to maintain their life and health, it's time for a time-out.

Paul Elvstrom learned something about the long, hard climb to the top of the sailing world in the late 1950s. Having already won several world championships and three Olympic gold medals, he was preparing for his fourth Olympic appearance when he felt that he was starting to crack under the pressure. After winning the Snipe World Championship, he decided that he would go to the Olympic Games in 1960 and then he'd have to stop sailing altogether in order to spare his nerves. He'd placed an expectation on himself for constant perfection, and would criticize himself harshly for any mistakes he would make. Having set such impossible standards for himself, Elvstrom was setting himself up for a crash. With each little error made, his self-admonition would detract from his focus, making recovery that much more difficult and further escalating the pressure.

Sure enough, Elvstrom suffered a nervous breakdown at the end of the 1960 Olympics, even after winning his fourth gold medal. He had reached a point to which many successful competitors can relate. Having put so much pressure on himself to always be the best, he had stopped enjoying the sport to which he'd devoted his life. However, he couldn't bring himself to turn his back completely on it, even though it was straining his family life, his mind, and his body. He took some time off from serious competition to simply observe regattas from his powerboat and reevaluate his plans for the future.

As it turned out, this was just what the doctor ordered. Elvstrom found that he was able to continue learning by watching races from the sidelines, without the pressure of competition. After a couple of years off, he was ready to get back into a boat and race again. Elvstrom continued to race over the years, winning many more championships, competing in the Olympics regularly through 1988, running a sail-making business and publishing books on the yacht racing rules. Without some time off to take a breath and regroup, the sailing world may have missed out on all the numerous contributions that this sailing legend made to the sport over the next few decades.

Richard Nixon learned something about the value of a time-out in the early 1960s. Despite a mixed record and a controversial career, it can be generally agreed upon that Nixon was an energetic campaigner who lived and breathed politics. He rose quickly in public life, first as a congressman and then a senator. At the young age of thirty-nine, he was elected vice president of the United States under Dwight Eisenhower and became the heir apparent to the presidency in the election of 1960. In a close election with John F. Kennedy, however, Nixon suffered his first major political defeat, for the biggest job of all. Bored quickly with life out of office, Nixon threw his hat into the ring of the 1962 race for governor of California. However, he was ill suited to the office having been away from California for so long, and lost handily to Edmund G. Brown. Nixon even excused himself from further political contests at the press conference following the loss, fuming, "You won't have Nixon to kick around anymore." It was then that Nixon's career was pronounced over by the media and the general public.

Nixon wasn't finished, however. He knew that he still had it in him to go for the presidency, but that John Kennedy's popularity would make him practically unbeatable in 1964. Lyndon Johnson's position as JFK's successor following his assassination was equally invulnerable. Nonetheless, Nixon used the time on the sidelines productively. He returned to practicing law in New York and campaigning for Republican candidates in the '64 election. Through his extensive professional networking and all the favors he had granted to the members of his party, he had begun to lay the groundwork for 1968. From there, things began to work out even better for him. The war in Vietnam was going badly under LBJ, and there was violent unrest domestically through race riots and antiwar demonstrations. When Nixon began his campaign officially, he was a familiar face from happier times, and a powerful symbol of law and order. While the Democratic Party fractured, the Republicans rallied behind Nixon, resulting in his ultimate victory in the November election. Had Nixon run again right away in 1964, he certainly would have been beaten by LBJ and would have had almost nowhere to go from there. By giving himself a "time-out" through what he called, "the wilderness years," he came back stronger and better prepared, and was able to finally achieve his goal.

Everyone faces some tough times in their careers as they reach for the next rung on their ladder. When a really low point is reached, whether it's from a crushing defeat, or if you're sacrificing too much, or if your heart just doesn't seem to be in it anymore, it can feel like the time has come to get off the stage for good. Sometimes, walking away is the best thing in the end. If you're feeling low about your place in whatever you're pursuing, and you're considering quitting, take a break before you do. Step back from the front lines and take a breath. Think about whether you genuinely love what you've been doing up to this point. Would you miss it if you stopped for good? If you could think of another way to go after your goal that didn't put too many burdens on you, would you try again? If you could find a way to increase your odds of winning by getting more help or finding more resources or taking a new approach, would you want to give it a shot? If you say yes to any of these questions, then it might not be time to quit, just time to take a time-out. In that time, take yourself out of the "hot seat," give yourself a reasonable amount of time to build up to another effort, and consider anything that might have held you back before and think of new ways to correct them. Most of all, consider what your priorities are in life and determine how you will find a balance between all the different things you'll need to juggle day to day. Even though a time can come when it feels like you're at the end of your rope, taking a time-out can help you regroup and come back smarter and stronger if you're willing to give it another try.

Balance is a basic principle in sailing. Every boat has an ideal balance, horizontally (pitch), laterally (yaw), and vertically (heel). When a boat is well balanced in each of these dimensions, it sails efficiently. For a boat to sail forward, there must be a balance between force of the wind blowing on the sails (the center of effort), and the force of the water against the keel (the center of lateral resistance). When these forces are in balance with each other, the boat stays on course. When they are out of balance, the boat wants to spin out of control. Likewise, we need balance in our lives between the outside forces pushing on us in order to stay on course. Each person's ideal balance point may be different, but we all have one that helps us to move forward efficiently. When those outside forces undergo a dramatic shift, we need to recalibrate in order to adapt, and that might even mean stopping what we're doing in the short run. If we stay aware of those forces, though, and make little adjustments as necessary, then there's a much better chance of staying in the race over the long haul.

TAKE RESPONSIBILITY

Success in sailing depends on so many variables that the lack of success can spur much discussion on what could have been the factors responsible. For reasons of frustration or ego, it's common to hear skippers who have had an unsatisfactory result on the water cite the influence of various contributing factors, such as faulty crew work, poor sails or equipment, a slow boat, or cruel fate. Outside factors may indeed have been relevant to the result, but by putting effort into the blame game, a skipper takes focus away from improvement for the next contest in order to assuage his own anxieties and frustrations. Some skippers playfully own up to their mistakes, noting that the problem on the boat may be "the nut holding the tiller." It's vital to be honest with oneself in looking back at an unfavorable experience, putting aside ego for a moment and taking responsibility for one's own mistakes.

A sailing team crosses the finish line together, whether in first or last place. Each member of the team has his or her own contribution to make to the effort. When an unfavorable finish stems from human error, though, the egos of the individuals can sometimes kick in and finger-pointing ensues. The avoidance of blame is a universal desire. Nobody wants to be known as the cause of disaster, for reasons of guilt or fear or pride. The fable of George Washington chopping down a cherry tree as a boy and admitting it to his father is told to children to encourage honesty and taking responsibility for their actions. It's considered exceptional for a child to admit to breaking something, or for an employee to proactively alert a supervisor of a mistake made, because most people genuinely fear being branded as incompetent, dishonest, or worse. Some might hope that their mistakes will go unnoticed, while others try to brush off mistakes already discovered onto another person. Taking ownership of a mistake makes it possible to move past it more quickly and productively. Sometimes the consequences are already past, and other times they are forthcoming, but the acceptance of responsibility for an error in action or judgment is the first step to making it right.

During the Iran-Contra affair of the 1980s, Ronald Reagan had to take responsibility for a scandal that had erupted within his administration. The original intent of the administration was to open relations with Iran by brokering a weapons shipment through Israel to an Iranian group that would use its influence to secure the release of American hostages being held in Lebanon. With the plan already underway, Oliver North, an aide to the NSC, later proposed a modification in which arms and portions of the funds from the sale of arms to Iran would be diverted to the anticommunist Contras of Nicaragua. The plan met with great NSC support, and Admiral John Poindexter went ahead and approved it without consulting Reagan. However, this action was contrary to both administration policy and the Boland Amendment, which had been passed by Congress to limit funding of the Nicaraguan rebels. When the scandal broke, Reagan assured the public that no trading of arms for hostages had taken place, but as the Tower Commission that Reagan had appointed to investigate the affair uncovered the facts, the president had to return to the airwaves to correct himself.

"I take full responsibility for my own actions and for those of my administration," he said. "As angry as I may be about activities undertaken without my knowledge, I am still accountable for those activities ... As the Navy would say, 'this happened on my watch.'" Due largely to the lingering mistrust of government fired by the Watergate scandal, the president needed not only to weed out any potential corruption in his administration, but to squash any perception of it by being forthcoming with the American people. "There are reasons why it happened," he said, "but no excuses." In claiming personal responsibility for the misdeeds of some in his administration, Reagan took the opposite approach to Richard Nixon's stonewalling through Watergate. He accepted criticism for failing to properly supervise or keep control of his subordinates' actions, and noted that the lack of proper record keeping of the decisions made throughout the scandal made it difficult to ascertain the details of the affair. "Rest assured," he told the television audience, "there's plenty of record keeping now going on at 1600 Pennsylvania Avenue." By cooperating fully with the Tower Commission, Reagan not only protected his presidency, but was able to start corrective measures to prevent future such occurrences.

Philosophies of responsibility in a race vary among sailing teams. Some sail under the philosophy that all blame and glory rests with the skipper. In other words, if the crew makes a mistake, the skipper should have trained them better or selected more experienced people; if a spinnaker tears, the skipper should have called for a heavier one for the conditions; if a fitting rips out of the deck, the skipper should have checked it before leaving the dock, and so on. Single-handed sailors have to race under this philosophy, as there is no one else to blame for anything that should go wrong. Other crews share positive and negative responsibility equally, with decisions made as a team and no individual holding the spotlight. Likewise, businesses can vary in their organization, with some personnel charts resembling a Christmas tree, with a chain of command cascading down from the CEO, and others resembling the Knights of the Round Table, with each individual accountable equally to all others. Reagan held the former philosophy, taking responsibility for the Iran-Contra scandal not only because he had missed the doings of those beneath him, but because it showed integrity and leadership. Similarly, Harry Truman famously had a plaque on his desk that read, "The Buck Stops Here," to remind him of the "endless chain of responsibility that binds him" as president. Being at the helm of a yacht, a company, or a country holds burdens of responsibility, even for those factors outside of one's own control. Like Shakespeare's King Henry IV said, "Uneasy lies the head that wears a crown."

It's a matter of honesty in the spirit of problem solving to place responsibility where it truly lies, which is particularly important when the responsibility lies with oneself. To take responsibility for mistakes made is productive as well as noble; it puts a stop to self-defeating practices and starts the process of problem solving for a better result next time. When things go wrong as they often can, take a look in the mirror before pointing a finger; it can have a big effect on how you approach a solution to your problem.

IF YOU CAN'T STAND THE HEAT, SPEND MORE TIME BEING HOT

In the challenger trials leading up to the 1987 America's Cup, the boat to beat from day one was *Kiwi Magic* from New Zealand, led by the twenty-four-year-old Chris Dickson. This was New Zealand's first foray into America's Cup competition, although the country and its new Cup team were brimming with sailing talent. While Dennis Conner's experienced *Stars & Stripes* team garnered much interest for its quest to regain the Cup for the US (having lost it to Australia in the previous match), New Zealand's superb performance in the early rounds made the outcome of the trials anything but obvious; *Kiwi Magic* went all the way through the round robins with a 37–1 record, losing only to *Stars & Stripes*.

When these two teams found themselves matched against each other for the challenger finals, both skippers showed great confidence, but *Stars & Stripes* took an early lead in the best four-of-seven series, winning the first two races. *Kiwi Magic* won the third race when *Stars & Stripes* suffered gear failure, but would lose the fourth with gear trouble of their own. Down 3–1, the *Kiwi Magic* crew had to win three races in a row or be eliminated. Halfway through the fifth race, *Stars & Stripes* was leading up the second beat when the headsail exploded into tatters. The American crew had practiced for this kind of situation and everyone knew their jobs, getting a new headsail up just in time to prevent *Kiwi Magic* from passing. Coming downwind to the final mark, *Kiwi Magic* was just seconds behind *Stars & Stripes*. Dickson, under so much pressure to win the race and survive another day, took the rounding a little too close and hit the mark. Under the rules, *Kiwi Magic* had to re-round the mark, and with only one leg to go, New Zealand's bid for the 1987 America's Cup was effectively over. *Stars & Stripes* sailed conservatively up the last leg to win the race and the right to challenge for the America's Cup.

At the press conference following, young Dickson was asked what had happened; how could a team that seemed so invincible at first go down in defeat at the critical moment? "The best boat—the best team won," replied Dickson graciously. "Thirteen years' beat thirteen months' experience." As Conner had put in more hours behind the wheel of a 12-meter yacht than any other skipper in the field, he had not only built a solid team and a solid program in the process, but had become used to racing in every possible condition, including situations of tremendous pressure. By contrast, the talented but considerably less-experienced Chris Dickson was still susceptible to uncharacteristic mistakes in the pressure cooker.

As anyone who's ever been in a stressful situation can recall, pressure under fire can lead to making mistakes. It's common and natural to be nervous before going into anything difficult, and even the most experienced experts in a given field, from performers to teachers to athletes, feel nervous before or during their moment in the spotlight. However, the veterans have the ability to get through those tense situations without signs of nervousness, and without making the same mistakes to which a novice can be susceptible. With the benefit of experience, nerves become less detrimental to performance when the pressure is on.

Experience can be the best cure for the tendency to crack under pressure, not because it eliminates nerves, but because it eliminates the aspect of the unknown. Without the fear of the unknown—the tendency to wander into worry—an experienced person is better equipped to execute their task despite the nervousness they still feel. They are able to focus more readily because they can act on "autopilot," having made a habit of their every move in various situations. They don't worry about "What ifs," or whether they will make a mistake; the hours that they've put in have whittled those fears away, leaving only the task at hand to focus on. The tendency to crack under pressure comes not from lack of competence, but from unfamiliar circumstances. When a person is able to become familiar with the conditions in which they are expected to perform, their ability to execute to their maximum potential is greatly improved.

Experience enables adaptation to a more stressful environment. People adapt to their changing environments on an ongoing basis. A person from a warm climate may visit a friend in a colder climate and say, "How can you live in these freezing conditions?" to which the friend responds, "What are you talking about? This is nice!" The more time we spend under certain conditions, the more those conditions become our standards of reality. When we step outside of that comfort zone, we have to adapt to be able to thrive.

Putting in the time to adapt outside of our comfort zone is how we can become more comfortable with what at first seems to be an impossible challenge.

Gymnast and gold medalist Mary Lou Retton faced a tremendous challenge in training for the 1984 Olympics, made even more difficult by having knee surgery just six weeks before competition began. Though an Olympic gold medal seemed to be an impossible dream, she remained committed through the hardships of training, knowing that backing off in her efforts could leave her one day wondering what might have been. The hours were long and the training was difficult, but by keeping her focus on the objective at hand, Mary Lou Retton was able to prepare herself thoroughly for a winning performance at the Olympic Games.

In a competitive world full of talented people with vast resources at their disposal, experience can make the difference in any endeavor. By focusing on the task at hand and enduring plenty of time outside of your comfort zone, you will gain the resilience necessary to succeed when your best performance is called upon. Get as much time under your belt as possible in your own "race conditions," and you'll perform much more smoothly when the pressure is on.

ADAPT TO CHANGE

Part of reactive learning is determining how to adapt to a changing environment. Sailors, like people in all walks of life, are constantly adapting to change. The sport of sailing is one that thrives on innovation, and so new techniques and technologies are always being explored. In order to stay competitive in this evolving field, sailors must be prepared to change with the times. Further, the racing rules of sailing are updated every four years, so sailors everywhere must learn what changes occur in order to adapt their tactics to the new regulations of the sport. Change happens throughout a sailboat race as well: the wind can change in its strength and direction, the direction of the current or the consistency of the water's surface may change, the positioning of the competition continuously changes, and even the course can change in some situations. Change is a fact of life for sailors. They must be constantly prepared to change gears, change course, change tactics, or change equipment in order to maintain an advantage. The need for anticipation of, and adaptation to, change is universal; the ability to implement successful change can make a positive difference in the growth of an individual, a family, or an organization, just as it can for an ambitious sailor.

Keep Your Eyes on the Horizon

Anticipation can be a facilitator of adaptation. When you have considered possible scenarios that could feasibly develop down the line, you can adequately prepare for them and be ready to adapt when the time comes. It may be light and sunny when a sailor leaves the dock, but it is only prudent to bring along the foul-weather gear should the clouds on the horizon grow more ominous. Conditions rarely are consistent throughout a season, a series, or a single race, so sailors must be prepared to meet a wide range of weather conditions through sail inventory, rig tune, deck layout, or even ballast. It is generally easier and more efficient to prepare for new wind than it is to adapt once it is upon you. By keeping an eye on the horizon, anyone can better prepare to weather the storms that can threaten them in their field.

Defense contractor Lockheed Martin was created in changing times, consisting of two separate entities trying to survive peacetime. With the fall of the Berlin Wall, the US defense industry contracted sharply, and thousands of defense contractors began to fall by the wayside through acquisition or dissolution. "Lockheed Martin learned many lessons as it added battle scars to its battle ribbons," wrote former CEO Norman Augustine. "The most important lesson became self-evident: there are only two kinds of companies—those that are changing and those that are going out of business."

Before their 1995 merger into Lockheed Martin, both Martin Marietta and Lockheed had endured and survived takeover attempts. They'd each taken on a lot of debt to remain independent and focused firmly on new defense initiatives, unfortunately just as the industry was about to contract. "The hard-and-fast lesson we learned is that forced restructurings, such as those that result from takeover attempts, usually signal problems ahead," said Augustine, who was the CEO of Martin Marietta at the time. "The trick is to recognize the warning and act on it." As military contracts dried up, the defense industry took on a Darwinian atmosphere in which only the strongest companies would be expected to survive; the smaller firms began seeking acquisition while the larger firms sought out merger opportunities.

By recognizing the need for change and planning for adverse contingencies, Martin Marietta was able to survive this tightening period in the industry. It had become apparent that the industry's M&A fever would require some careful advance planning. In 1994, a long battle ensued between Martin Marietta and Northrop, in an effort to purchase Grumman. Martin was outbid, but had already written a $50 million cancellation fee into the Grumman contract in anticipation of such a scenario. Rather than fight Northrop for Grumman, Martin took the fee and focused instead on other opportunities. It wasn't long before a new opportunity would emerge; later that year, Martin Marietta and Lockheed would announce plans to merge into the nation's largest defense contractor.

Part of handling change in any situation, be it athletics, business, or culture, is maintaining an awareness beyond our own small personal sphere. We need to watch what's happening around us and look for the little changes that tend to occur before the big changes come along. For a sailor, it might be by observing changes in the clouds, which could indicate a shift in the wind that has yet to reach him. For a company that sells snack foods, a spike in the sales of athletic wear among its target demographic could indicate that its customers are changing their health habits. When previously adversarial countries improve relations and start trading with each other, schools can expect demand to increase for language classes. We always need to pay attention to what we're doing in order to do well, but it's easy to be derailed by new realities if we fail to keep an eye on the bigger picture.

Fight Obsolescence

Sailing as a sport allows for gradual transitions to new technologies in order to keep costs down for competitors and prevent rapid obsolescence of expensive resources. When a fantastic new device or material becomes available, sailing rules may prohibit it at first to keep the playing field more level. Once the latest resources have been adopted, however, it's "out with the old, in with the new." For instance, flax sails were the norm in the early twentieth century, but today's sails are constructed of synthetic materials like Dacron, Kevlar, Mylar or carbon fiber, among others. Celestial navigation is a valuable skill in an emergency, but is no way to win an ocean race when GPS technology is available. While there is still a place in the sailing world for the "classics," a number of racing classes have evolved beyond their original construction, techniques, and methods in order to stretch the possibilities for each class and keep the racing interesting. Once a progressive change comes to a fleet, the sailors who embrace it and exploit its benefits will lead the pack, while those who are slow to adapt will struggle in the brave new world.

It doesn't help in the long run to master a skill that is losing its value. Throughout the history of business, companies that excelled at creating a product or delivering a service that was facing obsolescence have faced the choice of whether to change to meet the new reality or go out of business. Norman Augustine notes, "None of the companies that dominated the thriving ice-harvesting market in the nineteenth century converted to the refrigeration business. The Pony Express did not develop into a railroad. The producers of electromechanical calculators never made the technological leap into electronic computers." Clinging too long to an outmoded formula for success can lead to a quick reversal of fortune. As the times change, people and industries change with them.

Prepare for Change

The more complex a change needed aboard a sailboat, the more preparation for implementing it is needed between crew members. This is even more important when the process ahead is an unfamiliar one. Sailors new to ocean racing often are required to learn new skills to be ready to adapt to new conditions. For example, reefing a sail—reducing its exposed area to the wind—is a technique that needs to be done quickly, smoothly, and correctly the first time. If a reef is poorly made, the sail can come loose and be difficult or dangerous to get control of again. Therefore, sailors expecting the need to make this adjustment in the future take care to be prepared to execute it correctly.

When the time for change draws near in any effort, it is important to get people and resources together in order to more efficiently implement it. Communication is key through this period; everyone involved needs to share the same goals, understand their tasks and interactions in the effort, and understand the timing of the initiative. By going over the plan thoroughly ahead of time, nobody need be caught off guard when the time to act arrives. In many cases, preparation for change may consist of removing obstacles. Consider what it is that can hold you back from making the changes needed: Lack of funds? Lack of support? Opposition to the plan? Whatever stands in the way of making the transformation go as smoothly as possible, address it early. If someone needs to be convinced of the plan's value, communicate your reasoning. If you see financial hurdles ahead, look for solutions through additional support or budget restructuring. If you face competition that seeks to block your initiative, prepare to either confront or evade them in order to get it done.

ACT QUICKLY AND DECISIVELY

Tacticians in sailing act as the skipper's eyes on the course, making tactical suggestions based on what they see in the wind and the positioning of the other boats. Sometimes, emergency situations can arise when the tactician can't make a diplomatic suggestion, but may instead shout "We've got to tack right now!" in order to avoid an imminent collision. With an urgent need for a course change, the urgency comes through in the tactician's command. The skipper, in turn, should be able to trust his tactician enough to turn the wheel even if he can't see what the emergency is.

In any situation where quick change is needed, those whose contributions you depend upon must hear clarity in the decision and understand the need for fast action. If the group's leader is indecisive about the need to make a change or the details of its implementation, the effort will not be able to build sufficient momentum to carry it through to successful completion. There is a chance of the decision being wrong, but without clarity and decisiveness, the door is opened to chaos instead of focused effort.

Once the decision has been made to implement a change, action should be taken with all deliberate haste. Without a sense of urgency to the task at hand, the status quo may continue to be perceived as an acceptable standard, and opportunities for competitive advantage could be lost. When things have gone well for a while, it's too easy to assume that the way things have always been done is the way they should continue to be done. Make sure that high-priority change initiatives are understood to be high priority for the benefit of the group. Do not, however, treat every new initiative as an emergency, or you will succeed only in watering down the urgency that you are trying to convey, like the boy who cried "wolf."

STAY AHEAD OF THE CURVE

Without a spirit of innovation, a sailor may find himself standing still while the competition gains ground over time. Sailors may find that a certain formula for boat speed works very well for them and find it difficult to change it. "If it ain't broke, don't fix it," as the saying goes, but without keeping innovation going, there is no progress to be made. The winning formula can serve as the baseline through the process; if a new idea doesn't work, you can still return to the methods that worked well before and try something else.

Complacency is hard to detect until it has already settled in and had its consequences, however. By keeping new ideas flowing and remaining open to positive change, complacency can be guarded against while embracing progress. In the competitive business world, this is particularly important. The expectations of the marketplace and the capabilities of the competition continue to evolve and place new demands on businesses over time. Even with high-quality products and services, a strong and vital enterprise that neglects the perpetual pursuit of innovation can face an early extinction.

Just as leaders in other industries strive for constant innovation, sailmakers, boat builders, racers, and riggers are always trying new things to see where they can make improvements to equipment and techniques for better performance. They have their parameters within which they know they need to work, but when inspiration strikes, the most successful innovators don't delay giving their latest idea a try. Take some time away from distractions once in a while and brainstorm for some ideas for whatever it is you're looking improve. When you've got a list of several "no limits" ideas written down, cut out the ones that are impractical for whatever reason and spend some time considering the ones that could work out. Hidden within our minds are kernels of brilliance for innovation—it's up to us to make the effort to look for them and bring them to light in order to grow.

Change Together

Teams must be able to embrace change as a group to be able to implement it successfully. If there are people who will resist change, who don't know their roles, or are ill prepared to make it happen, then progress will be stifled. For example, a sailing team on a large racing yacht may find that a dying breeze has made their current choice of headsail unsuitable to the new conditions. The first step for the team is to recognize the problem, and that a change is needed. Next, the afterguard (decision makers) must call for the new sail to be set. Then, the crew must prepare the new sail and determine what their method of initiating the sail change will be; they can set the new sail while holding course, or while going through a maneuver. Finally, the crew must implement the jib change, each member performing their task in order to make the change as smooth as possible. In a matter of moments, the new headsail should be up and flying and the old one stowed down below. Throughout the process, the crew members should be communicating clearly and decisively, calling every step in the maneuver to each other so nobody acts out of turn. If the crew's roles are clearly defined and everyone knows how they are expected to contribute to the task of making the sail change, and the team communicates clearly, it should go off without confusion.

Any group of individuals that exist in a common purpose, whether it consists of two people or two hundred, will need to go through changes in sync with each other if the change is to be of real benefit. It is common for people to resist change because it seems unnecessary, unwise, or just inconvenient. This can be a problem that arises anywhere, including societies, governments, families, and businesses. In cultures around the world, the members of any generation are often baffled by the habits, beliefs, and styles both of their parents and of their own children. The changing times can make the cultural gap between generations apparent in a number of unique ways, and it is common for the elder generation to be more resistant to a changing cultural landscape than the younger generation coming of age within it.

The game of politics often matches two philosophies against one another; one advocating significant changes in current policies and the other in favor of a more measured approach. When families face a decision to make a change, such as moving to a new town, there will be members that are resistant to the new scenario while others can't wait to get going. Businesses often must face decisions whether to change their offerings or their infrastructure in order to keep moving forward. Change management consultant Paul Strebel wrote for the *Harvard Business Review*: "Top-level managers see change as an opportunity to strengthen the business by aligning operations with strategy, to take on new professional challenges and risks, and to advance their careers. For many employees, however, including middle managers, change is neither sought after nor welcomed. It is disruptive and intrusive. It upsets the balance."

In any of these cases, change can be met with resistance, as change can be very difficult to accept, to implement, or for some even to consider. Often such resistance comes from concerns over disruption to a comfortable environment that results in little payoff in the end. Nobody wants to see their efforts wasted, nor to take on a new challenge with no reasoning behind it or direction toward its accomplishment. When the need for change becomes apparent, group leaders need to gain the commitment of the team to make the necessary change happen. By communicating the need for change and outlining how it can be successfully implemented, the group can be set to its task as a unified team with a common purpose.

Members of large, complex, and well-established institutions often become so entrenched in the status quo that they resign themselves to the belief that change would be impossible. Not only is change possible even for the most complex organizations, it is in varying degrees absolutely inevitable. In the end, trying to resist change is like trying to hold back the tide. Change is a constant force in our world, in every aspect of our lives. Change can be pursued, or it can be thrust upon us, but it is to be expected because it is a natural phenomenon, on the water and off.

SEEK ADVICE FROM THE EXPERTS

Sailing is a sport that has been around for a very long time, so there are a lot of very knowledgeable veterans around the water, throughout the world. The sport also is a community in which each new generation learns from those who have gone before, as well as from peers. As every sailor continues to learn new lessons throughout their sailing career, there is always something of value for seasoned veterans to share with any eager up-and-comers who come looking for advice.

People in a variety of careers may find themselves in a situation in which they may benefit from another person's experience. Finding an experienced veteran who can give some insight to your situation can help you to avoid any of the mistakes or problems that they may have encountered. The toughest challenges that come up for us in the course of our lives and careers are seldom truly new; they're just new to us. More often than not, you won't have to look very far for advice from someone who's been there before. Look for opinions from the people you know in your field that may have been down the very same road. You might even start making new friends by asking for advice from someone of prominence in the field whom you haven't yet met. Politely approaching a pro for a dash of their wisdom can often pay off.

Making brief contact with an expert may provide an answer to one particular question, but one of the best long-term learning resources that anyone can have, whether they are a sailor or another athlete, an entrepreneur or any other kind of professional, is a coach. Most sailors at the top of their game, like any athlete, have a coach to guide and support them through their greatest challenges. There is much to concentrate on when preparing for a sailboat race, and the sailing coach can act as an extra set of eyes to filter important information to the sailor. The coach can offer a different perspective on sail trim and boat handling to the sailor, since these things can seem one way aboard the race boat and look very different from the coach boat; when you're too close to a problem, it can be much more difficult to see. The coach can also help coordinate the teamwork between the sailors on the boat to make sure that their actions and communication are in sync with one another to deliver better results.

Coaches don't simply lecture to their athletes. They must actively watch for the subtle flaws in performance, that the athletes are unable to notice for themselves, in order to make corrections. They must be able to recognize the athletes' strengths and train them to capitalize on them. They must be able to see and hear beneath the surface of what the athlete says and does, to expose the reality that underlies their performance. When the athlete is fatigued or frustrated, they look to the coach to get them back on their game. Keeping someone motivated won't come from a pep talk alone. An inspiring talk works well to lift spirits in the moment, but over the long run, motivation must come from seeing the progress being made. The most effective coaches keep their charges always on an upward curve, illustrating regularly how far they have come with each advance made in the process. Whenever we find ourselves struggling to keep our heads up through any grueling challenge, a moment's consideration of how much better we are today than we were when we started can give a mental boost that makes even the most challenging ordeals seem more worthwhile. A coach can bring those improvements to light, having seen firsthand every step made up the performance curve.

Augie Diaz found that, even for the highest performers, bringing in a coach can make a big difference: "In the 2001 Snipe Worlds in Punta del Este, we had a great team with Bill Hardesty, George Szabo, and a few other guys, but no coach. There were a bunch of us who were pretty well set up, but we were the only team there without a coach … the Brazilians had a coach, the Argentineans had a coach, the Uruguayans had a coach. The last day we were there, with any kind of a good day, Bill Hardesty would have won the event or maybe gotten second … he actually wound up fifth. I was sailing with Mark Ivey and we could have been fifth or sixth and we wound up eleventh. What happened was that the current was really weird that day, and as a team we were a little bit off. So I decided for the 2003 Worlds in Sweden that that wouldn't happen to me, so I hired a coach. And I got to thinking that the coach really shouldn't be just for me. I hired a local kid who knew the conditions really well, and I said, 'Do you mind coaching the whole team?' And he said, 'No, of course not.' So I got the group together and said, 'This guy is a local sailor, he's going to be coaching us as a team.'"

In finding a coach to support the whole US team, Diaz had not only found a valuable resource for himself, but he had boosted his own training partners' performance in the process: "Peter Commette and John Manderson were at the regatta, and they are both absolute brains, and they'd figured out the currents of the area. The weird thing about Sweden is that the water level in the Öresund is higher than at sea level, so the water is always draining toward the ocean, except for when there is a big high over the ocean and a big low at the end of the Öresund. And during the 2003 Worlds, we had such a day. That morning we had our briefing, and our coach said, 'Hey Guys, unlike every other day that we've had here, the current is going to be going in the other direction.' And John had actually already gathered some information on that, and Peter had a map of the bottom drawn in his boat … that was the level of detail those guys were putting in. That day, when the current switched direction, the Americans all finished in the top ten."

While the US team as a whole had a strong performance, Diaz sailed a consistently strong series to win the world championship, due in part to bringing in a coach to work with the group. "The lesson I learned was, sometimes you feel like you're giving a lot, but you get a lot more in return.

Clearly, it was a team effort, and the input that those guys had led to our results as a team, and led to me and Jon Rogers winning the regatta." For Diaz, this lesson also translated well into his professional life after winning the Worlds. "Sometimes, I find that if you give more—give the customer more than they're expecting, you'll get more back," he said. "We put that into our discussion in a bunch of our sales meetings, and it works, it really works."

For an individual seeking to take their game up a notch, a coach can offer an outside perspective and break the big picture down into focused performance initiatives. Organizations can similarly benefit from a coach, with the added bonus of having someone to help coordinate teamwork and communication for better efficiency. When you are using the services of a coach in your efforts, there are a few considerations to keep in mind through the process:

SELECT A COACH WHO CAN STRENGTHEN YOUR WEAK POINTS

Understand from the outset what it is that your coach brings to the table and consider how their experience can complement your needs. For example, if you have trouble performing under pressure, find someone who has been able to shine in stressful situations. If you have a hard time organizing all that you have on your plate, seek the advice of someone who has managed large and complicated projects successfully. Have a good understanding early on of where you are in need of improvement, and find a coach who has the ability to strengthen you in those areas.

KEEP UP THE COMMUNICATION

Both the coach and student need to understand what their expectations are and what they need from each other. It will be up to both of you to keep feedback going back and forth throughout the process. Regular meetings and habitual question-and-answer periods will sustain the flow of information in order to keep both you and your coach on task.

WORK TOGETHER TO MANAGE YOUR AREAS OF FOCUS

You need to let the coach know what is helping, what is confusing, or what is frustrating you so that they can direct their focus on the most pertinent issues for you. In turn, the coach needs to challenge, correct, and encourage you on an ongoing basis. The coach also can be a resource to help simplify complex undertakings through their own involvement, but you must let them know what your challenges are specifically so that they can provide assistance.

It takes motivation from within oneself to fuel great achievement, but a knowledgeable and compatible coach can provide a positive boost to help keep that motivation up and improve the speed and efficiency of the improvement process. Whether you're looking for a way to make a tough challenge more manageable or gain an edge over a tightly competitive field, a coach can help seemingly impossible tasks feel much more attainable; the tougher the environment, the more benefit a coach can provide. In the end, it's up to you to achieve your goals, but bringing a coach on board can make those goals more obtainable and make the journey more enjoyable, as well.

PROACTIVE LEARNING

Acquire new knowledge whilst thinking over the old,
and you may become a teacher of others.

—Confucius

Learning in a proactive way is a lifelong habit among the most successful people. It is an ongoing pursuit built on imagination, curiosity, ambition, and self-discipline. While reactive learning is based largely on reviewing past experiences and absorbing their lessons, proactive learning comes from seeking out new information and experiences. Research and learning in sailing and most other pursuits can be done through various means and media. Reading, attending seminars and classes, discussing ideas with colleagues, and experimentation are all elements of proactive learning. The sport of sailing, with the endless puzzles and possibilities that it entails, rewards those who take a proactive approach to their learning and improvement. Sailing champions at the top levels have been those who have constantly sought to raise the bar on their own performance, always striving to learn new things and gain new skills, always looking for that elusive extra quarter knot of boat speed.

For sailors looking to get into a new fleet with which they are relatively unfamiliar, some self-analysis can help them to craft their approach to learning, through a better understanding of their strengths and natural talents as well as their weaknesses. The first question anyone can ask themselves before starting their education in a new field is, "*Where do I stand?*" What do you already know about your subject matter? What have you seen and heard about it? What experience, if any, have you had thus far? How strong is your understanding of it? It's a natural tendency for many people to unconsciously assign themselves a higher degree of knowledge and experience than they actually have, due largely to the fact that they have not yet fully glimpsed the depth and breadth of knowledge yet to be gained in their field. It's a safe bet when starting to learn anything new to start at a more basic level rather than overwhelming yourself with more advanced concepts too soon. There may be some redundancy, but at least you'll be able to reinforce the fundamentals.

After getting an idea of where to start in the learning process, you'll want to get an idea of what methods will best serve you, asking yourself, "*How do I learn best?*" Can you recall information best through reading, observing, listening, or experiencing? For many people, one of these methods tends to be more effective than the others, although each has value. Through the course of our lives, we tend to get a general feel for the ways we best absorb new information. For instance, some students find difficult concepts easiest to grasp through visual aids, and others feel that their best way to gain mastery is through experience, by working through practice problems and other exercises. Finding ways to see, hear, and experience lessons in your field will give you more thorough exposure to new information. When time management becomes a factor, focus on the learning methods that are most effective for you.

Starting off on any new endeavor requires a proactive learning approach as part of the preparatory process. This essentially means that there will be homework before the first day of class. The greatest asset that anyone can have is useful information. Finding the information we need and putting it to good use through action is a giant leap toward success.

KNOW THE GAME

When getting into new territory, it's important to have a thorough understanding of the various aspects of the environment that you will be entering. For a person just learning to sail, or even an experienced sailor getting into a new fleet, there will be much to learn about the new setting into which they will step. Entering into a new endeavor, whether it's a new sport or a new job, requires technical know-how and general competence, but by learning the game as the insiders know it, the transition can be greatly eased.

KNOW THE LANGUAGE

Every career, every hobby, and every sport has a language to it. The language of any activity or industry isn't necessarily to be found in the dictionary or textbooks; it is determined and molded by those within it. Sailors have a language full of terminology that can be found in any sailing text. For instance, we don't say "rope" when we mean "line." Just to follow a sailing conversation, a newcomer would do well to understand, for example, how a word can have multiple meanings, like "tack": there's the action of tacking, the tack of a sail, and the angle of sailing on port or starboard tack. From year to year, however, new terms are simply invented by the sailors themselves and find their way into the popular sailing vernacular. They may be overheard on a boat, on the dock, or in the bar, and become a new and commonly used term. To really blend in with the veterans, the new sailor should be up to date with current sailing slang in order to go with the flow of a conversation among more experienced racers. Whatever field you're going into, whether you're an aspiring doctor, stockbroker, surfer, computer programmer, mechanic, film crew member, or any number of other careers, there is a unique language to be learned. Go beyond just what you see in books and learn the language of the game from the mouths of the experts themselves; you'll find that it becomes instinctive faster than you realize.

KNOW THE RULES

Every civilized organization of people has rules of some kind to keep a sense of order. Various laws and regulations apply to each career, and every sport has its rules of play. There are also the unwritten rules that groups go by. Over time, certain cultural guidelines tend to take shape, which create the standards of etiquette for people in a shared experience. Sailors at a big regatta, for example, often are rushed to get their boats in the water while many others wait behind them at the beach, the ramp, or the hoist. There's an expectation that the sailor will make an effort to move his trailer out of the way of the other boats trying to launch, even if he can't get it done that very second. He can ask a friend to help him out and reciprocate in kind, or he can tie his boat to the dock and move it himself. But if he just leaves it and expects someone else to move it for him, he may find it buried behind dozens of other trailers at the furthest corner of the lot when he returns.

Every sport has its rules of etiquette: surfers know not to drop in on another surfer once he catches a wave, golfers know not to cast their shadows over the line of another player's putt, and bowlers know to yield to the bowler in the next lane to the right if he wants to bowl at the same time. Travel for business or diplomatic matters requires advance understanding of local customs and practices, at the risk of being caught off guard by such cultural variations as the shortened personal space between conversing people in the Middle East, or greetings with a kiss in Europe. Pay close attention to your surroundings and take a cue from those with experience when you're on unfamiliar ground and are unsure what to do in a given situation. When in doubt, ask rather than guess; it's less awkward than guessing wrong.

KNOW THE STYLES

Not limited merely to attire, there are styles in every culture that are observed knowingly by the insiders and subject to being overlooked by newcomers. Such styles are not always practical, but it is wise to know what the rules of style are in your new environment in order to avoid making a spectacle of yourself. Sailors in small boats often have their own sense of style when it comes to something like their life jacket. Racing in many smaller one-design classes requires competitors to wear a life jacket, so the sailors generally want one that is not only functional and comfortable, but that looks good as well. Many experienced racers care much more about how they look in their gear than they might care to admit. The sleekest life jackets can cost more, but it is worth the price to look the part of an athlete rather than to go out on the water for a major race with the cheapest alternative.

Individuals in any given setting will find a certain style that suits their needs. Some cultures, such as a conservative office environment, prefer its members to have a more formal look through business attire; even the label on the clothing can make a difference to the more critical observer. In the most disciplined environments, such as a karate dojo or a military base, there is a uniform that is adhered to strictly. In some creative settings, you may find people who prefer wild and unconventional styles. Styles are always changing, for the individual, their immediate peer groups, and our culture at large. The challenge is to give the impression that you want to make by understanding what is acceptable and appropriate for your given situation. Once you grasp the big picture of what the parameters of style are for your particular environment, it becomes easier to bring out your own individuality within those boundaries.

KNOW THE PLAYERS

When you are coming into a new world in which you hope to thrive, it's important to start a mental file of its key players. There are two basic groups that you will want to get to know something about: the icons, that is, the top performers of your field (historical and present-day), and the local talent, the best and brightest in your community.

Icons are of value to study for the example they set. An entrepreneur, for instance, may want to learn more about successful entrepreneurs of today like Larry Page, Sergey Brin, or Bill Gates, as well as entrepreneurs of history like Henry Ford, Cornelius Vanderbilt, and Cyrus McCormick. Sailors often pick up stories of great sailors and great regattas past, not unlike a kid memorizing the players and statistics on his baseball cards. The stories of the greats who have gone before can be not only inspirational, but instructive as well.

Local talent is important to know about not just because there is some chance that you will meet and get to know them at some point, but because they influence your activities. Such people may be influential local business leaders or politicians, the top-ranked athlete at your local club, or even a person who simply is popular enough to have the ear of the community. These people are a hub of their world; they know what is going on behind the scenes, what the trends for their sport/industry/community are, and who the other key players are and will be. The sailing community is a tight-knit group that loves to teach within its own ranks; Olympic champions often are happy to give tips to eager ten-year-olds in the yacht club parking lot. If you have the opportunity to get to know the local talent, take advantage of it. Their experience and insight can be of such benefit to you that in time, you may be able to join their ranks. Whether you will eventually encounter the local talent as a protégé or a rival, it is wise to know who they are and how they operate, so that you may learn from them.

You can learn much from traditional means such as books, classes, and videos, but these information sources fall short in the timeliness of the information they give when compared to regular person-to-person contact. If you can get close to the daily happenings of your new endeavor, you will be able to pick up the language and culture faster, and assimilate into it. It is far easier to learn from others in a new job, sport, or hobby once you start to fit into that world. Get behind the scenes as soon as possible, and listen, observe, and absorb; you'll be in like a native in no time.

DON'T MAKE OTHER PEOPLE'S MISTAKES

In regattas with multiple fleets, there is often an opportunity for the sailors whose fleet will be starting after others to observe the action of the races preceding their own. It can be difficult to discern wind and wave patterns looking out over a large course sometimes, but watching a fleet work its way up a racecourse can provide some clues. For instance, if all the boats on one side of the course are heeling over more, it would indicate more wind on that side. A group of masts bouncing around more than the rest of the fleet's could indicate choppier water in a particular area. Perhaps a pattern develops where the boats that go up one side of the course tend to be behind at the first mark. These clues can help to reinforce a strategy for an upcoming race, or shed some light on race conditions that are difficult to discern at a glance. Thanks to the boats that start their races before her own, a discerning tactician will not have to repeat the mistakes of her predecessors on the course.

Most people who repeat others' mistakes of the past do so out of ignorance. Occasionally, an informed person simply ignores lessons of the past out of sheer ego or delusion. One such example is the repeated efforts made by European powers to conquer Russia in the eighteenth, nineteenth, and twentieth centuries, using similar methods only to arrive at the same failed result. In 1708, Charles XII of Sweden attempted an invasion of Russia, only to be defeated by Russian scorched-earth tactics and freezing weather that slowly killed off his men until they were forced to surrender. The size and geography of Russia, as well as the experience of Charles's army, would seem to indicate that an invasion of Russia would require lots of time and therefore ample reinforcements and plenty of warm clothing, but this lesson would be lost on two more would-be conquerors over the next two-and-a-half centuries.

In 1812, Napoleon Bonaparte decided to wage war against Russia and invaded from the west. As the Russian army withdrew eastward, Napoleon's troops pursued deeper into Russian territory, just as winter was arriving. His advisors warned him of the severity of the Russian winter, but Napoleon ignored them, leaving his soldiers without adequate clothing and the horses without proper shoeing. As a result, Napoleon's army was crippled by the harsh conditions and was unable to stand up to the Russians' retaliation on their own turf. Over 500,000 of Napoleon's troops died, deserted, or were captured before his forces beat a hasty retreat back to France.

This repetition of history should have been an ample lesson, but about 130 years later, Nazi Germany attempted the same move in 1941 under Operation Barbarossa, invading Russia from the western territories. Napoleon's fate was not far from the German army's thoughts, yet they would find themselves in the same position. As the campaign dragged on into October, Hitler had the upper hand and sought to take Moscow, but neglected to reinforce the Panzer divisions or resupply them with adequate provisions. Once again, winter began taking its toll on the invading forces, and the Russian defenders now had a fighting chance. As the Nazis closed within sixty miles of Moscow, Stalin ordered in the elite, winter-trained Siberian divisions away from the eastern front to defend the city. As temperatures dropped to -40°C, the Germans began to succumb to frostbite, having no winter shoes. This opened the door for the Siberians to stage a counteroffensive and defeat the German army.

Awareness of world history can be useful to anyone, even if it's simply as a point of reference from which to consider the issues of the day. Knowledge of the past need not be limited to world events, however; having an understanding of one's own ancestry and history of family health issues can be of enormous help in a practical and vital sense. Furthermore, learning from mentors and relatives, such as parents and older siblings, can be helpful along life's road, particularly in our younger years when much about the world and its challenges is still unfamiliar to us. There's no sense in making mistakes that can be avoided with a little more information. Pay attention to the experiences of others, and you can avoid some of the potholes they've hit along life's bumpy road.

TAKE NOTES

Every student knows the importance of taking notes in class. Every executive knows to have a notepad at hand in an important meeting. Sailors, too, know that to be able to remember the important points from every event, it's important to make notes for future reference. Peter Commette won a spot on the US Olympic Team in the Finn thanks in large part to some notes he'd made a year before: "At the Olympic Trials in 1976, no race was like the Pre-Trials the year before, which had been held at the same venue at the same time of year, except for the last race. I did not want to announce my entry into the class at the Pre-Trials—didn't want any fanfare. So, for the Pre-Trials, I rented a cottage away from the site, and rented a kid's small motorboat. I watched the entire series from a distance, semi-incognito and took copious notes. The next year, the notes on the weather did me no good until the final race, when they saved my series."

On the last day of racing at the trials, Commette found himself in close contention with a few other boats that harassed him all the way out to and around the racecourse, and he knew he couldn't afford a bad race. "All the time," he said, "I knew which way I would go anyway, because we finally had wind the same as the Pre-Trials." He remembered his notes from his observations at the Pre-Trials, stuck to the strategy he'd already determined on paper, and held off his most aggressive competitors to win the Trials and his spot on the Olympic sailing team.

When taking notes for learning in any enterprise, there are a few qualities of effective notes to keep in mind:

Clarity

It's one thing if nobody else can read your handwriting, but if even you can't understand what you've scribbled, there's a problem. In our haste to get our thoughts down on paper, sometimes we produce a manuscript that resembles chicken scratch or Egyptian hieroglyphs. You'll save some future confusion and frustration if you can make sure that your notes are legible enough to understand later. Try to return to the notes later the same day to revise or add to your earlier work. If you glance at your notes at the first opportunity after you're done adding to them and anything's not crystal clear, you'll want to remedy them right away while the information is fresh in your mind, rather than waiting until later and struggling to remember details.

Thoroughness

It's better to have as much information as you can get on the page than to be missing important details. Minutes of executive meetings are generally very thorough, noting those present, times of arrival and departure of attendees, and the contributions of individuals to salient points of the meeting. A sailor starting off in a new venue or in a new class of boat may find himself adding extra details about his boat, the weather, and various other factors, hoping to have as much information at hand as possible that can be scanned for the most important points later. When you are early in the learning stage of your field, whether you're a student starting a new semester, a new employee at a company, or an athlete at a performance clinic, you may find yourself less certain of what the most important things to make note of are, and which are less so. With time and practice, you'll be able to filter information to make your notes more effective.

Efficiency

Efficient notes are those that provide all the information that you're looking for and reduce the amount of extra information that isn't particularly relevant. This isn't to say that if you don't need some information in your notes at one time that you won't need it later. Don't be too hasty to chop down your notes at first until you've looked at possible scenarios down the line where extra tidbits might come in handy. Think to your future use of this information to know what is most critical and put a star or arrow next to the most vital pieces of data.

Accessibility

Before many small boat races, crews may take out a grease pencil and write compass headings and times right on the deck where they can see them. It's important to be able to find information quickly when you need it, so work on ways to put your notes together in a way that they will catch your eye and save you time in searching for facts. Indexing a notebook can be done in a number of ways: chronologically, by subject, by people, alphabetically, or perhaps geographically, if your notes relate to travel. Your methods will depend on your preference of mentally organizing this information; remember that they're your notes, so don't feel that you have to adopt someone else's ways of organizing if those methods don't work for you. Consider the use of color as an eye-catcher for your notes. Highlighting text is a good way to find the points most important to you, but using colors on pages or tab dividers is a good way to group your information into categories. The priority is to find a way that saves you time, so experiment with your organizational methods until you find a system you're comfortable with.

RECORDING INFORMATION

Sailors often augment their training by recording information about their sailing in any way possible. Note taking is the most cost-effective method, if less detailed. The most advanced racing yachts have computers aboard that record data such as load measurements, wind readings, and hull speed. This information is then analyzed by the design team and used to determine what configurations on the boat are improving overall performance. Between these two extremes are the more accessible and affordable methods of audio and visual recording. A sailing team that is able to film their training sessions is better able to analyze sail shapes, steering and boat-handling techniques, and tactical maneuvering after returning to the dock. Video plays a critical role in most sports, particularly those with a need for "instant replay." Coaches rely on video recordings in order to visually illustrate to their teams weak points that need improvement.

The learning of a new skill can be greatly reinforced by the use of video. It can point out subtle mistakes that we make but of which we remain unaware. For example, practicing a speech in front of others is a good form of preparation, but watching a video of that same performance can reveal fidgeting and verbal ticks (like "um") that escape our attention. Whenever possible and practical, try to acquire or produce a visual recording of your own performance or that of someone you are looking to study—it can make a big difference in your absorption of the information as well as the thoroughness of your analysis.

Audio recording is helpful to coaches, sailors, and race committees. Coaches can record their thoughts on a team's performance on audio throughout a race in order to refresh their memories for later discussion. A race committee trying to record the sail numbers of a large number of boats at the finish line may use recording devices to confirm the order of finishers. Audio recording can be used as a quick way to record an idea that comes to mind or a reminder of the day's to-do items. Reporters, attorneys, and students often need audio recorders just to be able to capture all the necessary information that they need in the course of their day. When you are expecting to need to record a vast amount of information faster than you can write, consider bringing along an audio recorder.

BRING THE BOSS ABOARD

Sailors aboard larger yachts are a part of a much more complex organization than those in smaller one-designs. For a long and complicated campaign like the America's Cup, the campaign manager is easy to imagine as a harried individual at a desk on shore, but this isn't always the case. Most winning America's Cup yachts of the modern era have had the syndicate head aboard the boat in some capacity while racing: Bill Koch shared the helm on *America³*, Peter Blake worked the traveler and mainsheet aboard *Black Magic*; Ernesto Bertarelli sailed as navigator, grinder, and helmsman aboard his various *Alinghi* yachts; and Larry Ellison and Russell Coutts sailed part-time aboard the trimaran *USA-17*. Each of these teams benefited from the presence of the boss aboard the boat, as this allowed each manager to see the action for himself and to make decisions for the management and funding of the team accordingly. By being able to listen and speak to the afterguard members throughout the racing and training, they were able to bridge the gap that so often exists between upper management and the rest of the "troops."

Having the boss involved in the day-to-day activity can be very beneficial to an off-water team as well. Every effective manager needs to keep their finger on the pulse of their organization, and many business leaders make it a habit to regularly get out of their offices and walk the floor. Henry Ford and John Rockefeller, for instance, were known to walk the floors of their factories, inspecting the production line and looking for ways to improve the operation. Ray Kroc habitually walked through his McDonald's restaurants to inspect the facilities for cleanliness. David Packard, cofounder of HP, was known for his "management by walking around."

In their book *In Search of Excellence*, Thomas Peters and Robert Waterman tell of how Ed Carlson, the CEO of United Airlines for much of the '70s, brought his management style from the hotel business to his tenure at United. "I travelled about 20,000 miles a year to express my concern for what I call 'visible management,'" Carlson said. "I'd get off an airplane, I'd shake hands with any United employees I could find. I wanted these people to identify me and to feel sufficiently comfortable to make suggestions or even argue with me if that's what they felt like doing … What I was trying to do was create the feeling that the chief executive officer of the company was an approachable guy, someone you could talk to ... If you maintain good working relations with the people in line positions you shouldn't have any trouble." Putting in "face time" not only keeps people on their toes, but also keeps morale up by conveying management's personal involvement. It's nice to drop in and say, "hello," but using one's eyes and ears in the process is how problem solving is facilitated; it's about more than staying in touch with people—it's about staying in touch with the issues.

It is to the boss's benefit to be accessible and involved on the front lines as an opportunity to learn more about the functions and needs of their organization without having to be told, often through varying accounts. The message meant for the boss can start with one person only to be contradicted by another with an opposing agenda, or diminished in effectiveness as the number of people passing the word on increases. There can be no covering up of mistakes or euphemistic descriptions of internal problems if the boss is right there to see it with the rest of the team. The "see no evil, hear no evil" approach will never serve a leader well in any profession. It's better to have accurate bad news than inaccurate good news, and the best way to get the latest news is firsthand, through fast, honest, and ongoing feedback. You might get some dissent from time to time among the group, but a bit of constructive criticism from smart people you can count on can go a long way.

The leader that remains isolated from the activities of his team deprives himself of a critical learning opportunity, and the team of a chance to contribute to its own development from within. The on-board boss can help his team to cross the finish line in first place for the day, but he can also take lessons back to the dock that will help his team to win the regatta. Likewise, the hands-on leader off the water is not only contributing on a day-to-day basis, but also to the long-term improvement of his organization through lessons learned in the trenches alongside his comrades.

TRAVEL

Top performers in any field often find that travel comes as part of the game. Top salespeople attend meetings, shows, and conferences throughout their territory or throughout the country. Top skiers go to the toughest slopes, year-round, all over the world. Top performers travel for months at a time to take their show on tour. For sailors, the need for travel also holds true for long-term success. Regattas are held all over the world all year long, wherever there is water and wind. To hone their skills enough to be ready for anything in competition, sailors must become comfortable leaving their home waters and attending events away from home as often as possible.

Besides the joy that many people get from the adventure of traveling to new places, sailors and non-sailors alike can reap a number of specific benefits from traveling to big events:

MEETING THE TOP PEOPLE IN THE FIELD

Whenever you leave your own backyard to attend a big event elsewhere, you get the opportunity to meet more of the top people in your field. Sailors meet other sailors, students meet other students, investors meet other investors, and sales reps meet other sales reps that they can network with and learn from. This is not only an opportunity to make contacts or gather information; it's also a way to make lasting and rewarding new friendships.

GAINING PERSPECTIVE FROM A NEW LOCALE

To a sailor, getting onto unfamiliar waters can be an immediate learning experience. A saltwater sailor can find a new feel from sailing in freshwater. An ocean sailor may find the shifting winds of lake sailing an entirely new experience. A lake sailor tackling the winding currents of Charleston harbor may have his hands full. Anyone can have their perspective turned upside down by a new environment. An American businessperson visiting Asia will learn a whole new repertoire of business etiquette. A politician traveling in the third world will gain new perspective as to the values and lifestyles of other cultures, and will have her eyes opened to the needs of the people of other nations.

Just about anyone may find that dining out can be a completely different experience when in a new country. When I was in Uruguay for a regatta, a teammate relayed an interesting story to me. Apparently, the manager of a local restaurant was worried that the US team was unhappy with the service at his establishment. He was wondering why we always asked for the check as soon as we finished a meal, paid, and then got up to leave almost immediately. To him, this was truly unusual. As it turns out, many South Americans prefer to stay at the table and chat for much longer after a meal than we Yankees do; we seem to be somewhat unique in our tendency to eat and run!

PICKING UP NEW IDEAS FROM OTHER PLACES

The modern sailing skiffs now seen in Olympic sailing evolved from the 18-foot skiffs of Australia, which have a history dating back to the 1890s. These lightweight, overpowered boats left their rules wide open for development; the boat needs to be eighteen feet long on the waterline, but there's plenty of flexibility in the design otherwise. As sailors from around the world began visiting Australia for sailing events, the sight of these speed demons inspired more high-performance dinghy designs that still exist and thrive today. Paul Elvstrom introduced a number of innovations in technique and rigging that he kept as secret as possible until their use in competition. Several standards of modern sailboat racing, such as the boom vang and hiking strap, were first observed by sailors watching Elvstrom go blasting past them at major international events.

The ancient Roman philosopher and theologian Saint Augustine of Hippo said, "The world is a book, and those who do not travel read only one page." All too often, we lose sight that the small portion of the planet that we occupy on a daily basis is only a tiny fraction of a larger world full of new wonders and experiences. Getting out and seeing more of the world will inspire you with new sights and methods, whatever your field. Consider how educational a trip to Europe can be for an American artist or chef. An architect may thrill to the building designs of Dubai or Hong Kong. An information technologist can broaden their view with time in India or Japan. And no financial wizard should miss an opportunity to visit New York. Look for opportunities in your own field to get some travel experience, and take full advantage. Remember to always travel with open eyes and an open mind, and you will return home filled with deeply rooted lessons that will serve you well for years to come.

NEVER STOP LEARNING

The sport of sailing, like any complicated endeavor, is without an upper limit to the knowledge available of it. No human being can sail an absolutely perfect race, and nobody will ever fully know all that there is to know about it. The very nature of the sport, driven as it is by the ever-changing elements, lends itself to an open-ended quest for learning. New technology may simplify many of sailing's more complicated challenges, but sailors continue to stretch themselves, learning new ways to harness these forces and exploit them to drive a sailboat to greater levels of performance. With each new lesson learned, more new questions arise. Sailors can definitely relate to the old familiar saying, "The more I learn, the more I realize how little I know."

It can be to anyone's benefit to pursue learning on an ongoing basis, not just about one thing, but about anything and everything of interest or of use to them. Learning new things doesn't just accumulate facts in one's head; it keeps the mind sharp, drives creativity, and opens horizons for new experiences. Professionals in every career often must be trained in new methods and techniques in order to stay current with best practices: lawyers continue to learn about legislation and regulations that are passed, doctors continue to learn about new technologies and techniques in their area of specialization, marketing managers learn about new tools and methods for promoting their company's offerings, and so on. Perhaps the learning you'd like to pursue is not in a professional capacity, but to acquire a new skill for fun, such as taking up a new sport or hobby; this can introduce you to new people with similar interests that can help drive and also benefit from your own learning. Perhaps you'd like to learn to play a musical instrument or learn a new language. Whatever interests you, put the time into learning more about it, and watch new doors open.

Knowledge truly is power, but only if actively and continuously pursued. If one does not make learning a lifelong habit, that power can wane over time. We may stop growing physically at a certain point in life, but we can continue to grow mentally for much longer. Keeping a mind-set open to learning, one of wonder and intrigue, brings out the spirit of youth, when all things are possible. Keeping the brain well fed and exercising it daily helps to keep it strong like any other muscle; by approaching learning in a youthful way, the mind can be kept young and sharp. Whether the next lesson you pursue is for your work or for your own personal interest, dive right in and keep asking questions. The more you learn, the more there will be to find out.

LEARNING ON YOUR OWN

The most common and straightforward way to learn on one's own is by reading. Sailing, like anything known to a large and diverse group of people, has been the subject of numerous books and magazines over the years, and entire libraries are devoted to the subject. Books abound on weather, oceanography, yacht design, boatbuilding, aerodynamics, hydrodynamics, tactics, fitness, and more. For the aspiring sailor, a look at any of these subjects can provide a better understanding of the underlying principles of the sport. With that foundation in place, the sailor becomes more imaginative and more adept at problem solving when called for.

Learning by reading isn't just about memorizing facts or mastering theories discussed in books; one must stay current on the news in their field as well. News cycles have been reduced over time, from weeks in the early days of printing to seconds in the modern mobile technology era. By understanding the foundation of your subject of interest and keeping up to date on the latest developments, you can gain insight into what the future may bring. In other words, if you understand what has been and what is, you can better imagine what will be.

Watching others is another way that learning can be pursued. If you can obtain a video of an expert in your field and watch them at work, there is much that can be absorbed by paying careful attention. Actors, athletes, and even attorneys have learned from the greats of their professions by watching the pros perform. An even better way to learn by observation is in the company of a master. If you can find a way to spend some time watching and learning from an expert in your field, you will have found a golden opportunity to learn that few get to take advantage of. Donald Trump has credited much of his success in real estate to learning at the feet of his father, listening to the discussions his father would have with contractors on the phone and tagging along to visit construction sites.

Reading and observation can be excellent ways to build up technical know-how, but there is no substitute for experience. Of the three main methods of learning—seeing, listening, and doing—the latter is often the most effective for building overall mastery. No amount of watching, reading, or listening to advice about sailing will improve one's sailing skills as much as the same amount of time spent on the water actually doing it. The well-built education in any subject consists of a combination of these disciplines; reading, listening, and observing make a solid foundation for a tower of experience that can be expanded to infinite heights. When you've had a chance to get out and add to your experience level, you learn new lessons, gain new instincts, and make corrections where they are needed.

LEARNING IN A GROUP

When someone sets about learning a new skill, they may prefer to go about it as part of a group rather than by studying solo. Learning alongside others can be more fun as well as more productive. For sailors, this may be done by attending a race clinic, or simply setting up practice sessions with skilled contemporaries. It gives the opportunity not only to compare one's own performance against someone else's, but it also opens up a conversation of ideas that can fire the imagination to new inspiration.

Managers may pursue group learning by developing what Peter Senge called in *The Fifth Discipline* "the learning organization—an organization that is continually expanding its capacity to create its future." A group setting lends itself to open discussion and shared experience, and therefore a way to learn from each other. Members of a group can offer different perspectives and ideas to spur creative thinking. This creative synergy is a key trait of the learning organization. "The discipline of team learning involves mastering the practices of dialogue and discussion," said Senge. "In dialogue, there is the free and creative exploration of complex and subtle issues, a deep 'listening' to one another and suspending of one's own views. By contrast, in discussion different views are presented and defended and there is a search for the best view to support decisions that must be made at this time." In essence, managers can lead their teams to greater productivity over the long run by learning in a group dynamic, somewhat similarly to how sailors, musicians, engineers, and many others may "talk shop" to learn from each other.

Being a part of a group for the experience of learning can have long-term benefits beyond the salient material of the group's study. The connections made to others in the process can lead to relationships that last for years. When friends from school, a clinic, a conference, or a seminar go their separate ways, they venture forth into new experiences that they will carry with them. These friends are your bridge to a wider world; their experiences can be shared with you, just as your experiences can be shared with them. Even via casual conversation, a friend's career or life lessons can be your lessons as well.

Technology continues to increase connectivity between individuals, and it is easier than ever to stay in touch with friends, colleagues, and mentors. Build a network of friends in your field of interest, and over time you will learn much with them and from them.

LEARN A LITTLE ABOUT A LOT

Competitive sailors, like many other athletes, often employ cross-training to build up their edge on the water. They may balance their physical training with running, cycling, aerobics, or tennis, for instance, in addition to their training on the water; this can provide better all-around fitness that can be of tremendous benefit when a long race becomes physically taxing. They may also sail in different boats in the course of their campaign; a single-handed dinghy sailor may step into a two-man keelboat or an offshore racing yacht once in a while and do quite well. Although the campaigning sailor must continue to develop specific muscles and specific skills for the particular class of boat that he intends to race to achieve his objective, it is to his benefit to go into the competition as a well-rounded sailor. Buddy Melges, Paul Elvstrom, Paul Cayard and Torben Grael are just a few of the very successful sailors who have raced a wide variety of boats throughout their careers to hone their skills. By diversifying the kinds of boats that they spent time in, these men and many like them have become better all-around sailors by being well-rounded.

Leading up to application for university admission, students are often encouraged to become better rounded by participating in extracurricular activities. If a person puts all of their focus into only one specific area, they may excel at it for a while, but may later find that by passing up opportunities to broaden their horizons along the way, they have cheated themselves out of rich experiences. An excellent science student may be able to become the most brilliant scientist in human history by focusing entirely on that one specific subject, but without building up any other interests, he may not be able to be at his best outside the laboratory; he might not even be able to carry a conversation about anything but his work. If you can be interested in a wider range of subjects, it not only stimulates intellectual and professional growth, but social interactions as well. By being interested, you become more interesting.

Few Americans stand out more in the variety of their pursuits than Thomas Jefferson. Jefferson had a curiosity about a wide range of subjects, and he pursued them with vigor. Although he is best remembered as a politician for his two terms as president of the United States, Jefferson was also a scholar, a scientist, an inventor, an architect, and a botanist. He was a voracious reader, and left his massive collection of books to the Library of Congress. His inquisitive nature made him one of the most successful and learned men in Virginia at a young age, and this natural curiosity led Jefferson to become one of the great visionaries of American history. By expanding his worldview and broadening his interests throughout his life, Jefferson not only benefited himself, but also those who have learned from his legacy.

Diversifying one's pursuits has a number of benefits. It exposes us to different perspectives and viewpoints, and can introduce new methods and theories that can be adapted as solutions to other problems. Aeronautical engineers have often been inspired to make better boats and planes by taking cues from nature; for example, by emulating the sleek lines of a porpoise or blue shark in a boat's design. It is not uncommon for the ways and methods of a culture, sport, business, or hobby to translate well into other areas to serve as solutions to frustrating dilemmas. Without an approach to learning that includes exposure to a variety of areas, a person who specializes in a very narrowly defined area of expertise cannot expect to solve problems as creatively and effectively as one who has some familiarity with a broader range of subject matter.

The additional benefit of "mixing it up" from time to time is that it keeps one's interest in and ability to focus on their chosen field from growing stale. A number of Olympic sailors who have emerged from long, focused campaigns have walked away from their efforts, successful or not, happy to never again set foot in the class of boat they raced hard for years. Burnout can set in when one focuses, laser-like, on one specific goal for too long without a break. It can be very refreshing to step away from the challenge at hand once in a while to get some variety. Just as our bodies require a balanced diet, our minds and spirits require a balanced approach to our labors. A Star sailor, for instance, can hop aboard a sailboard for a weekend and come back to his Star campaign mentally refreshed. It doesn't sacrifice focus on the overall goal to introduce some cross-training once in a while. On the contrary, it helps to maintain focus over the long run by keeping burnout from taking hold. Too much of anything for too long can get stale, but allowing a break once in a while can bring you back to your work with renewed energy and fresh ideas.

Even when we are zealously pursuing our greatest passion, it can be detrimental, spiritually and intellectually, to make that single pursuit the sole focus of our lives. By broadening our horizons and pursuing a variety, even a small variety, of interests, we can not only keep the fire in our belly from burning out, but also bring in new ideas from other areas to keep the fire burning even brighter.

NURTURE CREATIVITY AND INNOVATION

"Think outside the box" tends to be an overused phrase, but it has at least ingrained in the minds of executives, engineers, and problem solvers in every field the need for, and the benefits of, creative solutions. Sailing is a sport that has remained open to creative solutions over the years. Revolutionary new concepts have been introduced to sailing by borrowing them from other applications, combining elements to create something new, or making improvements to existing materials or practices. Sometimes such innovation has been pursued in the spirit of adventure and others from the necessity of problem solving. Creativity is an essential element of personal as well as professional growth. Just as sailors have stretched the boundaries of their imagination from time to time, so must we all in order to improve, evolve, and learn.

Creativity can be expressed in the combination of successful elements. Over time, sailing has found exciting new frontiers opened when combining disciplines together. When two Southern Californians, sailor Jim Drake and surfer Hoyle Schweitzer, put their heads together, they were able to develop the Windsurfer in the early 1970s. This simple concept, putting a sail onto a surfboard, gave birth to a global phenomenon, and by 1984, the young sport of windsurfing had been added to the Olympic Games. Kiteboarding (aka kitesurfing) resembles a mix of parasailing, wakeboarding, and windsurfing. Sailing has spread to every climate through similar creative solutions. For instance, you can blast across a frozen lake on an iceboat or over sandy terrain in a land yacht. Skateboards and recumbent cycles have been outfitted with sailing rigs, and concepts have been tried for sailing uphill in the snow. The notion of capturing the wind for forward motion has inspired innovation on a number of platforms, and will continue to do so over time.

Bringing two things together to create something new can work in all walks of life. Wrapping a waffle around a scoop of ice cream brought about the ice-cream cone, for instance. At the 1904 World's Fair in St. Louis, Missouri, Syrian immigrant Ernest Hamwi had a booth to sell "zalabia," a waffle-like pastry. When the ice cream vendor in the next booth ran out of paper dishes, Hamwi rolled up some of his pastries and gave them to him to use to serve ice cream. The creation proved so popular that Hamwi opened his own ice-cream cone company in 1910, and was issued a patent for a pastry cone–making machine in 1920. What had been an improvisation at the spur of the moment quickly turned into the new standard for eating ice cream, and remains so.

Creative approaches can help to break through barriers that once seemed impossible. Sailing, like motor racing, has a governing body to certify speed records as they are set. For many years, the notion of sailing at fifty knots seemed impossible, but the fifty-knot barrier has been broken. The boats that are created to set speed records are certainly innovative, if sometimes impractical; many record setters in the past have been able to only sail on one tack, and only in flat water. However, in September of 2009, an average speed record of 51.36 knots over 500 meters was set by a relatively traditional-looking trimaran, *l'Hydroptere*, skippered by Alain Thebault. The twist to *l'Hydroptere's* design is its hydrofoil appendages, which extend below its outer hulls. When the boat gains enough speed, the foils generate enough lift to boost the hulls out of the water, and the boat flies above the surface with minimal drag. This platform was not only effective for the speed record, but also versatile. Unlike previous speed record holders, *l'Hydroptere* is capable of sailing on open water, opening possibilities for other speed records in the future. The bar continues to be raised for sailing speed records; in 2012, the *Sailrocket 2*, piloted by Paul Larsen, set a new speed record of 59.2 knots, or just over 68 mph, going over 2.5 times the speed of the wind.

Taking performance to new levels can require inventive solutions to make success attainable. For example, film production studios continue to raise the bar for visual effects; and new technologies and techniques have had to be invented over the years, first to produce an effect for one particular film, and then for subsequent films that follow. Whether the audience was seeing a giant shark attacking a fishing boat, a squadron of fighters strafing a giant space station, a hero in a cape flying high over a city, or aliens leaping through treetops, the filmmakers had to develop new equipment and techniques to achieve the desired effect. Whenever an impossible objective is pursued, it tends to require the creation of new means to make it attainable. New technologies constantly arise to serve as the tools toward accomplishing something that hasn't been done before. To explore outer space and the deep sea, for instance, man had to develop new technologies. Barriers of all sorts have stood before mankind, only to be broken through its inventiveness and courage. If the imagination is allowed to wander beyond known boundaries, new possibilities open up to achievement and discovery.

Sometimes older ideas can be revamped into fresh new variations. Tom Perkins's superyacht, the *Maltese Falcon,* sports an innovative rig that is a modern take on the old square-rigger concept. Three twenty-stories high, freestanding masts carry fifteen massive sails amounting to nearly 26,000 square feet of sail area. The sails can be trimmed or furled by computer, reducing the need for numerous deckhands. To change the angle of the sails to the wind, the masts rotate on gears below deck. The method of furling and unfurling the sails is particularly creative. The sails themselves are stored inside the mast and emerge for use by commands from the cockpit's computer. With this creative solution, Perkins's design team had developed a system that took one operator instead of several to manage the sails and eliminated the danger factor of climbing the rig. In his desire to create and own "the perfect yacht," Perkins introduced a creative and fascinating take on classical principles to the yachting world.

Ideas that get left behind can be brought back to life when needed. In 2009, with concerns over carbon emissions and fuel economy taking priority in many consumers' minds, Ford Motor Company was reviewing concepts from the 1940s in order to reduce emissions and increase gas mileage, and found a workable fuel-injection design to use as the basis for new engine development. It goes to show the benefit of writing down your ideas as you think of them; even if you're unable to implement them right away, there may be a chance to bring them to fruition in the future.

Successful innovation is ultimately about using one's own creative capacity to explore ways to meet a need. Ideas may be extraordinarily original, or they may be inspired by methods, products, or concepts that already exist. You may have to invent something completely new to realize your goals, or you may be able to alter or combine existing platforms to meet your specific needs. Use your creative skills to reach beyond the boundaries in which you live and work through bold innovation. Whether your solutions to problems turn out to be evolutionary or revolutionary, a small step or a giant leap, pursuing creative innovation can vastly expand your potential.

LEARN BY TEACHING

Many of the top sailors in the sport are, or have been, instructors and coaches. No matter how many awards a coach has received in their own right, however, the most effective ones are those who are able to teach complicated concepts to students at a more basic level. Some top-flight racers have struggled to get their lessons across to their students, because they didn't sufficiently simplify the material to make it memorable. When any teacher neglects to do this, an opportunity to strengthen their own skills, as well as their students', can be missed.

Teachers carry on their shoulders the responsibility of deeply understanding and then clearly communicating subject matter to someone else. It can be a challenge to communicate a concept that is instinctual to you but completely foreign to your student in such a way that the novice will immediately understand. To do so requires looking at the subject matter from every angle. The successful teaching of sailing or any subject often requires breaking difficult subject matter into simple and memorable concepts, which will serve as the building blocks of more complex principles to be learned later. As in so many fields, the advanced theories and practices of sailing stem from the far less-complex fundamentals, and unless the student has mastered the basics, he will struggle to learn more advanced techniques.

By simplifying concepts to the point that anyone can understand them, the teacher becomes her own student, embedding the lesson deeply in her own mind before she has shared it with anyone else. Some simple maxims for beginner sailors have been created to get them started without overwhelming them. For example, the aero- and hydrodynamic forces at work on a sailboat are complex, but the beginner doesn't need to understand them when their first priority is to avoid crashing into something. This is why instructors provide helpful hints like, "tiller toward trouble." A handy phrase like this is easy to remember under stress, and has saved many paint jobs. The concept, however, is greatly reinforced in the mind of the teacher simply by teaching it to others, having not only clarified it in order to incorporate it into a lesson, but also having repeated it, perhaps several times a day. While the student will consciously recall the lesson when it's needed, the teacher will have it so distinctly burned into their mind that it is instinctive.

Teaching others can benefit the teacher in various forums. In teaching the basics of a subject, one is simply reinforcing material already well understood. The more advanced the material to be taught, the more it stokes the mental fires of the one teaching it, and the more the teacher learns in the process. When the subject matter is new to both teacher and student, the learning process is amped up further. Peer groups are often used in academia as a learning forum to discuss matters about which few people in the group have yet developed mastery, such as on current events or new scientific theories. This kind of learning keeps everyone in the group on their toes, stimulating learning at a more equal level for each individual. "To teach is to learn twice," wrote Neal Whitman in his academic monograph *Peer Teaching*. "Individuals who experience a course as a student and then return to the same course as a peer teacher develop an understanding of the material from two very different perspectives." Sailors acting as tuning partners employ a form of peer-to-peer learning, sharing their observations of a speed test with each other in order to raise the bar for both of them. This principle can be applied to any field of interest in which a person wishes to develop their knowledge and understanding of a topic alongside others.

There are many rewards to sharing knowledge with others that take an interest in your field of expertise: you will be helping to develop novice students into competent, informed, and enthusiastic performers and advocates; you will be interacting within, and helping to build, a community of people with a shared need or interest; and you will be strengthening your own grasp of the material that you teach as you refine your method of communicating it and deliver the lesson to your students. Whether you're instructing someone on how to sail, play the guitar, solve an equation, build a birdhouse, or anything else, teaching is a win-win situation for student and teacher alike.

ENJOY THE RIDE

Sailing, like any effort, athletic or otherwise, requires a love of the game to achieve real excellence. All too many professionals across the spectrum of careers have been plagued by frustration, boredom, anxiety, and failure by putting their efforts into something for which they hold no enjoyment. It is exceedingly difficult to put all of your attention and energy into any task that you don't care for. Conversely, when you pursue something that engages and excites you, the hours fly by and even difficult tasks are a pleasure.

People don't find success in an area that they lack passion for and are unable to have fun with. Sometimes they've gotten into the game for the wrong reasons and have realized later on that they are out of place. Other times, they have lost sight of the love they once had for their work and are now simply going through the motions. As you concentrate on getting the job done in your field, you need to remind yourself occasionally of why you're doing it— not only why it's important to you, but what sparked your passion for it in the first place. Ask yourself: What do you love about what you're doing? The faster you can answer, the better off you are. When you can stay in touch with your passion, working toward your goals stops being a chore and your true talents can come to the surface without being weighed down by stress.

The ability to have fun in any endeavor, regardless of the result, reduces the tension brought on by the pressure to succeed, and thus improves actual performance. Gary Jobson learned this during his college sailing years, when he went to the qualifiers for the Singlehanded Nationals. After struggling through the first two races, his coach, Graham Hall, told him to get back out and have fun, even though Jobson was more concerned about his lack of boat speed at the time. Hall's pep talk paid off; Jobson relaxed and decided to have fun with the racing, and was rewarded with ten straight wins as a result. When the competitor can embrace a spirit of enjoyment, the mind and body are better able to deliver a better performance.

Ted Turner was up against formidable opposition during the 1977

America's Cup defense trials. Although early trial racing had gone well for Turner and the *Courageous* crew, the all-important final selection trials would ultimately determine which team was chosen to defend the Cup. With the pressure mounting to keep his spot atop the leader board, Turner remarked, "I'm going to do something that no one has ever done before! I'm going to enjoy the final trials—win, lose, or draw—because I think that will increase our chances of winning." This philosophy made sense for Turner's crew (after all, the crew was unpaid, so they might as well have fun), and it proved effective. *Courageous* won the right to defend, and went on to win the Cup.

To truly be at your best through the ups and downs that invariably come with any challenge worthy of a mighty commitment takes honest, deeply rooted passion for the task at hand. Without a love of the game, it becomes a form of self-torment to try to make it through another month, another week, or another day of the same thing. If you love what you're doing, it gets easier to put in long hours, to suffer through disappointments, and to keep up your patience when it is most called for. When you're doing what you love, whether it's in an office, in a boatyard, on a stage, in a car, or anywhere, even the difficult moments can seem fun.

Being good at your job doesn't always mean that you have to take yourself too seriously. Even in the usually serious and sober environment of business, a sense of fun can benefit everyone. Southwest Airlines has maintained a loyal and productive workforce since its creation, largely due to its unconventional corporate culture. Former CEO Herb Kelleher espoused a philosophy that working at Southwest should be fun. The Southwest offices are a casual environment, and parties and practical jokes are common and encouraged. On the planes, flight attendants often dress up in themes (Kelleher himself dressed as Elvis to greet passengers at times) and may deliver a comedy version of the in-flight instructions (e.g., "If you'd like to smoke during the flight, you'll need to step outside.") Keeping the mood light at Southwest has helped the company achieve one of the lowest employee turnover rates in the airline industry and to stay profitable through some of the industry's toughest times.

There are jobs and tasks that have to be done seriously, of course. A lighthearted approach to work would not be particularly appropriate for certain careers, such as an undertaker, or a secret service agent. This doesn't mean that having a serious job means taking no satisfaction in it. Any job, no matter how sober, serious, uncomfortable, or depressing its tasks may be can bring satisfaction to the one who does it and knows that their job is important. You can love your work without being especially mirthful in it. To know that your efforts make a difference to someone else is something to smile about, even if you can't smile on the job. The guards at Buckingham Palace must surely take satisfaction in their job, although you won't see any toothy grins from them while they're on duty.

If you love what you're doing, you will be able to look back on the hardest moments of the journey, even if you haven't been particularly successful, and feel that your efforts have all been worthwhile. Everyone willing to work hard in a worthy effort deserves to derive satisfaction from it. If you can find joy in what you do, continue to love it through trials and hardship, and come away from the experience each day with a genuine sense that you belong where you are, then you have found an endeavor worthy of your time and labor. In the final analysis, this is the ultimate goal for so many talented individuals: to discover their true passion and make the very best of it.

CONCLUSION

AFTER WINNING THE 2010 AMERICA'S CUP, Oracle CEO Larry Ellison told the *Wall Street Journal*, "The America's Cup is like running Oracle. You have to have a large number of engineers—dozens. Then you need a factory to build the boats. Everyone sees the sailing teams, but there's an awful lot behind them." Meeting the logistical challenges of a major sailing campaign such as the America's Cup requires an ambitious nature, as well as the organizational and leadership skills that Ellison and his Cup-winning predecessors have possessed; leaders of large companies like Ted Turner, Ernesto Bertarelli, and Bill Koch. Other men of enterprise, such as Philippe Kahn, the inventor of the camera phone, and the late Roy E. Disney, have been as successful on the water as on land, both winners of the Transpac race from Los Angeles to Honolulu.

Many of the world's most successful business moguls have shown their winning ways on the water as well as in the boardroom. The synergies between the worlds of sailing and business allow the lessons of each to translate well to the other. However, these lessons are not limited to application in the corporate world; people of all ages and from all walks of life, such as students, artists, politicians, doctors, lawyers, other athletes, and so many more can learn and draw inspiration from sailing to apply to their own situation in life as they see fit.

You may not compete for an advantage every day in your life, but you will eventually face opposition that needs to be overcome, as everyone does. You may not be the key decision maker in your family or your workplace, but everyone eventually faces a difficult decision that only they can make. You may not currently be a member of a team or manage a large staff of employees, but you will need to work and play well with others in some capacity to achieve any degree of success in life. You may not be dealing with any major changes in your life and career right now, but change eventually will come in some form or another. You may not feel that risk assessment is a major concern in your daily life, but the most worthwhile pursuits in life—for love, for money, for happiness—all carry some degree of risk. How you weigh risk and get through it is up to you, but occasional uncertainty happens to be an absolute certainty in life. Inspiration for dealing with such commonplace challenges is where you find it, but this enduring and often complex sport of sailing can be an eye-opening source of motivation for tackling the issues that come at us from day to day.

Draw what you need from these pages to apply to your own life, and give consideration to the rest as food for thought. A sailor's approach to winning may not apply to every single situation that arises for you, but seeing issues through a sailor's eyes can give you a broader perspective in handling your own challenge with a well-considered and balanced approach. For the sailor that reads these pages, I hope that these lessons strike a chord to reinforce principles for success on the racecourse, and translate into greater success off the water as well. For the reader who has not yet had the pleasure of participating in this amazing sport, I hope that this introduction to the sailing world has proven informative as well as inspirational, and that you will not only apply these lessons to greater success in your own field, but that you may join us on the water soon.

Good luck and good sailing.

BIBLIOGRAPHY

BOOKS

Ainslie, Ben, and Nick Townsend. *Close to the Wind: The Autobiography of Britain's Greatest Olympic Sailor*. London, UK: Yellow Jersey Press, 2009.

Ali, Muhammad, and Hana Yasmeen Ali. *The Soul of a Butterfly: Reflections on Life's Journey*. New York: Simon & Schuster, 2004.

Allen, Frederick. *Secret Formula: How Brilliant Marketing and Relentless Salesmanship Made Coca-Cola the Best-Known Product in the World*. New York: Harper Collins, 1994.

Bartlett, John. *Bartlett's Familiar Quotations, 17th Ed*. Edited by Justin Kaplan. New York: Little, Brown and Company, 2002.

Bavier, Bob. *Keys to Racing Success*. New York: Dodd, Mead & Company, 1982.

Branson, Richard. *Business Stripped Bare: Adventures of a Global Entrepreneur*. London: Virgin Books, 2008.

Branson, Richard. *Losing My Virginity*. New York: Three Rivers Press, 1998.

Browne, Christopher H. *The Little Book of Value Investing*. Hoboken, New Jersey: John Wiley & Sons, Inc., 2007.

Canfield, Jack. *The Success Principles: How to Get from Where You Are to Where You Want to Be*. New York: HarperCollins, 2007.

Caswell, Christopher, ed. *The Sailing Fanatic: Timeless Reflections on Water, Wind, and Wave*. Guilford, Connecticut: The Lyons Press, 2006.

Chernow, Ron. *Titan: The Life of John D. Rockefeller, Sr*. New York: Vintage Books, 1999.

Chouinard, Yvon. *Let My People Go Surfing: The Education of a Reluctant Businessman*. New York: Penguin Books, 2006.

Churchill, Winston S. *A History of the English-Speaking Peoples, Vol. 2: The New World*. New York: Dodd, Mead & Company, 1966.

Collins, Jim. *How the Mighty Fall: And Why Some Companies Never Give In*. New York: HarperCollins, 2009.

Collins, Jim, and Jerry I. Porras. *Built to Last: Successful Habits of Visionary Companies*. New York: HarperCollins, 1994.

Conner, Dennis, and Michael Levitt. *The America's Cup: The History of Sailing's Greatest Competition in the Twentieth Century*. New York: St. Martin's Press, 1998.

Conner, Dennis, and John Rousmaniere. *No Excuse to Lose: Winning Yacht Races with Dennis Conner*. New York: W.W. Norton & Company, Inc., 1978.

Coutts, Russell, and Paul Larsen. *Russell Coutts: Course to Victory*. Auckland, New Zealand: Hodder Moa Beckett Publishers Ltd., 1996.

Doyle, Arthur Conan. *The Complete Sherlock Holmes*. New York: Barnes & Noble Books, 1992.

Eldred, Gary W. *Investing in Real Estate: 6th Edition*. Hoboken, New Jersey: John Wiley & Sons, Inc., 2009.

Elvstrom, Paul. *Elvstrom Speaks on Yacht Racing*. Edited by Richard Creagh-Osborne. Chicago: Quadrangle Books, 1970.

Forbes, Steve, and John Prevas. *Power, Ambition, Glory: The Stunning Parallels between Great Leaders of the Ancient World and Today … and the Lessons You Can Learn*. New York: Crown Business, 2009.

Freiberg, Kevin, and Jackie Freiberg. *Nuts! Southwest Airlines' Crazy Recipe for Business and Personal Success*. New York: Broadway Books, 1996.

Gilson, Clive, and Mike Pratt, Kevin Roberts, and Ed Weymes. *Peak Performance: Inspirational Business Lessons from the World's Top Sports Organizations*. Mason, Ohio: Thomson, 2000.

Giorgetti, Franco. *Sailing Yachts*. Vercelli, Italy: White Star Publishers, 2007.

Giuliani, Rudolph W. *Leadership Through the Ages: A Collection of Favorite Quotations*. Miramax Books, 2003.

Graham, Benjamin. *The Intelligent Investor, Revised Ed*. New York: HarperCollins Publishers, 2003.

Greene, Robert. *The 33 Strategies of War*. New York: Viking Penguin, 2006.

Grubb, Jake. *The Sailboard Book*. Newport Beach, CA: GrubbStake Media Ltd., 1984.

Hagstrom, Robert G. *The Essential Buffett: Timeless Principles for the New Economy*. Hoboken, New Jersey: John Wiley & Sons, Inc., 2001.

Hill, Napoleon. *The Laws of Success: The 21st-Century Edition*. Los Angeles, CA: Highroads Media, 2004.

Hoyt, Garry. *Go For the Gold*. Chicago: Quadrangle Books, 1971.

Jobson, Gary. *Gary Jobson's Championship Sailing: The Definitive Guide for Skippers, Tacticians, and Crew*. Camden, Maine: International Marine, 2004.

Jobson, Gary, Tom Whidden, and Adam Loory. *Championship Tactics: How Anyone Can Sail Faster, Smarter, and Win Races*. New York: St. Martin's Press, 1990.

Kaltman, Al. *Cigars, Whiskey, and Winning: Leadership Lessons from General Ulysses S. Grant*. Paramus, New Jersey: Prentice Hall, 1998.

Kaplan, David A. *Mine's Bigger: Tom Perkins and the Making of the Greatest Sailing Machine Ever Built*. New York: HarperCollins Publishers, 2007.

Kawasaki, Guy. *The Art of the Start: The Time-Tested, Battle-Hardened Guide for Anyone Starting Anything*. New York: Portfolio, 2004.

Keller, Kevin Lane. *Strategic Brand Management: Building, Measuring, and Managing Brand Equity*. Upper Saddle River, New Jersey: Prentice Hall, 2003.

Kennedy, Robert F. *Thirteen Days: A Memoir of the Cuban Missile Crisis*. New York: W.W. Norton & Company, Inc., 1971.

Koch, Charles G. *The Science of Success: How Market-Based Management Built the World's Largest Private Company*. Hoboken, New Jersey: John Wiley & Sons, Inc., 2007.

Kotler, Philip. *Marketing Management, 11th Edition*. Delhi, India: Pearson Education, 2003.

Kunhardt, Philip B., Jr., et al. *The American President*. New York: Riverhead Books, 1999.

Larsen, Paul C. *To the Third Power: The Inside Story of Bill Koch's Winning Strategies for the America's Cup*. Gardiner, Maine: Tilbury House Publishers, 1995.

Levitt, Michael, and Barbara Lloyd. *Upset: Australia Wins the America's Cup*. New York: Workman Publishing, 1983.

Livy. *The War with Hannibal*. Translated by Aubrey de Sélincourt. London: Penguin Books, 1965.

Mackay, Harvey. *Swim with the Sharks Without Being Eaten Alive: Outsell, Outmanage, Outmotivate, and Outnegotiate Your Competition*. New York: Ivey Books, 1988.

Maraniss, David. *First in His Class: The Biography of Bill Clinton*. New York: Touchstone, 1996.

Markham, Felix. *Napoleon*. New York: Penguin Books, 1966.

May, Ernest R. *The Kennedy Tapes: Inside the White House During the Cuban Missile Crisis*. Edited by Philip D. Zelikow. Cambridge, Massachusetts: Harvard University Press, 1997.

McCullough, David. *Truman*. New York: Simon & Schuster, 1992.

Melges, Buddy, and Charles Mason. *Sailing Smart: Winning Techniques, Tactics, and Strategies*. New York: Henry Holt and Company, 1983.

O'Neil, William J., ed. *Sports Leaders & Success: 55 Top Sports Leaders & How They Achieved Greatness*. New York: McGraw-Hill, 2004.

Packard, David. *The HP Way: How Bill Hewlett and I Built Our Company*. New York: HarperCollins, 1995.

Padover, Saul K. *Jefferson: A Great American's Life and Ideas*. New York: Penguin, 1970.

Perret, Geoffrey. *Jack: A Life like No Other*. New York: Random House, 2002.

Perry, Dave. *Winning in One-Designs, 4th Ed*. Portsmouth, Rhode Island: US Sailing, 2005. Available from US Sailing at 800-US SAIL-1, or www.ussailing.org.

Peters, Thomas J., and Robert H. Waterman Jr. *In Search of Excellence: Lessons from America's Best-Run Companies*. New York: HarperCollins, 2004.

Ray, Michael, and Rochelle Myers. *Creativity in Business*. New York: Doubleday, 1986.

Reeves, Richard. *President Kennedy: Profile of Power*. New York: Touchstone, 1994.

Ries, Al, and Jack Trout. *Positioning: The Battle for Your Mind*. New York: McGraw-Hill, 2001.

Rinzler, J. W. *The Making of Star Wars*. New York: Ballentine Books, 2007.

Rodgers, Nigel. *The History and Conquests of Ancient Rome*. London: Hermes House, 2006.

Safire, William, ed. *Lend Me Your Ears: Great Speeches in History*. New York: W.W. Norton & Company, Inc., 2004.

Schultz, Howard, and Dori Jones Yang. *Pour Your Heart Into It: How Starbucks Built a Company One Cup at a Time*. New York: Hyperion, 1997.

Schwarzenegger, Arnold, and Douglas Kent Hall. *Arnold: The Education of a Bodybuilder*. New York: Fireside, 1993.

Sefton, Alan. *Sir Peter Blake: An Amazing Life*. Dobbs Ferry, New York: Sheridan House, 2005.

Senge, Peter M. *The Fifth Discipline: The Art & Practice of the Learning Organization*. New York: Doubleday, 1990.

Shirer, William L. *The Rise and Fall of the Third Reich: A History of Nazi Germany*. New York: Simon & Schuster, 1960.

Smith, Lawrie. *Tuning Your Dinghy*. London: Fernhurst Books, 1985.

Somerset, Anne. *Elizabeth I*. New York: Anchor Books, 2003.

Sorensen, Theodore C. *Kennedy*. New York: Konecky & Konecky, 1965.

Stannard, Bruce. *Stars & Stripes: The Official Record*. San Diego, California: Dennis Conner Sports, Inc., 1987.

Starnazzi, Carlo. *Leonardo: Codices & Machines*. Florence, Italy: Cartei & Bianchi, 2006.

Thompson, Arthur A., and A. J. Strickland III. *Crafting & Executing Strategy, 12th Ed.* New York: McGraw-Hill, 2001.

Tillman, Dick. *The Complete Book of Laser Sailing*. Camden, Maine: International Marine, 2005.

Twiname, Eric. *Sail, Race, and Win*. Boston, Massachusetts: SAIL Books, 1982.

Tzu, Sun. *The Art of War*. Edited by Thomas Cleary. Boston, Massachusetts: Shambhala Publications, 2000.

Walker, Stuart H. *Advanced Racing Tactics*. New York: W.W. Norton & Company, Inc., 1976.

Walker, Stuart H. *Positioning: The Logic of Sailboat Racing*. New York: W.W. Norton & Company, Inc., 1991.

Walker, Stuart H. *The Tactics of Small Boat Racing*. New York: W.W. Norton & Company, Inc., 1966.

Walker, Stuart H. *Winning: The Psychology of Competition*. New York: W.W. Norton & Company, Inc. 1986.

Walton, Sam, and John Huey. *Made in America: My Story*. New York: Doubleday, 1992.

Welch, Jack, and John A. Byrne. *Jack: Straight from the Gut*. New York: Warner Books, 2001.

Whitman, Neal A. *Peer Teaching: To Teach is to Learn Twice.* ASHE-ERIC Higher Education Report No. 4. Washington, D.C.: Association for the Study of Higher Education, 1988.

Yeh, Raymond T. *The Art of Business: In the Footsteps of Giants.* With Stephanie H. Yeh. Olathe, Colorado: Zero Time Publishing, 2004.

Business: The Ultimate Resource, 2nd Edition. Cambridge, Massachusetts: A&C Black Publishers Ltd., 2006.

PRINT ARTICLES

Adams, Ed. "Primed for the Big One." *Sailing World,* April 1992, 13–17.

Adams, Ed. "Wave Dancing." *Sailing World,* September 1995, 43–47.

Altman, Dan. "Is Trading Right For You?" *Technical Analysis of Stocks & Commodities,* November 2009, 96–98.

Augustine, Norman R. "Reshaping an Industry: Lockheed Martin's Survival Story." *Harvard Business Review on Change,* 1997, 159–165.

Everson, Darren. "Ellison on His America's Cup Win." *Wall Street Journal,* Feb 17, 2010, Sect. D:8.

Gorman, Ed. "The World's Best Sailor." *Sailing World,* November/December 2009, 60–63.

Lashinsky, Adam. "The Decade of Steve: How Apple's imperious, brilliant CEO transformed American business." *Fortune* 160, November 23, 2009, 92–100.

McKee, Jonathan. "Olympic Coaching in the '90s." *Sailing World,* April 1992, 8–11.

Pemerantz, Dorothy. "A Star is Born." *Forbes* 185, March 15, 2010, 60–64.

Retton, Mary Lou. "Living Beyond Your Comfort Zone." *Peter Lowe's Success Yearbook,* 1999, 53.

Sheahan, Matthew. "Mystery Boat takes 49er Gold!" *Yachting World* 160, October 2008, 26–27.

Strebel, Paul. "Why Do Employees Resist Change?" *Harvard Business Review on Change,* 1996, 141.

Symes, Bill. "Champions." *The Laser Sailor,* Fall 2009, 23.

WEB SOURCES

"About EcoBoost," Ford Motor Company, accessed February 15, 2010, http://www.fordvehicles.com/technology/ecoboost/about.

"America's Cup," accessed February 14, 2010, http://www.americascup.com.

"An Interview with Paul Elvstrom," Sailpower.com, accessed August 3, 2009, http://www.ybw.com/sp/features/Elvstrom.

"Anthony Fokker, Biography," Spartacus Educational Publishers Ltd., accessed January 5, 2013, http://www.spartacus.schoolnet.co.uk/FWWfokker.htm.

"Banana Republic," Gap, Inc.—Our Brands, accessed November 17, 2009, http://gapinc. com/public/OurBrands/brands.shtml.

"Banana Republic Inc.," Funding Universe, accessed November 17, 2009, http://www. fundinguniverse.com/company-histories/Banana-Republic-Inc-Company-History.html.

"Beijing Olympics Results," ISAF, accessed January 21, 2010, http://www.sailing.org/ olympics/resultscentre.php.

"Francis Drake Biography," Biography.com, accessed May 21, 2013, http://www.biography. com/people/francis-drake-9278809?page=3.

"Howard Schultz, Starbucks," Myprimetime.com, accessed November 30, 2009, http:// www.myprimetime.com/work/ge/schultzbio.

"Ice Cream Cone," The Great Idea Finder, accessed March 1, 2010, http://www.ideafinder. com/history/inventions/icecreamcone.htm.

"Investor Relations—FAQ's," Royal Caribbean Cruises Ltd., accessed December 15, 2009, http://phx.corporate-ir.net/phoenix.zhtml?c=103045&p=irol-faq#23203.

"Leonardo da Vinci—Renaissance Man, Artist," Museum of Science, Accessed November 10, 2009, http://www.mos.org/leonardo/artist.html.

"Muggsy Bogues Player Profile," NBA.com, accessed January 6, 2013, http://www.nba. com/playerfile/muggsy_bogues/index.html.

"Stephen King, Recipient of the National Book Foundation's Medal for Distinguished Contribution to American Letters Award, 2003," NationalBook.org, accessed June 4, 2013, http://www.nationalbook.org/nbaacceptspeech_sking.html#.UbEeP9zn9dg.

"The Duryea Brothers—Automobile History," About.com, accessed June 3, 2013, http:// inventors.about.com/od/dstartinventors/a/DuryeaBrothers.htm?p=1.

"The Nobel Peace Prize 2007," Nobel Foundation, accessed March 4, 2010, http:// nobelprize.org/nobel_prizes/peace/laureates/2007/index.html.

WEB ARTICLES

Baker, James V. "The Video Game Industry: Nintendo Back in the Lead." SeekingAlpha. com. Article published July 13, 2007. Accessed December 7, 2009. http://seekingalpha. com/article/40770-the-video-game-industry-nintendo-back-in-the-lead.

Carter, Robert. "Boat Remains and Maritime Trade in the Persian Gulf During the Sixth and Fifth Millennia BC." *Antiquity* 80, no. 307 (March 2006). Accessed January 6, 2013. http://www.academia.edu/173149/Boat_remains_and_maritime_trade_in_the_Persian_ Gulf_during_the_sixth_and_fifth_millennia_BC.

Donovan, Mark. "For Years, Stephen King's Firestarter was Wife Tabitha; Now She Burns to Write, Too." *People*, May 18, 1981. Accessed June 5, 2013. http://www.people.com/ people/archive/article/0,,20079300,00.html.

Gerstner, Joanne C. "Anna Tunnicliffe: Floating to Victory." US Sailing. Article published August 11, 2009. Accessed January 21, 2010. http://www.sailing.teamusa.org/ news/2009/08/11/anna-tunnicliffe-floating-to-victory/14946.

Hornyak, Tim. "Sailrocket 2 Breaks Sailing Speed Record at 68 mph." CNET.com. Article published November 20, 2012. Accessed January 6, 2013. http://news.cnet.com/8301-17938_105-57552488-1/sailrocket-2-breaks-sailing-speed-record-at-68-mph.

Kiley, David. "Detroit Finds Green in Recycled Fuel-Economy Ideas." Bloomberg Businessweek. Article published February 12, 2009. Accessed February 15, 2010. http://www.businessweek.com/magazine/content/09_08/b4120064139211.htm?chan=magazine+channel_what%27s+next.

Kotelnikov, Vadim. "Case Study: Canon Production System." Ten3 Business E-Coach. Accessed March 3, 2010. http://www.1000ventures.com/business_guide/cs_efficiency_canon_ps.html.

Lynch, Jack. "Lockheed and Martin Marietta Set to Merge in $10 Billion Deal." New York Times. Article published August 30, 1994. Accessed May 30, 2013. http://www.nytimes.com/1994/08/30/business/lockheed-and-martin-marietta-set-to-merge-in-10-billion-deal.html.

McDowell, Edwin. "Royal Caribbean and Celebrity in Definitive Merger Agreement." New York Times. Article published July 3, 1997. Accessed November 30, 2009. http://www.nytimes.com/1997/07/03/business/royal-caribbean-and-celebrity-in-definitive-merger-agreement.html?pagewanted=1.

McNamee, Gregory. "Olympic Moments: Lawrence Lemieux Saves Lives." Encyclopedia Brittanica Blog. Online. Article published August 22, 2008. Accessed July 13, 2012. http://www.britannica.com/blogs/2008/08/olympic-moments-lawrence-lemieux-saves-lives-1988.

Perry, Dave. "Fitting Pieces into the Puzzle." Southport Sailing Foundation. Copyright 1985. Accessed February 18, 2010. http://www.cleverpig.org/back/pages/article_2.pdf.

Peter, Ian. "The History of Email." Net History. Copyright 2004. Accessed December 16, 2009. http://www.nethistory.info/History%20of%20the%20Internet/email.html.

Ryan, Monique. "Laird's Laws." Outside magazine. Article published June 5, 2007. Accessed November 30, 2009. http://www.outsideonline.com/fitness/Laird-s-Laws.html.

Schuster, Mike. "Rags to Riches CEOs: Howard Schultz." Minyanville. Article published November 18, 2009. Accessed December 14, 2009. http://www.minyanville.com/articles/print.php?a=25353.

Sheahan, Matthew. "World Sailing Speed Record Smashed." Yachting World. Article published September 6, 2009. Accessed February 24, 2010. http://www.yachtingworld.com/performance-world/news/417577/world-sailing-speed-record-smashed.

Sims, Calvin. "Northrop Bests Martin Marietta to Buy Grumman." New York Times. Article published April 5, 1994. Accessed May 30, 2013. http://www.nytimes.com/1994/04/05/business/northrop-bests-martin-marietta-to-buy-grumman.html.

Summers, Judith. "Broad Street Pump Outbreak." UCLA Department of Epidemiology/School of Health. Accessed January 6, 2013. http://www.ph.ucla.edu/epi/snow/broadstreetpump.html.

Tichy, Noel, and Ram Charan. "Speed, Simplicity, Self-Confidence: An Interview with

Jack Welch." Harvard Business Review. Article published September, 1989. http://hbr.org/1989/09/speed-simplicity-self-confidence-an-interview-with-jack-welch.

Viner, Brian. "Iain Percy & Andrew Simpson: 'We Can't Rely on Razzmatazz to Wow the Crowds at 2012.'" The *Independent*. Article published September 18, 2009. Accessed October 29, 2009. http://www.independent.co.uk/sport/olympics/iain-percy--andrew-simpson-we-cant-rely-on-razzmatazz-to-wow-the-crowds-at-2012-1789330.html.

"Biography: Gore's Road from Tennessee to the White House." CNN.com. Article published June 16, 1999. Accessed December 18, 2012. http://www.cnn.com/ALLPOLITICS/stories/1999/06/16/president.2000/gore.biography.

"Croatian 49er Sailors Presented With Fair Play Award." ISAF. Article published December 1, 2008. Accessed December 18, 2009. http://www.sailing.org/olympics/26778.php.

"Lemieux's Sportsmanship Still Recognized." The *Edmonton Journal* on Canada.com. Article published March 13, 2008. Accessed July 13, 2012. http://www.canada.com/edmontonjournal/news/sports/story.html?id=063e5f99-458f-47c2-b6c2-0e34056bb81f.

"Virgin Ads Too Sexy for Mississauga, Calgary." TheSpec.com. Article published January 7, 2010. Accessed January 11, 2010. http://www.thespec.com/article/700921.

FILM & TELEVISION

America's Cup: The Walter Cronkite Report, directed by James R. Donaldson III. Fairwind Productions, Ltd., 1988.

America's Cup '88: The Official Video, directed by Mark Kirsch. ESPN/Warren Miller Sports Films, 1988.

Anthony Fokker: The Flying Dutchman, produced by Mike Welt. Lucasfilm Ltd., 2007.

Aussie Assault, directed by Harvey Spencer. Sportsmaster Programs, 1984.

Big Mac: Inside the McDonald's Empire, produced by Mitch Weitzner. CNBC, 2007.

Black Magic: The Team New Zealand Story, directed by Glen Sowry. Television New Zealand, 1995.

"Coca-Cola: The Real Story Behind the Real Thing," *Biography on CNBC*. CNBC, November 24, 2009.

"Donald Trump," A&E *Biography*, directed by Elizabeth Jane Browde. A&E Television Networks, 1995.

Facing Ali, directed by Pete McCormack. Lionsgate/Spike TV and Muhammad Ali Enterprises, 2009.

Freedom, directed by Dick Enersen. Offshore Productions, 1981.

"Ice Cream," *Modern Marvels*. The History Channel, March 4, 2010.

Jimmy Carter, directed by Adriana Bosch. WGBH Boston, 2002.

"Napoleon Bonaparte: The Glory of France," A&E *Biography*. A&E Television Networks, 1997.

New York: A Documentary Film, directed by Ric Burns. Steeplechase Films/WGBH Boston, 2003.

Nixon, directed by David Espar. WGBH Boston, 1990.

Ray Kroc: Fast Food McMillionaire, produced by Greg Weinstein. A&E Television Networks, 1998.

Reagan, directed by Adriana Bosch and Austin Hoyt. WGBH Boston, 1998.

The 1992 America's Cup, directed by Jamie Reynolds. ESPN, 1992.

The Ascent of Money, directed by Niall Ferguson. Chimerica Media Ltd./WNET.org, 2009.

The Best Defense, directed by Dick Enersen. Offshore Productions, 1978.

The Greatest Race of the Century: The 1983 Official America's Cup Challenge, directed by Lucinda Constable. Xerox Corporation, 1983.

The Kennedys, directed by James A. DeVinney, David Espar, Marilyn H. Mellowes and Phillip Whitehead. WGBH Boston, 1992.

The World at War: Barbarossa, produced by Jeremy Isaacs. A&E Television Networks, 1974.

Winning & Reinvention. Success Television, 2008.

INTERVIEWS

Commette, Peter: December 17, 2012

Diaz, Augie: January 7, 2013

Perry, Dave: August 30, 2013

Reynolds, Mark: January 4, 2013, January 7, 2013

Szabo, George: January 8, 2013

ACKNOWLEDGEMENTS

SAILORS EVERYWHERE CAN UNDERSTAND THE VALUE of surrounding themselves with helpful, capable, energetic people, whether onboard or ashore. In that spirit, I set out from the start to talk to people who could keep me on track to bring this book to life. Although I've been writing for many years, no such project I've undertaken has been quite like the process of publishing my first book. Socrates said that true wisdom is in knowing that you know nothing, and for me, recognizing early on how much I had to learn about this process was an important step towards finding experienced and talented people from whom I could learn along the way.

I'd like to thank Jared Kuritz and Antoinette Kuritz for keeping me on course from the start, and helping me to keep all the moving parts of this project running smoothly. Their expertise and advice through the writing and publishing process have been enormously beneficial in exploring these new waters.

I would also like to thank:

The Monkey C Media team of Jeniffer Thompson, Chad Thompson, Aleta Reese, Julio Pompa Frizza, Matthew Gross, and Sophia McLane, for their excellent work done in the design and development of this book and my website.

Mary Altbaum, for her meticulous attention to detail in the copyediting of the manuscript.

Annie Gardner, for making time in her impressively packed schedule to review the manuscript and write the foreword.

Interviewees Peter Commette, Augie Diaz, Dave Perry, Mark Reynolds, and George Szabo, for granting me their time and sharing their experiences and insights.

Lisa and Tom, for being a willing sounding board and constant source of moral support. As always, I am deeply grateful for the love and encouragement of my wonderful family and friends.

PERMISSIONS

ABOUT THE AUTHOR

PRIOR TO WRITING *PLOTTING THE COURSE*, Rick Arneson had a lifetime of sailing experience, growing up in the San Diego Yacht Club junior sailing program. Before starting a college sailing team during his freshman year at Pepperdine, he'd won state and district championships, match-raced 12-meter yachts in the World Scholar-Athlete Games, and taken a gold medal at the AAU Junior Olympics. He would bring his experience to coaching sailors at the club, high school, and collegiate levels, including Stanford University, Orange Coast College, and UC Irvine. Since 2003, he has been a member of the U.S. Snipe team at three World and two Western Hemisphere championships. He has been a marketing professional in a range of industries, and a contributing writer to *Sailing World* and various other sailing publications. He holds B.S. and M.B.A. degrees from Pepperdine University.